# The WASHINGTON ❧ INN ❧ Cooks for Friends

### 350 Favorite Recipes from Cape May's Premier Restaurant

*Michael Craig with Mimi Wood*
*Art by Alice Steer Wilson*

LOVE
· THE ·
COOK
BOOKS

*Cape May, New Jersey*

The Washington Inn is located in Cape May, New Jersey. This national historic landmark city is famous for its hundreds of beautifully restored Victorian homes. Situated on the southern tip of the state, where the Atlantic coastline meets the Delaware Bay, Cape May is renowned as a major site of bird migration every Fall and Spring.

The Washington Inn is located in Cape May's historic district.
To make a dinner reservation or arrange a catered event, please call (609)884-5697.

Copyright © 1998 by Michael Craig

Love the Cook Books
801 Washington Street
Cape May, New Jersey 08204
www.washingtoninn.com

Cover and interior art: Alice Steer Wilson
Editor: LaVonne Carlson-Finnerty
Contributing writer: Elizabeth George
Indexer: Nanette Cardon
Contributing designer: Debra Borg

ISBN 0-9665244-0-3

Printed in the United States of America

10 9 8 7 6 5 4 3 2 1

Cataloging-in-Publication Data is available upon request
from the Library of Congress.

# Table of Contents

# Dedication

To our friends, guests and employees,
who have helped make our restaurant successful.

# Acknowledgments

We would like to thank the people who helped us
with their expertise and advice.
Debra Borg, Lavonne Carlson-Finnerty,
Heidi Cummings of Inkwell, Sue and Mike Kelly,
Candice Hawkins of Typographical Solutions,
Anita Hirsch, Tim Joyce Photography, Martha Kesler
and all of our friends who encouraged us
to make this happen.

The Washington Inn and the Craig family came together in the spring of 1978. Our family included Toby, myself and our three children, Michael, David and Betsy. Lola, our daschund, was also part of the entourage.

The inn included a dining area, six guest rooms with baths, and a tiny two-bedroom apartment on the third floor. The inn had been operating on a plan that provided the guests with both breakfast and dinner. We continued operating that same way for the first two years. At times we all became housekeepers, bellhops, dishwashers and cooks who prepared two meals a day for our guests!

The joining of the Craigs and the Washington Inn was exciting, if not overwhelming. Living in the crowded third floor accommodations was a real lesson in togetherness. We quickly learned the dynamics of balancing both family and business, which to this day helps us support and encourage each other. The kids worked in the restaurant during the summer and after school and sports each day. We all worked together and the business started to grow. At that time, Cape May was still much of a summer resort, so we closed the inn in October. In the winter, after all the summer guests had gone, we would move to the second floor and choose our own bedrooms and baths. Normal at last!

The Washington Inn's evolution to a restaurant started our very first year when we added a "new member" to our family. We hired a chef named Isadore. He came from Savannah, Georgia, and had a southern cooking background. We also added fresh rolls and cinnamon buns to the bread baskets, candles and fresh flowers to the tables and carpeting to the floor. Each year we changed a little more, always putting the emphasis on fresh, well prepared food, a welcoming atmosphere and, most important, pleasing our guests.

Our inn became solely a restaurant when we gave up the guest rooms in 1980—letting our family's living quarters grow too! We all moved into the second floor. The children were delighted to have a living room, dining room and even our own kitchen. One of our biggest challenges was keeping Lola from sneaking downstairs into the dining room during evening business hours. She usually tried to make a grand entrance at around seven o'clock—sticking her nose through the staircase banister to watch the goings on.

In 1980 another big change came to the restaurant when we purchased a liquor license from a local tavern. The whole family was involved in creating the new addition to the Washington Inn. Toby had the idea and executed the plans to build a bar from a huge old armoire that his grandmother brought from Germany. The base of the bar came from antique doors gathered from local builder-friends. The 30 coats of varnish came from the rest of our family. Friends would stop by and give a hand in every way possible, from fixing lunches and libations to lending the tools of a woodshop for Toby's use.

When the Washington Inn re-opened in the spring of 1981, a new Victorian lounge and adjoining porch added a new dimension to its ambiance. We were growing each year and building a wonderfully loyal clientele as well. Many of our regular customers became our friends, as did most of our employees. Our employees also took part in the changes, growing and developing their skills in creating a fine restaurant. As always, our priorities remained great food, a beautiful setting and our guests' satisfaction.

Having a liquor license opened up the opportunity to create and develop a wine cellar. Our plan was to develop our restaurant as a wine destination. We wanted our guests to be able to get as excited about the wines we served as they did about the food, ambiance and service. Both Mike and David became very knowledgeable about wine. For two years, they drove to New York City every week to pour wine for the Windows on the World wine course. They took trips to California and Europé to find new wines to put on the list. Over the years, their choices have received high accolades. Our restaurant has benefited from their expertise by having an award-winning wine cellar that contains 8,000 bottles of hand-picked wines.

We are fortunate that each of our children, after finishing college and stints in Europe, returned to the Washington Inn to help it continue to grow and improve. Everyone in the family has brought new ideas and touches that make the restaurant better. We can truly say we are a family business. And a business that knows how lucky it is and appreciates the guests who walk through our door.

The joining of our family and the Washington Inn back in 1978 has taken many turns and presented many opportunities to the Craig family. And in every decision and change we have made, we always put improving our guests' experiences first. To this day our family and employees enjoy making our guests feel welcome and special. This philosophy has enabled us to give a wonderful dining experience to many, many guests over the years and has given us the opportunity to meet some very special people. Through the years we also have been blessed to have had a wonderful staff, who have become family to us. They have helped us to implement great ideas and achieve the high standards that our guests expect. Without these people, our restaurant would not be so special.

This cookbook, *The Washington Inn Cooks for Friends,* was conceived and developed, again, with our guests in mind. We are presenting our most popular dishes over the years, from appetizers to desserts—and have put a homemade spin on them for your enjoyment. We include wine suggestions, cooking tips and ideas for entertaining, so you can enjoy your time in the kitchen and create your own great memories along the way. Enjoy!

Rona Craig

*Basics*

These crunchy croutons
are made with two
complementary kinds of
bread—sourdough and
pumpernickel. San Francisco
is known for its sourdough, a
bread with a slightly sour,
tangy flavor that's made with
a yeast starter. Pumpernickel,
a coarse dark bread that gets
its dark color from molasses,
also has a slightly sour taste
and is made with rye and
wheat flours. Home bread
bakers can make their
sourdough using packages of
dry sourdough starter.

# *Washington Inn Croutons*

$^1/_4$ *cup butter, melted*
$^1/_4$ *cup olive oil*
*1 tablespoon garlic powder*
*1 tablespoon dill, dried*
*1 tablespoon basil, dried*
$^1/_2$ *teaspoon salt*
$^1/_2$ *teaspoon white pepper*
*5 cups sour dough and pumpernickel bread, cut into $^3/_4$-inch cubes*
$^1/_4$ *cup Parmesan cheese, grated (optional)*

1. Mix the butter, oil and seasonings in a large bowl.

2. Add the bread cubes to the oil mixture and toss. Place them on a
   baking sheet.

3. Bake them in a preheated 350°F oven until they are golden brown,
   approximately 5 to 8 minutes.

4. For cheese croutons, toss the baked croutons with the Parmesan
   cheese as soon as you remove them from the oven.

5. Store the croutons in an airtight container.

**Makes 5 cups**

# Roasted Garlic

*4 heads fresh garlic*
*4-5 grinds of fresh black pepper*
*$1/2$ teaspoon kosher salt*
*1 sprig fresh rosemary*
*1 sprig fresh thyme*
*$1/4$ cup olive oil*
*$1/2$ cup chicken stock (see page 5) or water*

1. Cut the pointed tops off of the garlic heads to expose the cloves. Place the heads stem-side down, in a small casserole dish.

2. Season them with salt and pepper, then lay the herbs on top. Pour the olive oil over this.

3. Pour the stock or water around the garlic, then cover the pan with a double thickness of foil.

4. Bake in a preheated 350°F oven for approximately 1 hour. The garlic should be tender when touched with a fork.

**Makes 4 garlic heads**

**Roasting Garlic**

It is important to choose a casserole dish where the garlic can fit snugly. Too large a pan allows the liquid to evaporate too quickly. A small Pyrex casserole dish works nicely, and even an omelette pan will do.

## Chicken Soup Remedies

A good chicken stock is the basis for chicken soup, nicknamed Jewish penicillin and widely held to be the cure-all for colds. But is there any truth to its healing benefits? Yes! Researchers have found that the combination of a hot liquid coupled with chicken soup's savory aroma helps open up clogged nasal passages, albeit temporarily. And the psychological boost of sipping something warm and homemade also helps people feel better.

# Basic Chicken Stock

*3 pounds chicken bones, back, neck and wings*
*2 large onions, peeled*
*2 large carrots*
*2 celery stalks*
*1 bay leaf*
*1 bunch parsley stems*
*12 peppercorns, whole*
*4 quarts cold water*

1. Under cold running water, rinse the bones well.

2. Cut the onions, carrots and celery into large squares. Avoid using the darker celery leaves, as they can impart a bitter taste to the stock.

3. Place the bones, vegetables, herbs and spice into a 6-quart stockpot. Add the cold water and bring to a boil. Skim the impurities from the surface.

4. Reduce the heat and simmer for at least 2 to 3 hours, up to 6 hours. Continue to skim off the impurities throughout the cooking process.

5. Strain the liquid and cool it in a refrigerator. (Discard the bones and vegetables.) Stock keeps for 1 week in the refrigerator and 3 weeks in the freezer.

**Makes approximately 3 quarts**

# Basic Vegetable Stock

2 leeks, cleaned
1 medium-size onion, peeled
2 celery stalks
2 carrots
1 turnip
1 parsnip
1 potato
$^1/_2$ pound mushrooms
2 tablespoons vegetable oil
9 cloves garlic, finely chopped
$^1/_2$ teaspoon white pepper
1 bay leaf
fresh herbs
4 quarts cold water

1.  Cut the leek, onion and celery into $^1/_2$-inch pieces. Cut the carrot, turnip and parsnip into half rounds. Cut the potatoes into quarters and the mushrooms in half.

2.  Heat the oil in a heavy 6-quart stockpot. When the oil is hot, add the leeks, onions and carrots. Cook over medium heat for 5 minutes.

3.  Add the celery, turnip, parsnip, potato, mushrooms, garlic, pepper and bay leaf. Add the water and bring it to a boil. Reduce the heat and simmer for about 35 minutes.

4.  Strain the stock into a container. (Discard the vegetables.) Refrigerate. Stock keeps for 1 week in the refrigerator and 3 weeks in the freezer.

**Makes approximately 1 gallon**

## Hearty Winter Roots

Two root vegetables—turnips and parsnips—add flavor to this hearty stock. Though best known as winter vegetables, turnips and parsnips are available year-round. When selecting either, choose ones that are small to medium in size as they have a delicate, sweet taste. Both turnips and parsnips can last in the refrigerator, when wrapped in plastic, for up to 2 weeks. Besides being a handy staple for winter soups and stews, these "roots" are tasty when boiled, baked, buttered or mashed.

## Basic Shrimp Stock

3 tablespoons olive oil or
  vegetable oil
3 pounds shrimp shells, raw
  or cooked
1 medium onion, chopped
1 clove garlic
2 cups carrots, sliced
1 cup celery, roughly
  chopped
1 leek, cleaned and sliced
1 tomato, chopped
1 bay leaf
1 sprig fresh thyme
3 tablespoons tomato paste
2 cups white wine
10 cups water

1. Heat the olive oil in a
   large stockpot over
   medium heat. When the
   oil is smoking hot, quickly
   add the shells. Cook them
   for 5 minutes, until they
   are crispy and brown.

2. Add the onions, garlic,
   carrots, celery, leeks, fresh
   tomato and herbs. Cook
   them over medium heat
   for 8 minutes. Add the
   tomato paste.

3. Add the wine and water,
   and bring to a boil. Lower
   the heat and simmer for
   an hour, reducing the
   broth by one-third.
   (Continue to reduce the
   stock if you want a more
   concentrated flavor.)

4. Strain, then freeze or
   refrigerate.

**Makes 1¹/₂ quarts**

# Basic Fish Stock

2 pounds fish bones, tails and heads (gills removed)
1 small onion, peeled
1 celery stalk
1 tablespoon butter
¹/₂ cup dry white wine
7-8 cups cold water
2 parsley stems, leaves removed
¹/₂ bunch fresh thyme
12 peppercorns, whole

1. Clean the fish bones thoroughly under running water. Cut the onion
   and celery into small dice.

2. Melt the butter in a heavy 6-quart stockpot. When it is hot, add the
   onion and celery. Sweat the vegetables over medium heat, stirring
   occasionally, for 3 to 5 minutes, until the onions are translucent.

3. Place the bones on top of the vegetables and cover them with a piece
   of parchment paper. Reduce the heat to low and sweat the bones for
   5 minutes. Remove and discard the parchment paper.

4. Add the wine and bring it to a simmer. Add enough cold water to
   cover the bones completely.

5. Add the remaining ingredients and simmer uncovered for 25 minutes.
   Skim off the impurities throughought the cooking time.

6. Strain the stock through a fine china cap or strainer. Cool completely.
   Cover and store in the refrigerator. Stock keeps for about 1 week in
   the refrigerator in an airtight container and about 4 weeks in the
   freezer.

**Makes approximately 6 to 7 cups**

# Basic Beef Stock

*10 pounds beef bones including marrow, cut into 3- to 4-inch pieces*
*2 onions*
*2 carrots*
*2 celery stalks*
*2 tablespoons tomato paste*
*cold water, several quarts*

*Herb-Spice Mix*
*2 bay leaves*
*10 parsley stems*
*4 cloves garlic*
*$1/2$ teaspoon peppercorns, whole*
*3 sprigs of thyme*

1.  Preheat the oven to 350°F. Place the bones in a roasting pan in the oven for about 30 minutes.

2.  Cut the onions, carrots and celery into 2-inch pieces to make the mirepoix. Avoid using the darker celery leaves, as they can impart a bitter taste to the stock.

3.  After roasting the bones, remove them from the oven and brush them with tomato paste, coating every side. Add the mirepoix and stir.

4.  Put this mixture back into the oven for 20 minutes, stirring the bones and mirepoix every 5 minutes.

5.  Take the pan out of the oven and transfer the bones and mirepoix into an 8-quart stockpot. Drain off the fat from the roasting pan. Deglaze the pan with a little red wine, and add this to the stockpot. Add the herb-spice mix and enough water to cover the bones. Bring this mixture to a boil.

6.  Reduce the heat and simmer for 8 to 12 hours. Skim off the impurities throughout the cooking time.

7.  Strain the stock through a strainer, discarding the bones and vegetables. Refrigerate. Stock keeps for 1 week in the refrigerator and 3 months in the freezer.

**Makes 1 gallon**

## Mirepoix Means…

Mirepoix is a classic French cooking term that refers to a combination of chopped, aromatic vegetables that are used for flavoring. The combination typically includes 2 parts onions to 1 part celery and 1 part carrots. It is used most often to flavor meats and stocks.

## Base Basics

For any recipe requiring a base or demiglace, you can continue reducing the stocks described in this chapter or you can have this demiglace base already made aheat to eliminate the need for heavy reducing when you are busy cooking a meal.

## Veal or Beef Demiglace

1. To reduce a stock, use a large, thick-bottom pot.

2. Let the stock boil, then lower the heat and reduce it until you have a nice, thick sauce-like consistency (approximately 1 hour). This process concentrates the flavors of the stock and creates a great base for sauces.

3. Once the demiglace cools down, refrigerate it for up to 2 weeks or freeze it in an ice cube tray for 2 months. The cubes are easy to use: Just heat them up in the same pan you'll use for cooking. They also eliminate waste by enabling you to use only the exact amount you need.

**2 quarts of stock makes 2 cups of demiglace**

# Basic Veal Stock

*10 pounds veal bones*
*3 carrots, roughly sliced*
*3 stalks celery, chopped*
*2 medium onions, sliced*
*3 heaping tablespoons tomato paste*
*water, several quarts*

*Herb-Spice Mix*
*1/2 bunch fresh parsley*
*1 bunch fresh thyme*
*10 whole peppercorns*
*1 tablespoon dried thyme*
*3 bay leaves*
*6 garlic cloves, whole*

1. Spread the thawed veal bones onto a roasting pan. Roast them in a 400°F oven until they become a dark even brown color. Remove the bones from the oven and put them in a large stockpot. Drain the fat. Set aside the pan.

2. In a large sauté pan, over medium heat, sauté the vegetables until they begin to soften and change color. Turn up the heat and caramelize the vegetables until they are brown.

3. Add the tomato paste and continue to cook until the mixture is a mahogony color. Be careful not to scorch the pan.

4. Put the vegetable mixture in the pot with the bones. Add enough water to cover the bones. Deglaze the roasting pan with the remaining water, then add it to the pot. Add the spices and herbs.

5. Slowly bring the stock to a boil, then lower the heat and simmer. Cook the stock for 6 to 8 hours. Throughout cooking, continue skimming the surface as the fat and debris rise, to keep the stock clear.

6. Strain the stock into another pot. You can put this on the stove and reduce it further to concentrate the flavors. Cool to room temperature, then refrigerate or freeze in small containers.

**Makes 1 gallon**

# Béchamel Sauce

*2 tablespoons onions, chopped*
*4 tablespoons butter*
*5 tablespoons flour*
*2 cups half-and-half*
*salt and pepper, to taste*

1. In a saucepan, sauté the onions in the butter until they are translucent.

2. Add the flour and stir well. Cook for a few minutes until a nice paste forms.

3. Add the half-and-half. Whisk until the mixture is thick and smooth.

4. Let it simmer for 30 minutes.

5. Strain the sauce, then season it with the salt and pepper.

**Makes 2 cups**

**The Perfect Sauce**

Named for its creator, Louis de Béchamel, a 17th-century financier and courtier, this French sauce is made by stirring milk into a butter-flour roux. Béchamel sauce varies in thickness, depending on the proportion of flour and butter to milk. It is a perfect sauce to bind, coat or thicken foods and its mild, unobtrusive flavor makes it ideal to add to any dish. After cooking béchamel sauce, you can prevent a skin from forming on top by placing a piece of wax paper directly over its surface.

## Beurre Blanc Basics

Meaning "white butter" in French, this sauce is a staple at the Washington Inn. It makes the perfect fish sauce because it is both light and rich. It offers a perfect balance that does not overpower the delicate taste of the fish.

There are two ways to make beurre blanc: with cream, or without it. The traditional way omits the cream so that the essence of the reduction is infused into the whipped butter; it is more tricky and delicate. The addition of cream helps stabilize the sauce and gives it a silky quality. We use the cream when we make our beurre blancs.

The trick is to keep the butter emulsified into the cream or the reduction. Keep the sauce warm, but never bring it to a boil or it will separate. To prevent separating, take the pan off the heat. Add a bit more butter to cool down the mixture, then continue whipping it.

To keep the sauce warm until you are ready to use it, place it in a well cleaned coffee thermos.

# Classic Beurre Blanc

*1 cup white wine*
*1/4 cup shallots, chopped*
*1 ounce white wine vinegar*
*1/2 cup cream*
*2 sticks butter (1/2 pound), softened*
*salt and pepper, for seasoning*

1. Reduce the wine, shallots and vinegar in a saucepan until almost all of the liquid evaporates.

2. Add the cream and continue to reduce, over medium heat, until it has a sauce-like consistency. Turn the heat down to low.

3. Cut the butter into small pieces and whip it into the cream with a wire whisk.

4. Do not allow the pan to get too hot, or the sauce will separate.

5. Season with salt and pepper.

**Makes 1 cup**

# Compound Butters

## Merlot-Shallot Butter

*1 stick butter ($^1/_4$ pound), softened*
*$^1/_4$ cup red wine*
*$^1/_4$ cup shallots, chopped*
*salt and pepper, for seasoning*

1.  In a small saucepan, simmer the shallots and wine over medium heat until the wine reduces and only about 2 tablespoons remain.

2.  Place them in a food processor fitted with a steel blade. Add the butter and season with salt and pepper. Purée.

3.  Shape the butter into a log and wrap it in plastic wrap or parchment paper.

4.  Refrigerate or freeze.

## Jalapeño Butter

*2 sticks butter ($^1/_2$ pound), softened*
*4 tablespoons jalapeño peppers, seeded and chopped*
*3 tablespoons mint, chopped*
*2 tablespoons chives, chopped*
*salt and pepper, for seasoning*

1.  Place all of the ingredients into a food processor fitted with a steel blade. Purée.

2.  Shape the butter into a log and wrap it in plastic wrap or parchment paper.

3.  Refrigerate or freeze.

**Flavored Butters**

These flavored butters are easy and fun to make. You can be very creative with inventing new combinations. When you are looking for a new and easy topping at dinnertime, place a dollop or slice of butter on top of chicken, fish or beef to make a simple meal extra special. These butters also can complete beurre blancs to intensify their flavor. Several of our favorite butter recipes are featured here.

## Make a Butter Log

Butters can be made and refrigerated for over 1 month. Give them an attractive look by using plastic wrap or parchment. Tear off a sheet of plastic wrap or parchment, sized about 8 by 15 inches. After processing the butter, place the butter onto the sheet of wrap using a rubber spatula. Cover the butter with the wrap, then form it into a roll. Tighten the wrap to form a log about 2 inches in diameter and 11 inches long. Twist the ends. A log can be refrigerated or frozen.

# Olive Butter

*4 tablespoons butter (2 ounces)*
*¹/₂ cup pitted black olives, chopped*
*1 anchovy fillet*
*¹/₂ teaspoon fresh garlic*
*pepper, for seasoning*

1. Place all of the ingredients into a food processor fitted with a steel blade. Purée.

2. Shape the butter into a log and wrap it in plastic wrap or parchment.

3. Refrigerate or freeze.

# Fresh Lime Butter

*2 tablespoons lime juice*
*1 stick butter (¹/₄ pound)*
*1 tablespoon lime zest, chopped*
*2 teaspoons shallots, chopped*
*salt and pepper, for seasoning*

1. Place all of the ingredients into a food processor fitted with a steel blade. Purée.

2. Shape the butter into a log and wrap it in plastic wrap or parchment.

3. Refrigerate or freeze.

# Tarragon Butter

*1 stick butter (¹/₄ pound)*
*¹/₂ cup fresh tarragon, chopped*
*1 tablespoon white wine*
*salt and pepper, for seasoning*

1. Place all of the ingredients into a food processor fitted with a steel blade. Purée.

2. Shape the butter into a log and wrap it in plastic wrap or parchment.

3. Refrigerate or freeze.

# Orange Citrus Butter

*1 stick butter (¼ pound)*
*3 tablespoons orange zest*
*2 tablespoons orange juice*
*1 tablespoon shallots, chopped*
*1 tablespoon Grand Marnier*
*salt and pepper, for seasoning*

1. Place all of the ingredients into a food processor fitted with a steel blade. Purée.

2. Shape the butter into a log and wrap it in plastic wrap or parchment.

3. Refrigerate or freeze.

# Caper-Mustard Butter

*1 stick butter (¼ pound)*
*2 tablespoons Dijon mustard*
*1 tablespoon capers, drained and chopped*
*pepper, for seasoning*

1. Place all of the ingredients in a food processor fitted with a steel blade. Purée.

2. Shape the butter into a log and wrap it in plastic wrap or parchment.

3. Refrigerate or freeze.

# Anchovy Butter

*1 stick butter (¼ pound)*
*18 anchovy fillets, rinsed and dried*
*1 teaspoon lemon zest, chopped*
*1 teaspoon shallot, chopped*

1. Place all of the ingredients in a food processor fitted with a steel blade. Purée.

2. Shape the butter into a log and wrap it in plastic wrap or parchment.

3. Refrigerate or freeze.

**Grand Flavor**

Grand Marnier is a clear, dark golden-colored brandy-based French liqueur that is flavored with orange peel. It is often used in cooking, especially desserts, as well as for serving as an after-dinner cordial. Here, its flavor is layered with orange zest and juice to create a rich butter that is just as perfect on fish as on crêpes or pancakes.

## Fruit Preserves

Preserves are made by cooking fruit along with sugar and usually pectin. Preserves feature medium-sized chunks of fruit, unlike jams, which are cooked until the fruit is very soft, almost like a purée. Jelly is different from both, in that it is made from fruit juice and is cooked firm to hold its shape out of the jar. For these butter recipes, where fruit is called for, you can use preserves or chopped fresh or frozen fruit interchangeably.

# Strawberry Butter

*4 sticks butter (1 pound), softened*
*1 cup strawberry preserves*

1. Using a food processor or mixer, mix together.

2. Chill and serve.

# Maple Butter

*2 sticks butter (1/2 pound), softened*
*1/4 cup Vermont maple syrup*

1. Using a food processor or mixer, mix together.

2. Chill and serve.

# Blueberry Butter

*2 sticks butter (1/2 pound), softened*
*1/2 cup blueberries, fresh or frozen*

1. Using a food processor or mixer, mix together.

2. Chill and serve.

# Cinnamon Honey Butter

*2 sticks butter (1/2 pound), softened*
*1/4 cup honey*
*2 teaspoons cinnamon*

1. Using a food processor or mixer, mix together.

2. Chill and serve.

# Horseradish Butter

*4 sticks butter (1 pound), softened to room temperature*
*¹/₂ cup horseradish, grated*

*Reduction Ingredients*
*¹/₄ cup red onion, puréed*
*1 tablespoon garlic, chopped*
*2 tablespoons Dijon mustard*
*2 ounces A-1 Sauce*
*2 ounces Worcestershire sauce*
*¹/₂ cup red wine*
*dash of Tabasco*
*1 tablespoon black pepper*

1. Mix all of the reduction ingredients together. Simmer them in a saucepan until the mixture is reduced by half.

2. Cool the mixture to room temperature.

3. Add the butter and horseradish. Blend well.

4. Place the butter mixture on plastic wrap or parchment paper. Roll it into 2 logs.

5. Freeze or refrigerate the butter until ready to use. The butter stays fresh for 1 week in the refrigerator and 6 weeks in the freezer.

**Makes 1 pound (2 logs)**

### Where's Worcestershire?

Worcestershire sauce, which is used to add zing to meats, gravies, soups and Bloody Marys, was first bottled in Worcester, England, although the English originally created it in India. This zesty sauce is traditionally made with garlic, soy sauce, tamarind, onions, molasses, lime, anchovies, vinegar and spices.

## Making Mayonnaise

Mayonnaise can be used as a spread, dressing or sauce and is the base for tartar sauce and remoulade. Homemade mayonnaise lasts only 3 to 4 days and should be kept tightly covered in the refrigerator. The maximum time any dish made with homemade mayonnaise can be outside of the refrigerator is 2 hours—and only 1 hour when temperatures are 80°F or higher. Mayonnaise can be flavored with chopped herbs, curry, horseradish cream and even mustard.

# Mayonnaise

*3 egg yolks*
*$^1/_4$ teaspoon mustard*
*$^1/_2$ teaspoon salt*
*freshly ground pepper, to taste*
*2 tablespoons white vinegar*
*$^3/_4$ cup olive oil*
*$^3/_4$ cup vegetable oil*

1. Whisk together the egg yolks, mustard, salt, pepper and 1 tablespoon of vinegar.

2. Add the oil in a slow steady stream, allowing the eggs to slowly incorporate the oil.

3. Add the rest of the vinegar when the mixture is nice and thick.

**Makes approximately 2 cups**

# Peppercorn Dressing
## with Spring Mix

*1 egg*
*¹/₃ teaspoon salt*
*1 teaspoon black peppercorns, cracked*
*3 tablespoons onions, puréed and juice drained*
*1¹/₂ cups vegetable oil*
*¹/₄ cup white vinegar*
*3 cups fresh greens, spring mix*
*bacon, cooked crisp and crumbled, for topping*
*Romano cheese, freshly grated, for topping*

1. In a food processor, purée the egg, salt and pepper. Add the onions. Purée the mixture until it becomes fluffy and thick.

2. With the processor on, add the oil to the mixture in a steady stream.

3. When the mixture starts to thicken, add the vinegar slowly to thin the dressing to the right consistency. You may not need the full cup.

4. Toss the greens with the dressing.

5. Sprinkle the bacon and cheese on top, to your liking.

**Makes 2 cups**

### The Origins of Peppercorns

There are three basic types of peppercorns—black, white and green. Black pepper corns have the strongest flavor of the three—a hot taste with a slight sweetness. Green peppercorns, the soft under-ripe berry of the pepper plant, are usually preserved in brine. White peppercorns have a mild flavor and are used in white sauces or light colored foods instead of dark pepper.

## Blue Cheese Basics

Blue-green veins give blue cheese its distinctive appearance and strong flavor and aroma, which becomes bolder when aged. The most popular varieties of blue cheese include Gorgonzola, Roquefort and Stilton. Besides getting crumbled over salads or as part of a dressing, blue cheese is delicious eaten with apples and pears or served with Port or a dessert wine at the end of a meal.

# Balsamic Blue Cheese Dressing

*1 cup olive oil*
*$^1/_3$ cup balsamic vinegar*
*1 tablespoon Dijon mustard*
*1 tablespoon white wine*
*1 tablespoon lemon juice*
*salt and freshly ground pepper, for seasoning*
*$^1/_4$ cup blue cheese, crumbled*

1. Whisk all of the ingredients—except the cheese—together.

2. Five minutes before serving, add the crumbled blue cheese and mix well.

**Makes 1$^1/_2$ cups**

# Mimi's Swiss Vinaigrette

*3 egg yolks*
*3 tablespoons Dijon mustard*
*1 cup vegetable oil*
*3 tablespoons white vinegar*
*1 cup vegetable bouillon*
*salt and freshly ground pepper, for seasoning*
*pinch of nutmeg*

1.  In a food processor, purée the egg yolks and mustard until the mixture gets fluffy and thick.

2.  With the processor on, add the oil to the mixture in a steady stream.

3.  When the mixture starts to thicken, add the vinegar.

4.  To thin the dressing to the right consistency, slowly add the vegetable bouillon. You may not need to use the full cup.

5.  Season with the salt, pepper and nutmeg.

6.  Let the flavors blend for at least 15 minutes, before serving.

**Makes 2 cups**

**Various Vinaigrettes**

A basic vinaigrette consists of oil, vinegar (3 parts oil to 1 part vinegar), salt and pepper, but it can be enhanced by spices or fresh herbs, or in this case made creamy with egg yolks. Most vinaigrettes can be stored, tightly covered in the refrigerator, for up to 2 weeks. Before adding one to a salad, whisk the dressing to rebalance the ingredients or keep it in a jar with a tightly fitting lid so that you can shake to blend it.

# Raspberry Vinaigrette

*¹/₄ cup raspberries, frozen and thawed*
*1 teaspoon Colman's mustard*
*3 egg yolks*
*1 tablespoon shallots, chopped*
*1 cup soy oil*
*1 tablespoon sugar*
*¹/₄ cup cider vinegar*
*1 tablespoon fresh thyme, chopped*
*salt and freshly ground pepper, for seasoning*

1. In a food processor, purée the raspberries and mustard.

2. Add the egg yolks and shallots and continue to purée until the mixture gets fluffy and thick.

3. With the processor on, add the oil to the mixture in a steady stream. The mixture will start to thicken.

4. In a separate bowl, dissolve the sugar in the vinegar.

5. Add the sugared vinegar to the dressing in the food processor.

6. Add the thyme, then season with the salt and freshly ground pepper.

7. Let the flavors blend for 15 minutes before serving.

**Makes 1¹/₂ cups**

# Honey Poppy-Seed Dressing

*³/₄ cup honey*
*1 teaspoon granulated garlic*
*1 teaspoon dry mustard*
*1 teaspoon salt*
*¹/₃ cup Champagne or white wine vinegar*
*1¹/₂ tablespoons onion, puréed*
*1 tablespoon parsley, chopped*
*1 cup vegetable oil*
*1¹/₂ tablespoons poppy seeds*

1.  Combine the honey, garlic, mustard, salt, vinegar, onion purée and parsley in a food processor.

2.  In a steady stream, slowly pour the oil into the mixture.

3.  Transfer the mixture to a bowl. Add the poppy seeds and mix well.

4.  If the dressing is too thick, cut it with water or vinegar.

**Makes approximately 2 cups**

**Poppy Seed Tips**

The blackish-blue poppy seed, with its crunchy texture and nutty flavor, can be purchased whole or ground in most supermarket spice sections. Poppy seeds have a high oil content: To prevent them from turning rancid, store them in an airtight container in the refrigerator for up to 6 months. Toasting poppy seeds is the best way to bring out their flavor.

# Honey Mustard Sauce

*¹/₄ cup brown mustard*
*¹/₄ cup Dijon mustard*
*6 tablespoons white vinegar*
*6 tablespoons honey*
*1 cup vegetable oil*
*2 tablespoons brandy*
*1 cup fresh dill, chopped*
*salt and pepper, to taste*

1. Whisk together the brown mustard, Dijon, white vinegar and honey.

2. In a steady stream, whisk in the oil.

3. Add the brandy and dill. Season with salt and pepper.

**Makes 3 cups**

# Caramel Sauce

*12 ounces granulated sugar*
*1 teaspoon lemon juice*
*¹/₂ cup water*
*1¹/₂ cups heavy cream*
*2 ounces (4 tablespoons) butter*

1. In a heavy saucepan, combine the sugar, lemon juice and water. Bring this mixture to a boil, but do not disturb the pan.

2. Cook the mixture until it turns a caramel color. Carefully remove it from the heat.

3. Carefully stir in the heavy cream and butter.

4. This sauce is best served warm. Store it covered in a cool (not cold) place. To thin it, just add a little milk and stir. It can be reheated in a microwave.

**Makes 2 cups**

**A Word of Caution**

Make sure that you slowly add the cream to the sugar. Adding it too quickly makes it bubble and splash. Extreme care should be taken.

## Who Said Plain Old Vanilla?

Serve this simple, intensely flavored sauce on chocolate desserts, bread puddings, or over fresh fruit.

## Really Raspberry

Fresh raspberries aren't often readily available. A 16-ounce bag of frozen raspberries works just fine for this recipe.

# Vanilla Sauce

*16 ounces half-and-half*
*6 egg yolks*
*1/2 cup sugar*
*2 teaspoons vanilla extract*

1. Scald the half-and-half in a thick-bottom saucepan.

2. Whip the yolks and sugar together until ribboned. Add the extract.

3. Slowly temper the egg mixture with the scalded half-and-half mixture.

4. Return the mixture to a low heat and cook until thickened. Cool.

5. Store the mixture in the refrigerator for up to 2 or 3 days.

**Makes 2 cups**

# Raspberry Sauce

*16 ounces frozen raspberries*
*3/4 cup super fine (quick dissolving) sugar, available at your*
*    supermarket*

1. Purée the fruit and sugar to create a liquid.

2. Strain any seeds through a sieve to make this sauce perfectly smooth.

**Makes 2 cups**

# Sweet Pastry Dough

*8 ounces butter, softened to room temperature*
*4 ounces sugar*
*pinch of salt*
*1 large egg*
*12 ounces flour*

1. Using a mixer, combine the butter, sugar and salt until they are smooth and evenly blended.

2. Stir in the egg. Mix until it is absorbed.

3. Add the flour until a ball forms and the mixture is well blended.

4. Cover it with plastic wrap. Chill for a minimum of 2 hours.

5. Roll out the dough. Form it to fit into a tart pan.

**Makes 1 crust**

**Keep It Cool**

One trick to working successfully with dough is to keep it cool. Once you take the chilled dough out of the refrigerator, work quickly and handle it as little as possible. The warmer it gets, the less stiff (and manageable) it remains.

Hors D'Oeuvres

Mimi's Bruschetta - 29

*Marinated Tomatoes - 30 • Olive Pesto - 30 • Herbed Cream Cheese - 31 • Grilled Sourdough Bread - 31*

Tuna Dip Croutons - 32

Roasted Eggplant Croutons - 33

Eggplant and Goat Cheese Canapés - 34

Mediterranean Canapés - 35

Mediterranean Mushrooms - 36

Stuffed Mushrooms with Crab Imperial - 37

Lobster Asparagus Mousse - 38

Salmon Mousse Canapés - 39

Gravlax on Pumpernickel - 40

Coquille on Horseback - 41

*Horseradish Cream - 41*

Clams Casino - 42

Deviled Clams - 43

Crispy Shrimp Appetizers - 44

Grilled Shrimp with Horseradish, Mustard and Bacon - 45

Shrimp Pancakes - 46

Tzatziki Sauce - 47

Shrimp and Prosciutto Puffs - 48

Spanikopita - 49

Marinated Lamb Kebabs - 50

Grilled Filet Mignon Carpaccio - 51

Duck Breast Prosciutto Canapés - 52

Maple Chicken Lollipops - 53

Grilled Chicken Saté - 54

*Peanut Dipping Sauce - 54*

Thai Stuffed Endive - 55

*Coconut Chili Sauce - 55*

Stuffed Belgian Endive with Gorgonzola and Pecans - 56

Risotto Cakes - 57

Roquefort Grapes - 58

Baked Mussels with Hazelnut Butter - 59

Roasted Red Skin Potatoes with Caviar - 60

## Bruschetta Basics

Here is a great coffee table appetizer and Grange restaurant favorite. These recipes are for several toppings that can be used together or individually on the grilled bread of the bruschetta—all are wonderful! Make the toppings ahead of time, then grill just before guests arrive.

# Mimi's Bruschetta

*Decorative salad greens, such as oriental kale or radicchio*
*Marinated Tomatoes (see page 30)*
*Olive Pesto (see page 30)*
*4 bulbs Roasted Garlic (see page 4)*
*Herbed Cream Cheese (see page 31)*
*Grilled Sourdough Bread (see page 31)*

1.  Line half a plate with decorative salad greens.

2.  Arrange the Marinated Tomatoes, Olive Pesto, Roasted Garlic and Herbed Cream Cheese on the leaves.

3.  Place the Grilled Sourdough Bread on the other side of the plate.

**Makes 12 hors d'oeuvres**

## Wine Notes

 A light Sauvignon Blanc from New Zealand can have great minerally herb flavors that complement all of the different toppings.

# Marinated Tomatoes

*2 cups very ripe tomatoes, chopped*
*1 tablespoon garlic, chopped*
*¹/₄ cup olive oil*
*2 tablespoons balsamic vinegar*
*2 tablespoons fresh basil, sliced in chiffonade*
*¹/₄ teaspoon salt*
*a few grinds of fresh black pepper*

1. Mix all of the ingredients together in a bowl.

2. Allow them to marinate at room temperature for a few hours before serving.

# Olive Pesto

*¹/₂ cup black olives, pitted*
*¹/₄ cup pimento-stuffed green olives*
*2 cloves garlic*
*1 tablespoon capers*
*1 anchovy fillet*
*1 tablespoon parsley, chopped*
*2 to 3 large basil leaves*
*¹/₈ teaspoon black pepper*
*¹/₄ teaspoon salt*
*2 to 3 tablespoons olive oil*

1. Place all of the ingredients—except the olive oil—in the bowl of a food processor. Pulse until all are combined to a coarse paste.

2. With the machine running, add the olive oil through the feed tube.

**Jersey's Best**

Marinated tomatoes taste best when made with perfectly ripe Jersey tomatoes!

**Balsamic Vinegar**

We use quite a lot of this vinegar as it adds a nice zip to sauces, oils and vinaigrettes. The vinegar is made in Italy from a recipe that is hundreds of years old. White grape juice is boiled over a fire for a day and then transferred to wood vats for aging. The vinegar is transferred to different types of wood as it ages. Traditional aged balsamic is both delicious and expensive. It has a complex, syrupy sweet richness. Commercial brands tend to be more watery and less complex in flavor, so we often reduce them down to concentrate the flavors.

**Wine Notes**

Try a Sancerre from France, which has minerally herb flavors. Or try a New Zealand Sauvignon Blanc.

# Herbed Cream Cheese

*1 8-ounce package of cream cheese, room temperature*
*¹/₄ teaspoon granulated garlic*
*1 teaspoon dried marjoram*
*¹/₂ teaspoon thyme*
*10 grinds of fresh black pepper*

1. Combine all of the ingredients in the bowl of a food processor.

2. Blend until the mixture is smooth.

3. If necessary, thin with a bit of olive oil.

# Grilled Sourdough Bread

1. Slice a loaf of sourdough bread on the diagonal, allowing 2 or 3 slices per person. Each slice is approximately ¹/₃-inch thick.

2. Brush these lightly on one side with olive oil.

3. Grill over an open flame or toast in the oven under the broiler, with the oil-brushed side toward the flame.

# Tuna Dip Croutons

20 French bread croutons (see sidebar)
chopped parsley or capers, for garnish

*Dip*
*1/2 pound fresh tuna, cooked*
*1/2 cup butter*
*juice of 1 lemon*
*salt and pepper, for seasoning*

1.  Purée all of the dip ingredients in a food processor.

2.  Spread the dip on the croutons, and place them on a serving tray.

3.  Garnish with chopped parsley or capers.

**Makes 20 croutons**

---

**French Bread Croutons**

To make French bread croutons, cut a loaf of French bread into thin slices (about 1/4-inch each) and lightly butter both sides of the slices. Because French bread is round, the cut slices create round croutons. You can cut them into smaller cubes and remove the crusts, if desired. Bake the bread on a baking sheet in a preheated, 350°F oven, turning the rounds or cubes over until evenly browned on all sides.

To flavor the croutons, a minced clove of garlic or finely chopped fresh herbs can be mixed into the butter before spreading it on the bread.

**Wine Notes**

 A light Beaujolais or Dolcetto is the perfect match for this spread.

## Toasted Bread Basics

Toasted bread with a variety of savory toppings is quickly becoming a favorite at restaurants. When served on a larger piece of bread, this tasty snack is called bruschetta. A smaller piece is called crostini. This version takes the traditional tomato topping and adds smoky roasted eggplant purée, which is perfect for spreading on bread. Garlic fans can cut slits into the eggplant before roasting them and fill them with sliced garlic for even more flavor.

## Wine Notes

 The wine Arneis from Piedmont, Italy, is light-bodied with crisp almond and apple flavors. Also try a grassy Sauvignon Blanc from the Central Coast of California.

# Roasted Eggplant Croutons

*3 large eggplants*
*1 cup olive oil*
*1 1/2 tablespoons garlic, chopped*
*1/4 cup red wine vinegar*
*2 tablespoons capers, drained and chopped*
*2 anchovy fillets (optional)*
*salt and freshly ground pepper, for seasoning*
*1/4 cup parsley, chopped*
*25 French bread round croutons, freshly toasted (see page 32)*
*1 cup fresh tomato, chopped*

1. Preheat the oven to 400°F.

2. Prick the eggplants, then cook them in a 400°F oven for 1 hour. Remove them when they are soft and cooked all the way through.

3. Sauté the garlic in 1 tablespoon of olive oil for 1 minute, until soft. Do not overcook or brown.

4. Scoop out the eggplant pulp and place it in a food processor with the garlic. Pulse it until the mixture is roughly puréed.

5. Add the remaining olive oil, vinegar, capers, anchovies and parsley. Season with the salt and pepper.

6. Refrigerate for 1 hour.

7. Spoon the mixture onto the croutons. Top with the tomatoes and serve.

**Makes 25 croutons**

# Eggplant and Goat Cheese Canapés

*¹/₄ cup fresh basil, chopped*
*2 teaspoons balsamic vinegar*
*¹/₃ cup olive oil*
*salt and pepper, for seasoning*
*1 large eggplant, cut lengthwise into 6 ¹/₂-inch slices*
*¹/₄ cup sun-dried tomatoes, cut finely, julienne style*
*¹/₈ cup roasted peppers, cut finely, julienne style*
*9 ounces goat cheese, softened*
*1 cup cilantro, chopped*

1. Combine the basil, vinegar and olive oil in a mixing bowl.

2. Season with salt and pepper.

3. Heat the grill or broiler.

4. Brush the eggplant slices with the oil mixture.

5. Grill or broil the eggplant until the slices are golden brown (approximately 4 minutes per side). Be careful that you do not burn them.

6. Combine the tomatoes, peppers and goat cheese.

7. Spread the cheese mixture over the eggplant slices. Roll them inward, lengthwise.

8. Cut the rolls on a bias.

9. Dip the ends in the cilantro, then place them on a platter. Refrigerate for 30 minutes.

**Makes 12 canapés**

## Care for a Canapé?

The word canapé appears often when talking about hors d'oeuvres. Although it typically refers to a piece of bread topped with any delicacy, it can mean any tasty tidbit served as an appetizer or hors d'oeuvre. This recipe uses eggplant, instead of bread, as a foundation for the filling.

When this recipe refers to cutting the eggplant rolls "on a bias," it's suggesting that you slice the roll at an angle rather than at a straight up-and-down, perpendicular cut. The angled cut creates added visual appeal.

## Wine Notes

Try a Graves-like white wine, such as a Sonoma Sauvignon Blanc or a Sémillon blend from Washington State.

## Marinate Means...

*Webster's* uses the word "pickle" as one definition for "marinate." More commonly, marinate means to allow an ingredient to season in a special dressing in order to absorb the additional flavors.

In this recipe, when marinating the tomatoes, you can put the mixture in the refrigerator or leave it at room temperature.

## Wine Notes

 A lighter style red, such as a Dolcetto or Beaujolais, served chilled, is a good selection.

# Mediterranean Canapés

*5-10 plum tomatoes*
*1¹/₂ cups olive oil*
*1 cup balsamic vinegar*
*1 teaspoon fresh garlic*
*2 sprigs rosemary, finely chopped*
*salt, to taste*
*black pepper, to taste*
*1 loaf French bread baguette, thinly sliced*
*4 tablespoons butter, melted*
*granulated garlic, to taste*
*20 slices of cheese (provolone, mozzarella, or fontina), ¹/₄-inch slices*
*¹/₄ cup fresh parsley, finely chopped, for garnish*

1.  Slice the plum tomatoes lengthwise to get about 8 slices per tomato.

2.  Marinate the tomatoes in the olive oil, balsamic vinegar, fresh garlic, rosemary, salt and pepper for a minimum of 5 hours.

3.  Brush the bread slices with butter, then season them with salt, pepper and granulated garlic.

4.  To create the croutons, spread the slices out on a baking sheet and toast them in a 375°F oven until they are golden and crisp (approximately 5 to 10 minutes).

5.  When the croutons have cooled, place a slice of drained, but still moist, tomato on each crouton. Cover each with a half slice of cheese.

6.  Place these croutons in a 375°F oven until the cheese melts.

7.  Remove them from the oven and sprinkle with the chopped parsley.

8.  Place them on a tray and serve while hot or until they reach room temperature.

**Makes approximately 30 canapés**

# Mediterranean Mushrooms

*1 tablespoon olive oil*
*¹/₂ cup onion, diced*
*2 tablespoons white wine*
*1 cup heavy cream*
*¹/₂ tablespoon garlic*
*3 tablespoons sun-dried tomatoes, moistened and chopped*
*6 cups spinach, packed and chopped*
*¹/₂ cup Romano cheese*
*1 egg*
*4 tablespoons bread crumbs*
*salt and freshly ground pepper, for seasoning*
*30 mushrooms, medium to large, cleaned*

1. Sauté the onion in ¹/₂ tablespoon of the oil. Add the wine and reduce. Add the cream and reduce until it thickens (approximately 15 minutes). Cool.

2. In a separate pan, sauté the garlic, tomatoes and spinach in the remaining oil. When soft, remove this mixture from the heat and squeeze out any excess water.

3. Combine all of the ingredients—except the mushrooms—and mix well. (Add more cream if the spinach mixture seems too dry.)

4. Preheat the oven to 375°F.

5. Remove the mushroom stems.

6. Stuff the caps with the spinach mixture and place them on an ungreased baking sheet.

7. Bake for 10 to 12 minutes. Serve hot.

**Makes 30 hors d'oeuvres**

## Fresh Mushrooms

To choose the freshest mushrooms for this tasty treat, look for ones with their tops tightly curved underneath. If you can see too much of the mushroom's gills, they are older. Older mushrooms have a stronger taste that can overpower other foods. They are better suited for soups or dishes where you want a strong mushroom flavor.

Assemble the mushrooms ahead of time, place them on a baking sheet, then pop them in the oven just before guests arrive.

## Wine Notes

A Soave or Orvieto from Italy goes well with these Mediterranean components. The citrus fruit of these wines cleanses the palate nicely.

## Crab Meat Galore

On the East coast the leading fresh variety of crab meat sold is Atlantic blue crab, while on the Pacific coast Dungeness dominates. Most frozen crab meat is from Alaska king crabs or snow crabs, which are harvested in the north of either coast. Both of these varieties are available year-round.

## Wine Notes

 This dish is rich, and needs rich flavors to stand up to and complement it. Try a medium-bodied Chardonnay from Australia or California.

# Stuffed Mushrooms
## with Crab Imperial

*3 tablespoons butter*
*$^1$/8 cup onion, diced*
*$^1$/8 cup red pepper, diced*
*$^1$/8 cup green pepper, diced*
*1 teaspoon dry mustard*
*2 tablespoons white wine*
*1 cup mayonnaise*
*1 egg*
*$^1$/2 pound crab meat*
*salt and freshly ground pepper, for seasoning*
*30 mushrooms, medium to large, cleaned*

1. Sauté the onions and peppers in butter until al dente.

2. Add the mustard and wine and reduce. Cool.

3. Add the mayonnaise and egg, and mix together with a whisk.

4. Fold the mixture into the crab meat.

5. Season with the salt and pepper.

6. Preheat the oven to 375°F.

7. Remove the mushroom stems.

8. Stuff the mushroom caps with the crab mixture. Place them on an ungreased baking sheet.

9. Bake for 15 minutes, until golden brown.

**Makes 30 hors d'oeuvres**

# Lobster Asparagus Mousse

1¹/2 cups fresh, cooked or canned asparagus
2 envelopes gelatin
¹/2 cup water
1 can (8 ounces) cream of asparagus soup
1¹/2 pounds cream cheese
1 teaspoon celery seed
¹/2 cup onion, chopped
1 cup mayonnaise
11 ounces lobster meat, in small chunks
¹/2 teaspoon salt
¹/4 teaspoon white pepper
French bread round croutons (see page 32)

1. Purée the asparagus in a little liquid (a few tablespoons of water or canning juices work fine).

2. Sprinkle the gelatin in ¹/2 cup of water. Set aside.

3. Combine the soup, cream cheese and gelatin over low heat, stirring until blended and smooth. Remove it from the heat.

4. Add the purée and stir.

5. Add the remaining ingredients and stir.

6. Pour the mixture into a decorative mold.

7. Refrigerate overnight.

8. Unmold the mousse and decorate it as you like.

9. Serve with toasted French bread crouton rounds.

**Makes 20 servings**

## Molding a Mousse

This impressive party dish is easy to make if you have the right mold. The best way to quickly chill, set and release a gelatin-based mousse is by using a copper, tin or stainless steel mold. Choose a mold with simple, clean lines, as these reproduce neatly when the filling is released. Decorative molds are available in all kinds of shapes. Pick something seasonal for a holiday gathering or something classic, such as a fish or star mold, for other occasions.

## Wine Notes

 A medium- to full-bodied Sonoma Chardonnay is rich enough to balance with the lobster.

## Making a Pastry Bag

If you don't have a pastry bag, a sealable plastic bag also works when making these canapés. Fill the bag with the salmon mousse, seal, then snip off a corner of the bag with scissors. Squeeze the bag gently to pipe mousse onto each crouton. This method works for almost any spread that requires a pastry bag, but the results are not as fancy. This homemade technique just doesn't have the same decorating effects that the special tips on a pastry bag can produce.

## Wine Notes

 A sparkling wine from Sonoma-Mendocino cuts through the rich flavors of the smoked salmon.

# Salmon Mousse Canapés

*1/2 pound smoked salmon*
*3/4 cups heavy cream*
*salt and pepper, to taste*
*pinch of cayénne pepper*
*1 loaf of French bread*
*4 tablespoons butter, melted*

1. Place the smoked salmon in a food processor on high speed.

2. Add the cream slowly. Season with the salt and peppers.

3. Chill for 1 hour.

4. Preheat the oven to 375°F.

5. Slice the bread at a slight angle to make 1/4-inch croutons.

6. Brush both sides of the bread with the melted butter. Bake them until they are golden brown (approximately 10 to 15 minutes). Cool.

7. With a pastry bag, pipe the mousse onto each crouton.

8. Garnish with fresh herbs.

**Makes 25 canapés**

# Gravlax on Pumpernickel

*¹/₄ cup salt, kosher*
*3 tablespoons white peppercorns*
*5 tablespoons sugar*
*1 4-pound salmon fillet, with the skin on*
*4 bunches of fresh dill, with the large stems removed*
*pumpernickel bread, sliced into 50 small rounds*
*Honey Mustard Sauce (see page 23)*
*fresh dill, for garnish*

1. Mix the salt, pepper and sugar. Rub the salmon completely with this mixture.

2. Place the salmon, skin-side down, in a baking pan.

3. Lay the bunches of dill on top of the salmon, covering it completely.

4. Place another pan on top of the salmon. Place something heavy on top of this second pan to weigh it down.

5. Refrigerate for 6 hours. Drain the liquid from the baking pan and flip the fish over. (The dill is now on the bottom of the pan.) Replace the weight and refrigerate for 48 to 72 hours.

6. Drain the liquid, remove the weight and pat the salmon dry.

7. Slice the salmon on the bias, diagonally.

8. Place each slice onto a bread round.

9. Top with a dollop of Honey Mustard Sauce.

10. Garnish with fresh dill.

**Makes 50 canapés**

---

**Gravlax Facts**

Gravlax is raw salmon traditionally cured in the Swedish style using salt, sugar and dill, then sliced paper thin and served on good dark bread. Only buy the freshest fish to make this easy-to-prepare delicacy. To slice the cured salmon as thin as possible, use a long, thin-bladed knife. Special smoked salmon knives are available in most kitchen stores.

Once made, gravlax, covered well, keeps several days in the refrigerator. You also can find gravlax at gourmet markets and specialty stores.

**Wine Notes**

 Sparkling wine is my favorite with cured salmon. Try a dry Spanish Cava or a dry sparkling Chenin Blanc from Vouvray.

## Tips for Buying Scallops

*Coquilles* is the French name for scallops. Fresh scallops should have a sweet smell; they should not have any fishy aroma.

Fresh scallops have a dry or sticky type of appearance. Avoid scallops that are bright white and have a bloated look to them. Fish purveyors may soak the scallops to give them extra weight and to help preserve them.

Soaked scallops shrink up considerably during cooking. These scallops also are difficult to brown and sear because of all the liquid that comes out. Quick cooking is best for scallops.

Do not overcrowd the scallops in the pan if you are attempting to sear and brown them.

## Wine Notes

 A clean, crisp Pinot Grigio or Pinot Bianco from Italy are delicious. Also try a dry Pinot Blanc from Alsace.

# Coquille on Horseback
## with Horseradish Cream

*12-18 slices of bacon, best quality*
*24 medium sea scallops*
*Horseradish Cream (below)*
*fresh parsley, chopped, for garnish*

1. Place the bacon on a baking pan and bake at 350°F, until it is half cooked, not crisp. Let it cool, then cut the strips in half.

2. Wrap the bacon around the scallops, and place these on the baking sheet. Use a toothpick to hold them together if needed.

3. Bake in a 400°F oven for 10 to 15 minutes, until the bacon is crisp. Remove from the oven.

4. Spoon the Horseradish Cream onto the plate and arrange 4 scallops on top.

5. Garnish with the chopped parsley.

## Horseradish Cream

*1 cup sour cream*
*¹/₂ cup mayonnaise*
*¹/₂ cup horseradish, drained*
*dash of Worcestershire sauce*
*juice of ¹/₂ lemon*
*salt and pepper, for seasoning*

1. Using a wire whisk, mix together all of the ingredients.

2. Refrigerate for 1 hour to blend the flavors.

**Serves 6**

# Clams Casino

*¹/₂ pound bacon, chopped*
*1 large onion, chopped*
*1 green pepper, chopped*
*1 red pepper, chopped*
*juice of 2 lemons*
*2 tablespoons Worcestershire sauce*
*dash of Tabasco*
*¹/₂ teaspoon dry mustard*
*salt and pepper, for seasoning*
*25 top neck clams, shucked*

1.  Cook the bacon in a large pan, sautéing it until brown.

2.  Add the onions and peppers. Sauté for 5 minutes.

3.  Season with the lemon juice, Worcestershire sauce, Tabasco, mustard, salt and pepper.

4.  Let the mix cool.

5.  Preheat the oven to 450°F.

6.  Top each clam with 1 heaping tablespoon of the mix.

7.  Bake for 15 minutes. Put under the broiler for a few minutes to finish them off with a crisp top.

**Makes 25 clams**

## Opening Clams

Colorful and appealing, this restaurant favorite is just as easy to enjoy at home because you can assemble the clams and then bake them just before serving. Open the clams using a clam knife or any sturdy short-bladed knife. Hold the clam in the palm of one hand and, with the other, insert the knife between the two shells near the hinge. Run the knife between the shells, using a twisting motion to pry the shells apart.

## Wine Notes

A young crisp Chablis from Burgundy (from a Chardonnay grape) has the acidic backbone that works beautifully with the salty richness of the clams.

# Deviled Clams

## Deviled Means...

This clam dish is a traditional East Coast favorite. The term "deviled" is used to describe dishes that contain dry mustard, Worcestershire sauce, Tabasco and pepper. In our area, deviled clams and crabs are very popular.

*2 cups clam juice*
*12 clams, top necks, shucked and chopped, reserve the clam shells*
*1 small onion, finely diced*
*$^1/_4$ cup white wine*
*$^1/_2$ cup butter*
*1 large rib celery, finely diced*
*1 green pepper, finely diced*
*2 teaspoons dried mustard*
*dash of Tabasco*
*dash of Worcestershire sauce*
*1 teaspoon ground thyme*
*2 teaspoons salt*
*freshly ground pepper, for seasoning*
*$^1/_2$ cup flour*
*1 cup bread crumbs*

1. Heat the clam juice and chopped clams to a boil. Remove from the flame and strain. Reserve the juice.

2. In a medium saucepan, reduce the onions in the wine until they are just moist. Add the butter, celery and peppers. Cook until tender, for about 4 minutes.

3. Add the mustard, Tabasco, Worcestershire, thyme, salt and pepper.

4. Slowly add the flour into the butter-vegetable mixture to create a thick roux.

5. Slowly add the clam juice into the roux. Mix it until it is well blended and thick.

6. Add the cooked clams and mix well. Cook for approximately 10 minutes. Cool the mixture.

7. Fill the clam shells, giving them a smooth finish. Sprinkle with bread crumbs. Dollop with butter if you desire.

8. Bake for 15 minutes at 350°F.

**Makes 24 hors d'oeuvres**

## Wine Notes

 A Loire Valley Sauvignon Blanc matches the sea flavors of the clams. Sancerre, Pouilly Fumé or Menetou Salon are all fine choices.

# Crispy Shrimp Appetizers

*25 shrimp, peeled and deveined, 21-25 count*
*3¹/₂ tablespoons olive oil*
*3¹/₂ tablespoons vegetable oil*
*²/₃ cup fine bread crumbs*
*¹/₂ teaspoon garlic*
*1 tablespoon parsley*
*³/₄ teaspoon salt*
*freshly ground pepper, for seasoning*

1. Rinse and dry the shrimp. Place them in a bowl.

2. Add the oils to the shrimp and toss.

3. Slowly stir in the bread crumbs to give the shrimp a nice, light coating.

4. Add the remaining ingredients and mix well.

5. Marinate for 30 minutes.

6. Preheat the broiler.

7. Place the shrimp on skewers.

8. Cook the shrimp for approximately 2 minutes on each side. Be careful not to burn the coating.

9. Serve with wedges of lemon or your favorite dip.

**Makes 25 hors d'oeuvres or 5 appetizers**

---

**The Best Bread Crumbs**

The best bread crumbs are homemade. To make your own, take some good stale bread and place slices of it on a baking sheet in a warm oven (about 200°F) for an hour or two until the bread dries out, but is not brown. Take the bread out and grind it into crumbs in a food processor. If a recipe calls for toasted bread crumbs, spread the crumbs on a baking sheet and bake at 375°F for 10 minutes. You can season the bread crumbs with any flavor you like by heating them in a skillet with butter, fresh or dried herbs, or grated cheese.

**Wine Notes**

 Try a crisp Pinot Bianco from the Friuli area of Italy. The citrus fruit works well with the garlic and shrimp flavors.

# Grilled Shrimp
## with Horseradish, Mustard and Bacon

*20 shrimp, peeled and deveined, 21-25 count*
*2 tablespoons olive oil*
*3 tablespoons mustard*
*3 tablespoons horseradish*
*1/2 teaspoon garlic*
*1 tablespoon parsley*
*fresh pepper, for seasoning*
*2/3 cup bread crumbs, fine*
*8 slices of bacon*
*2 lemons, sliced, for garnish*

1. Put the bacon in a preheated 350°F oven for 10 minutes. Remove it and cut it into thirds.

2. Dry the shrimp and place them in a bowl.

3. Add all of the ingredients—except the crumbs and bacon. Toss.

4. Slowly add the bread crumbs to give the shrimp a nice light coating.

5. Wrap each shrimp with bacon. Secure it with a toothpick, if necessary.

6. Place the shrimp on a hot grill.

7. Cook the shrimp for 2 minutes on each side. Be careful not to burn the bacon.

8. Serve on a platter with fresh sliced lemon.

**Makes 20 shrimp**

# Shrimp Pancakes

*3 tablespoons olive oil*
*3 tablespoons onion, finely chopped*
*2 tablespoons parsley, chopped*
*1/8 teaspoon paprika*
*6 tablespoons flour*
*7 tablespoons water*
*3/4 teaspoon salt*
*1/2 teaspoon baking powder*
*1/2 pound shrimp, chopped*
*oil for frying (approximately 1/2 cup)*
*Tzatziki Sauce (see page 47)*

1. In olive oil, sauté the onions until they are soft and lightly browned.

2. Add the parsley and paprika.

3. In a bowl, mix the flour, water, salt and baking powder.

4. Add the onion mixture and shrimp. Mix.

5. Heat the additional oil, approximately 1/2 cup, in a skillet until hot.

6. Drop the batter into the pan, a few tablespoons at a time. Flatten the cakes to 2-inch rounds.

7. Remove the cooked pancakes to a paper towel, then place them on a platter. Serve hot with Tzatziki Sauce.

**Makes 10 small pancakes**

**A Mediterranean Mix**

This Spanish recipe is from Cádiz, a spanish town that sits on the Mediterranean Sea. It is famous for its seafood and for being sacked by other countries. We serve this with the Tzatziki Sauce (see page 47). Even though the sauce is Greek, it maintains the Mediterranean theme.

**Wine Notes**

I enjoy this dish with a Muscadet from France. Its high acidity and lemony flavors create a natural contrast to the cakes.

**Amazing Tzatziki**

This dip is a refreshing Greek mixture made of yogurt and cucumber. It goes great with seasoned croutons or makes a tasty dip for vegetables. Tzatziki also is a wonderful complement to fish, lamb and barbecued meats. To make a nice base for a vegetable salad, just toss vegetables, cooked al dente, into the sauce.

# Tzatziki Sauce
## (Yogurt and Cucumber Dressing)

6 cucumbers, peeled, seeded and grated
1 tablespoon kosher salt
1 pint yogurt
1 cup sour cream
1 tablespoon red wine vinegar
$^1/_2$ cup extra virgin olive oil
1 teaspoon sugar
2 teaspoons fresh garlic, chopped fine
1 tablespoon fresh dill, chopped

1.  Mix the cucumbers and salt. Let sit for at least 3 hours.

2.  Rinse the salt off the cucumber and pat it dry or let it drain thoroughly.

3.  Combine all of the ingredients and serve.

**Makes 1$^1/_2$ pints**

# *Shrimp and Prosciutto Puffs*

*1 egg*
*2 tablespoons cold water*
*8 ounces cooked shrimp, roughly chopped*
*¹/₂ cup Parmesan cheese, grated*
*¹/₄ cup Monterey Jack cheese, grated*
*3 ounces prosciutto ham, sliced and chopped*
*freshly ground pepper, for seasoning*
*4 puff pastry squares, each 5"x 5"*

1. Make an egg wash by beating together the egg and water.

2. Mix the shrimp, cheese and ham together. Season with the pepper.

3. Lay out the puff pastry squares and cut each square into 4 smaller squares, forming a total of 16 2- by 2-inch squares.

4. Place a dollop of the shrimp mix in the center of a square. Pull the corners of the square together and pinch.

5. Brush the folds with egg wash, then seal the edges. Make sure that the seal is good.

6. Place the pastries seam-side down on a cookie sheet. Bake in a 450°F oven for 15 minutes. Serve hot.

**Makes 16 puffs**

## Lovely Layers

Puff pastry combines butter and flour in a special way, by placing a chunk of butter in the middle of rolled out dough, folding it, and then rolling it out again. The process of folding the dough and rolling it out is repeated several times, to create hundreds of light, flaky layers with butter between each one!

If this sounds complicated to you, don't despair! You can buy pre-made puff pastry. Both homemade and store-bought puff pastry freeze well.

## Wine Notes

A Pinot Gris or Pinot Blanc from Oregon cuts the richness of the prosciutto and cheese flavors.

**Phyllo Facts**

Spanikopita is the traditional Greek spinach and cheese pie made with phyllo dough, which is available frozen at most grocery stores or fresh from Greek or Middle Eastern bakeries.

Phyllo can be tricky to work with—the key is to keep the sheets from drying out. If using frozen phyllo, thaw it, still wrapped, in the refrigerator for several hours or overnight. Once the phyllo is thawed, unwrap it and remove the number of sheets required for the recipe. Rewrap the remaining phyllo and return it to the refrigerator or freezer. Stack the sheets you are using on plastic wrap. Cover the stack with another sheet of plastic to seal in the moisture, then cover this wrap with a damp towel. Remove the sheets one at a time and always recover the remaining stack. Phyllo left uncovered dries immediately and cracks.

**Wine Notes**

 Try a dry white Graves or a Napa Valley Sauvignon Blanc with a nice herbal character.

# *Spanikopita*

*¹/₂ cup onion, diced*
*1 tablespoon butter*
*1 stick (¹/₄ pound) butter, melted*
*1 pound fresh spinach, cleaned and chopped*
*1 cup feta cheese*
*pinch of nutmeg*
*juice of 1 lemon*
*1 egg, whole*
*salt and pepper, for seasoning*
*10 sheets phyllo dough*

1.  Sauté the onion in 1 tablespoon of butter until it is translucent. Add the spinach to the butter and sauté it until cooked.

2.  In a mixing bowl, crumble the feta, then add the onion and spinach mixture. Mix in the nutmeg, lemon juice and egg. Season with the salt and pepper.

3.  Lay out 1 sheet of phyllo and brush it with melted butter. Place another sheet of phyllo on top and brush it with butter. Repeat this process one more time so you have a stack of 3 sheets. Cut this stack into 4 lengthwise strips.

4.  Place approximately 2 tablespoons of the spinach mixture on the lower right-hand corner of 1 strip.

5.  Fold the corner containing the mixture into a triangle, which you keep folding up the entire lenth of the strip, just like a paper football. The corner containing the mixture folds up and across to the opposite edge, always maintaining a right angle where the next fold occurs. The final fold forms a right triangle.

6.  Brush melted butter on both sides of this triangle.

7.  Use the remaining 3 strips to make 3 more triangles. Then continue repeating steps 3 through 6 until you have a total of 20 triangles.

8.  Place the triangles on an ungreased baking sheet and bake in a preheated, 350°F oven until golden brown (approximately 10 to 15 minutes).

**Makes 20 triangles**

# Marinated Lamb Kebabs

*¹/₄ cup olive oil*
*juice of 1 lemon*
*¹/₈ cup fresh rosemary*
*¹/₂ tablespoon salt, kosher*
*freshly ground pepper, for seasoning*
*2 pounds lamb, cut into ³/₄-inch cubes*
*2 cups onion, cut into ³/₄-inch cubes*

*40 wooden skewers, soaked in water for 3 hours*

1.  Mix the olive oil, lemon, rosemary, salt and pepper.

2.  Toss in the lamb cubes and marinate overnight.

3.  Place the cubes of lamb and onion onto the skewers.

4.  Place them on a hot grill and cook for 4 minutes, turning frequently.
    (Watch that the skewers do not burn.)

**Makes 40 pieces**

## Simple Accompaniments

A quick turn on the grill is all it takes to make these easy kebabs. Marinating them the night before ensures that the lamb is tender and flavorful. Serve these kebabs with warm pita bread, Tzatziki Sauce (see page 47) and a salad of cucumbers, red onions, and tomatoes topped with some crumbled feta cheese and a red wine vinaigrette.

## Wine Notes

 A medium-bodied Zinfandel with a dry berry fruit from the Northern California Coast is tannic enough to hold up to the flavors of the marinade.

# Grilled Filet Mignon Carpaccio

*1 pound filet mignon*
*salt and pepper, for seasoning*
*30 French bread round croutons, toasted (see page 32)*

## Sauce
*2 tablespoons white vinegar*
*3 tablespoons dill gherkins, chopped*
*1 cup parsley, chopped*
*1/2 tablespoon garlic, chopped*
*1 anchovy fillet*
*1/4 cup capers, drained*
*2 tablespoons onion, chopped*
*3 tablespoons Dijon mustard*
*6 tablespoons olive oil*

1. Mix and chop all of the sauce ingredients in a food processor, except for the oil.

2. Pour the olive oil into the processor in a slow, steady stream. (The resulting sauce should have a creamy consistency.)

3. Season the filet mignon with salt and pepper. Place it on the grill and cook it for 20 minutes, turning frequently. After removing, let it stand to reach room temperature.

4. Cut the filet mignon into thin slices. Place the slices on the croutons.

5. Top with a dollop of the sauce.

6. Place the croutons on a serving tray.

**Makes 30 croutons**

## Serving Suggestions

We usually serve grilled carpaccio on toasted French bread. It also tastes delicious served on a bed of arugula or watercress with shaved aged Parmesan or over thinly sliced tomatoes and red onions. For a wonderful, simple meal, serve carpaccio over a bed of greens topped with a drizzle of extra virgin olive oil and freshly ground black pepper.

## Wine Notes

Try an Italian Chianti, Sangiovese or medium-bodied Super Tuscan with this dish.

# Duck Breast Prosciutto Canapés

*1 1-pound duck breast*
*1 tablespoon kosher salt*
*¹/₂ teaspoon dried thyme*
*¹/₂ teaspoon fresh rosemary, finely chopped*
*1 bay leaf, ground with a mortar and pestle*
*1 teaspoon coriander seeds*
*1 teaspoon black peppercorns, coarsely ground*
*25 French bread round croutons (see page 32)*

*1 package cheesecloth*

1. Trim the duck breast of the excess skin, tenderloin and fat.

2. Combine the spices and herbs. Be sure to use 1 tablespoon of salt for each pound of duck breast.

3. Rub the salt mix into the duck breast.

4. Place the seasoned duck on a plate and wrap it tightly with plastic wrap. Let it sit in the refrigerator for 48 hours.

5. Using a paring knife, scrape off the salt rub.

6. Wrap the duck well with cheesecloth. Hang it in the refrigerator for 21 to 30 days.

7. Remove the cheesecloth and scrape off any white bloom. Trim the fat.

8. Wrap in plastic wrap and freeze.

9. Slice paper thin while still frozen. Serve on croutons.

**Makes 25 hors d'oeuvres**

## Homemade Prosciutto

This is a make-ahead hors d'oeuvre—for the truly adventurous!

## Wine Notes

 An earthy Pinot Noir from Oregon pairs nicely with the salty flavors of the duck.

**True Tamari**

Tamari is the Japanese variety of soy sauce, the type served with sushi and sashimi. Slightly different than Chinese soy sauce, it has a thicker consistency, darker color and more mellow flavor. Made from soy beans, tamari soy sauce is used for dipping as well as basting.

# Maple Chicken Lollipops

*3¹/₂ pounds chicken wings, cut into halves at the joint*
*¹/₄ cup toasted sesame seeds*

## Marinade
*2 teaspoons garlic, chopped*
*¹/₄ cup green onions, chopped*
*¹/₂ teaspoon ginger, grated*
*1 cup maple syrup*
*¹/₄ cup tamari (good quality soy sauce)*

1.  Mix all of the marinade ingredients together for 1 hour.

2.  Sort the chicken wings, using the "mini drums" for this recipe. (You can use the wing tips for making stock.)

3.  Loosen the meat from the knob by cutting around the bone.

4.  Pull the meat down so that it looks like a lollipop.

5.  Marinate the chicken with the meat facing down (to prevent the bones from getting in the marinade).

6.  Preheat the oven to 375°F.

7.  Place the wings on a baking sheet and bake for 15 to 20 minutes.

8.  Remove them from the oven. Sprinkle the seeds over the wings. Serve immediately.

**Makes 40 wings**

**Wine Notes**

 An off-dry Vouvray from the Loire Valley of France matches up nicely with the maple flavors of this glaze.

# Grilled Chicken Saté
## with Peanut Dipping Sauce

*3 chicken breasts, boneless, 8 ounces each*
*salt and freshly ground pepper, for seasoning*
*Peanut Dipping Sauce (below)*
*1 cup chopped greens, such as a spring mix*

*25 wooden skewers, soaked in water overnight*

1. Cut the chicken breasts into 1¹/₂-inch cubes. Season with the salt and pepper.

2. Put the chicken onto skewers and place them on a hot grill. (Be careful not to burn the wooden skewers.)

3. Place the chicken over the chopped greens on a round serving tray, with a bowl of Peanut Dipping Sauce in the center.

## Peanut Dipping Sauce

*1¹/₂ cups peanut butter*
*4 tablespoons unsalted peanuts, chopped*
*¹/₂ tablespoon sugar*
*1 tablespoon lemon juice*
*¹/₄ cup cream of coconut milk*
*¹/₄ cup soy sauce*
*¹/₃ cup water*
*¹/₂ teaspoon cumin*
*¹/₂ teaspoon coriander*
*pinch of garlic powder*
*pinch of red pepper flakes*

1. In a saucepan, simmer all of the ingredients over a low heat for a few minutes.

2. Serve warm or at room temperature.

**Makes 25 hors d'oeuvres**

**Saté Sides**

This is the best recipe for saté that we have used. It has good depth of flavor and is perfect for hors d'oeuvres. Also known as satay, the term refers to marinated cubes of meat, fish or poultry threaded on skewers and grilled. This Thai favorite is traditionally served with peanut sauce, usually on a bed of shredded carrots and bean sprouts. A side dish of paper-thin sliced cucumber in a light vinaigrette makes a wonderful accompaniment. Several satays together can be served as a main dish.

**Wine Notes**

Try a Chenin Blanc with a crisp, minerally character, such as one from Vouvray or California.

## Thai Ingredients

This recipe comes from Chef George Pechin of Peaches Restaurant, a famous Cape May establishment. We served these for Mimi's wedding. They are always a favorite!

Thai fish sauce is often considered the single most important ingredient in Thai cooking. Made from anchovy extract and sea salt, it is used in many traditional Thai dishes, such as pad Thai.

Another important Thai ingredient used in this recipe is lemongrass. The herb is available fresh or dried in Asian markets. It is used to make tea and to flavor soups and other dishes. Lemongrass has long, thin gray-green leaves and a scallion-like base.

## Wine Notes

Alsatian wines go well with this dish. Try a Gewürztraminer, Riesling or Sylvaner. Their dry crisp fruit holds up to the strong Thai flavors.

# Thai Stuffed Endive
## with Coconut Chili Sauce

Coconut Chili Sauce (recipe below)
4 heads Belgian endive, separated
$^1/_2$ cup coconut, toasted
$2^1/_2$ tablespoons pine nuts, toasted

## Filling
$^3/_4$ cup shrimp, cooked and chopped
3 tablespoons lime, unpeeled and finely diced
3 tablespoons fresh ginger, chopped finely
3 tablespoons shallots, chopped finely
3 tablespoons lemongrass, minced
2 tablespoons serrano chili, finely diced

1. Combine all of the filling ingredients. Let them sit for 30 minutes.
2. Spread the chili sauce on the endive.
3. Stuff the endive with the filling.
4. Top with the coconut and pine nuts.

## Coconut Chili Sauce

2 tablespoons butter, melted
$^1/_4$ cup honey
1 teaspoon roasted chili paste
$^1/_4$ cup coconut, unsweetened and flaked
2 tablespoons fish sauce
2 tablespoons peanuts, unsalted and ground

1. Combine all of the ingredients.
2. Bring them to a boil and simmer for 5 minutes, stirring frequently.
3. Cool.

**Makes 50 hors d'oeuvres**

# Stuffed Belgian Endive
## with Gorgonzola and Pecans

*¹/₂ cup Gorgonzola cheese*
*¹/₂ cup sour cream*
*2 heads of Belgian endive*
*¹/₂ cup pecans, toasted, coarsely chopped*
*24 johnny-jump-up flowers or chopped parsley, for garnish*

1.  Combine the cheese and sour cream. Keep the mixture crumbly.

2.  Cut off the stems and separate the endive leaves.

3.  Spoon a teaspoon of the cheese mixture on top of each endive leaf.

4.  Sprinkle them with the pecans.

5.  Garnish with the flowers or parsley.

6.  Place on a serving tray and serve.

**Makes 24 to 28 hors d'oeuvres**

---

**A Pleasant Surprise**

Don't be afraid to experiment with unusual additions as garnish. In this dish, the tiny flowers can inspire a tremendous response. So be bold...but don't serve anything poisonous—and don't use your neighbor's flowers!

**Wine Notes**

 These delicious hors d'oeuvres work with many wines. Try a dry Vouvray or a Pinot Gris from Oregon.

## Wine Notes

 Try Santorini, a crisp, dry wine that our friends Harriet and Jim Hill introduced to us—from the Greek Island of Santorini.

# Risotto Cakes

1 tablespoon butter
$^1/_2$ onion, chopped
1 teaspoon garlic, chopped
8 ounces arborio rice
$^3/_4$ cup white wine
3 cups chicken stock, well seasoned (see page 5)
$^1/_4$ cup sun-dried tomatoes, moistened, chopped
$^1/_4$ cup fresh basil, chopped
$^1/_2$ cup Parmesan cheese
1 egg yolk
2 ounces heavy cream
1 cup flour
egg wash (4 eggs and 1 cup of milk)
2 cups white bread crumbs, fresh
3 cups vegetable oil

1. Melt the butter in a heavy saucepan over medium heat. Add the onions and garlic. Sauté them until translucent, but do not brown the garlic.

2. Add the rice and sauté for 1 or 2 minutes, until it is opaque and starts to make a clicking sound.

3. Slowly add the white wine, stirring constantly until the rice absorbs the liquid.

4. Add the chicken stock slowly, stirring and adding only enough to be absorbed by the rice. Continue this process until the rice is cooked al dente.

5. Add the tomatoes, basil and cheese.

6. In a separate pan, combine the yolk and cream. Temper (by adding a little rice to help it cool off first), then add to the rice mixture.

7. Cool the mixture and divide the rice into 20 portions. Shape into small cakes. Dip each cake in the flour first, then the egg wash and then the crumbs.

8. Over a medium-high heat, fry the cakes in a deep pan with oil for several minutes, until golden brown.

**Makes 20 cakes**

# Roquefort Grapes

*8 ounces cream cheese*
*8 ounces Roquefort or blue cheese*
*2 tablespoons heavy cream*
*1 pound seedless grapes, washed and separated*
*8 ounces walnuts or pecans, finely chopped*

1. Soften the cream cheese in a mixing bowl.

2. Add the Roquefort and heavy cream.

3. Roll each grape in the cheese mixture until each one has a nice thick coating.

4. Place the nuts in a large bowl. Toss in the individual grapes and coat them well.

5. Roll each grape in your hand to form a neat ball.

6. Chill for 20 minutes.

7. Put them on plates and garnish with fresh flowers.

**Makes 50 hors d'oeuvres**

## A Brand New Taste Treat

Grapes and cheese make a classic combination, but this inventive appetizer takes it to a whole new level with the contrast of the sweet grapes and intensely flavored Roquefort cheese. Serve them on glass plates or in champagne glasses as an appetizer or at the end of the meal as a cheese course in lieu of dessert.

## Wine Notes

An off-dry German Riesling, or even a Washington State Riesling, makes a great apertif wine for these hors d'oeuvres.

## A Note on Hazelnuts

The hazel tree is native to Europe and the eastern Mediterranean. The nut is high in fat, which can be used to produce an excellent salad oil. Hazelnuts are essential in making various confectionary, including certain types of chocolate, nougat and pastry.

### Wine Notes

 An Italian white called Greco de Tufo is dry and rich enough to hold up to these bold flavors. Try a dry Spanish white wine from the Penédes area.

# Baked Mussels
## *with Hazelnut Butter*

*24 large mussels, cleaned, debearded and scrubbed*
*8 tablespoons butter, softened*
*2 tablespoons white wine*
*1 garlic clove, chopped*
*1 tablespoon fresh parsley, chopped*
*1 teaspoon lemon juice*
*12 tablespoons bread crumbs*
*1 tablespoon hazelnuts, chopped*
*salt and pepper, for seasoning*
*1 lemon, sliced, for garnish*

1.  In a large stock pot, steam the mussels until they are just open (approximately 5 minutes). Save the broth for future soups and stocks.

2.  Cool the mussels and pull the meat out. Separate the 2 shells and place the mussel meat in 1 of the halves.

3.  Preheat the oven to 450°F.

4.  Whip the softened butter with wine, garlic, parsley and lemon juice.

5.  Fold in the crumbs and hazelnuts. Season with salt and pepper.

6.  Generously spread the butter mixture over the mussels.

7.  Place on a baking sheet and bake until bubbling and golden brown.

8.  Serve on a platter with lemon slices.

**Makes 24 hors d'oeuvres**

# Roasted Red Skin Potatoes
## with Caviar

*10 red skin potatoes*
*4 tablespoons olive oil*
*salt and pepper, for seasoning*
*1 cup sour cream or crème fraîche*
*1 teaspoon lemon juice*
*6 tablespoons chives, chopped*
*2 ounces caviar*

1.  Preheat the oven to 425°F. Cut off both ends of the potatoes so that they can stand up.

2.  Rub the potatoes with olive oil. Season them with salt and pepper.

3.  In a roasting pan, bake the potatoes for 40 minutes, until they just turn soft.

4.  While the potatoes are baking, whisk together the sour cream, lemon juice and half of the chives. Season well with salt and pepper.

5.  Allow the potatoes to cool just enough to handle them.

6.  Carefully cut them in half. With a melon scoop, scoop out the center of each potato half. Be careful not to remove too much.

7.  Spoon a dollop of the sour cream mixture onto each potato.

8.  Spoon a generous amount of caviar on top of each potato.

9.  Sprinkle the remaining chives on top for garnish.

**Makes 20 hors d'oeuvres**

**Faux Crème Fraîche**

To taste true crème fraîche, you would need to travel to Normandy, France. However, you can find American versions in specialty shops. Or, you can make your own by combining 1 cup of heavy cream with 1 teaspoon of buttermilk and heating it to no more than 85°F. Remove it from the heat and let it stand at room temperature until it thickens. Then you can stir it and refigerate.

**Wine Notes**

 Try a sparkling wine from Washington state or from the Anderson Valley in California.

*Appetizers*

Brandywine Mushrooms - 63
Mushroom Strudel - 64
Mediterranean Strudel - 66
Tomatoes and Mozzarella - 68
*Balsamic Vinaigrette - 68*
Spinach-Artichoke Rillettes - 69
Roasted Stuffed Pepper - 70
*Tapenade - 71*
Asparagus Crespelle - 72
*Crêpes - 73 • Asparagus Filling - 74 • Truffle Butter Sauce - 74*
Grilled Asparagus Wrapped in Prosciutto - 75
Goat Cheese Ravioli with Smoked Chicken - 76
*Goat Cheese Filling - 77 • Fennel Purée - 77 • Tomato Coulis - 78*
Soft Polenta with Taleggio Cheese and Shiitakes - 79
Dickens Escargot - 80
*Brie Butter - 81*
Clams Galway - 82
*Casino Butter - 83*
Mussels Mariniere - 84
Grilled Calamari with Arugula - 85
*Lemon Vinaigrette - 85*
Crab Louis - 86
*Louis Dressing - 86*
Crab Meat Caponata - 87
Crab Cakes - 88
*Roasted Red Pepper Cream Sauce - 89*
Crab and Shrimp Cake - 90
Doug's Barbecued Shrimp - 91
Poached Oysters with Stilton Cream - 92
Blue Point Oysters with Spinach and Crab Meat - 93
Star of Asia - 94

# Brandywine Mushrooms

*3 cups button mushrooms, cleaned*
*1 cup smoked ham, diced*
*2 cups heavy cream*
*1 cup fresh tomatoes, chopped*
*1 tablespoon tomato paste*
*3 tablespoons scallions, green part only, sliced*
*salt and freshly ground pepper, for seasoning*
*chives, chopped, for garnish*

1. Combine the mushrooms, ham and cream in a saucepan. Bring them to a simmer. Add the tomatoes and tomato paste.

2. Simmer until the cream is reduced to a sauce-like consistency.

3. Add the scallions.

4. Season with the salt and pepper.

5. Serve in 4 soup bowls, garnished with the chives.

**Makes 4 appetizers**

# Mushroom Strudel

*10 phyllo sheets*
*¹/₂ pound butter, melted*

*Filling*
*3 tablespoons butter*
*1 pound mixed shiitake, crimini and button mushrooms,*
  *cleaned and chopped*
*¹/₂ cup green onions, chopped*
*¹/₂ cup onions, chopped*
*8 ounces cream cheese*
*¹/₂ cup sour cream*
*salt and pepper, for seasoning*
*³/₄ teaspoon garlic powder*
*¹/₂ teaspoon caraway seeds, toasted*
*3 teaspoons parsley, chopped*

1. Melt 3 tablespoons of butter in a sauté pan over medium heat. Add the mushrooms and onions. Sauté them until the vegetables are soft and all of the liquid evaporates. It is important that the cooked mushrooms are dry, so that the phyllo dough does not become soggy.

2. Transfer the mushrooms to a bowl. Stir in the cream cheese and sour cream.

3. Season with salt and pepper to taste. Add the garlic powder, caraway seeds and parsley.

4. Allow the mixture to cool before assembling.

**Makes 5 appetizers**

## Tips for Shiitakes

If using shiitake mushrooms, be sure to remove the stems, as they tend to be very tough.

## Wine Notes

 This dish goes well with both red and white wine. Try a light Pinot Noir or a herbaceous Californian Sauvignon Blanc.

# Mushroom Strudel

To Assemble:

1. Preheat the oven to 400°F.

2. When you unwrap the phyllo sheets from the package, you have a rectangle of layered dough.

3. Lay out 1 sheet of phyllo and brush it with melted butter. Place another sheet of phyllo on top and brush it with butter. Repeat this process one more time so you have a stack of 3 sheets. Cut this stack into 4 lengthwise strips.

4. Place approximately 2 tablespoons of the cooled mushrooms on the lower right-hand corner of 1 strip.

5. Fold the corner containing the mixture into a triangle, which you keep folding up the entire lenth of the strip, just like a paper football. The corner containing the mixture folds up and across to the opposite edge, always maintaining a right angle where the next fold occurs. The final fold forms a right triangle.

6. Brush melted butter on both sides of this triangle.

7. Use the remaining 3 strips to make 3 more triangles. Then continue repeating steps 3 through 6 until you have a total of 20 triangles. Place the triangles on an ungreased baking sheet and bake until golden brown (approximately 10 to 15 minutes).

**Makes 20 triangles**

# Mediterranean Strudel

*10 phyllo sheets*
*¹/₂ pound butter, melted*

*Filling*
*1 small red onion, sliced*
*2 tablespoons olive oil or butter*
*1 can (12 ounces) artichoke bottoms, sliced*
*1 roasted green pepper, seeded and sliced*
*1 roasted red pepper, seeded and sliced*
*1 roasted yellow pepper, seeded and sliced*
*1 bunch scallions, thinly sliced on an angle*
*¹/₄ cup black olives, chopped*
*2 tablespoons garlic, chopped*
*2 tablespoons fresh basil, chopped*
*2 tablespoons fresh oregano, chopped*
*4 tablespoons extra virgin olive oil*
*3 tablespoons red wine vinegar*
*pinch of crushed red pepper*
*salt, to taste*
*15 grinds of fresh pepper*

1. Sauté the red onions in 2 tablespoons of olive oil or butter. Cool.

2. Mix all of the vegetables, olives, garlic and other herbs in a bowl.

3. Stir in the extra virgin olive oil and vinegar.

4. Season with the crushed red pepper, salt and pepper.

## Herbs: Fresh vs. Dried

Try to find fresh herbs for this recipe as they heighten its flavor tremendously. When buying fresh herbs, look for green and fragrant herbs with no sign of yellowing or wilting. Fresh herbs are highly perishable. To store them, place the stems in a jar with 2 inches of water, drape a plastic bag loosely over the leaves and change the water every 2 days. Herbs should keep for up to 1 week in the refrigerator this way.

You can use dried herbs in this recipe, but substitute 1 teaspoon of dry herbs for each tablespoon of fresh.

## Wine Notes

Try a dry rosé from the south of France or the Loire Valley.

# *Mediterranean Strudel*

## To Assemble:

1. Preheat the oven to 400°F.

2. When you unwrap the phyllo sheets from the package, you have a rectangle of layered dough.

3. Lay out 1 sheet of phyllo and brush it with melted butter. Place another sheet of phyllo on top and brush it with butter. Repeat this process one more time so you have a stack of 3 sheets. Cut this stack into 4 lengthwise strips.

4. Place approximately 2 tablespoons of the cooled vegetable mixture on the lower right-hand corner of 1 strip.

5. Fold the corner containing the mixture into a triangle, which you keep folding up the entire lenth of the strip, just like a paper football. The corner containing the mixture folds up and across to the opposite edge, always maintaining a right angle where the next fold occurs. The final fold forms a right triangle.

6. Brush melted butter on both sides of this triangle.

7. Use the remaining 3 strips to make 3 more triangles. Then continue repeating steps 3 through 6 until you have a total of 20 triangles. Place the triangles on an ungreased baking sheet and bake until golden brown (approximately 10 to 15 minutes).

**Makes 20 triangles**

# Tomatoes and Mozzarella

*3 very ripe Jersey tomatoes, thickly sliced*
*12 ounces fresh mozzarella cheese, thickly sliced*
*Balsamic Vinaigrette (below)*
*1 small red onion, sliced into rings*
*fresh basil leaves, for garnish*
*freshly ground pepper, for seasoning*

1.  Place several slices of tomato and mozzarella flat on each of 4 salad plates. Arrange the slices in alternating order, for added visual appeal.

2.  Drizzle the Balsamic Vinaigrette over the top.

3.  Lay slices of onion on the top. Garnish with fresh basil leaves and pepper.

**Makes 4 appetizers**

# Balsamic Vinaigrette

*1 shallot, chopped*
*1 tablespoon white wine*
*1 teaspoon lemon juice*
*1¹/₂ ounces white wine vinegar*
*¹/₂ cup balsamic vinegar*
*1 cup fresh basil, chopped*
*1 tablespoon fresh parsley, chopped*
*pinch of garlic powder*
*1¹/₂ cups olive oil*
*dash of hot sauce*
*salt and freshly ground pepper, to taste*

1.  In a bowl, whisk together all of the ingredients for the vinaigrette.

2.  Let sit for 30 minutes to allow flavors to blend.

**Makes 3 cups**

---

**Tips for Slicing Tomatoes**

For this recipe, do not slice the tomatoes until you are ready to serve them. Otherwise, the flavorful juices leach out and the seeds fall out. And remember: Jersey tomatoes are always the best when serving fresh tomatoes.

**Wine Notes**

 Try a medium-bodied, crisp Italian Gavi or a Vernaccia.

### Substitutions, Please

You can be creative with this appetizer by substituting ingredients. Change the type of cheese. Add sun-dried tomatoes or wild mushrooms. If you want to make this dish into an entrée, add cooked chicken.

### Wine Notes

 Try this dish with a dry rosé from Provence or a white wine from Cassis.

# *Spinach-Artichoke Rillettes*

*1 cup white wine*
*1 shallot, chopped*
*1 clove garlic, chopped*
*3 tablespoons butter*
*3 tablespoons flour*
*2 cups heavy cream*
*salt and pepper, for seasoning*
*1 pound fresh spinach, chopped, cooked and well drained*
*2 cans (8 ounces) artichoke hearts*
*1 cup Romano cheese, grated*
*French bread croutons, baked until crisp (see page 32)*

1.  In a small saucepan, heat the wine, shallot and garlic. Simmer until the mixture is reduced to almost dry.

2.  Add the butter and cook for 1 minute.

3.  Sprinkle with flour and stir well, until it makes a smooth paste. Add the heavy cream and bring it to a simmer.

4.  Simmer for about 20 minutes, until the raw flour taste is gone. Season with salt and pepper, to taste.

5.  Strain and cool the mixture.

6.  Drain the artichoke hearts. Set aside 6 small artichoke hearts and slice the rest.

7.  When the mixture is cooled, add the spinach, sliced artichokes and $^1/_2$ cup cheese.

8.  Place the spinach cream mixture into 6 ramekins and top each with the 6 artichoke hearts. Sprinkle the remaining cheese on top.

9.  Bake in a preheated 350°F oven for 10 to 15 minutes, or until hot and bubbling.

10. Serve with French bread croutons or bread sticks

**Makes 4 appetizers**

# Roasted Stuffed Pepper

*¹/₂ cup balsamic vinegar*
*4 red or yellow peppers with tops cut off, roasted, seeded and peeled*
  *(see sidebar)*
*8 slices fontina cheese*
*8 tablespoons goat cheese*
*4 thin slices prosciutto ham, chopped*
*8 tablespoons Tapenade (opposite page)*
*2 tomatoes, halved, sliced and marinated (see page 30)*
*2 cups mixed greens*

1. Reduce the balsamic vinegar by half over low heat on the stove. Cool.

2. Preheat the oven to 375°F.

3. Stuff each pepper with 2 slices of fontina cheese, 2 tablespoons of goat cheese, 1 slice of prosciutto ham, 2 tablespoons of Tapenade and 1 tablespoon of tomatoes.

4. Place the peppers, open side up, on a baking sheet.

5. Bake the peppers for 15 to 20 minutes.

6. Divide the greens onto 4 plates, then place 1 pepper on each.

7. Drizzle the reduced vinegar over the top and serve.

**Makes 4 appetizers**

## Roasting Peppers

You can roast peppers in a few different ways. Before roasting them, make sure the peppers are dry.

If you have a gas stove and proper ventilation, the stove top is a fast and easy way to roast them. Set the pepper directly on the burner with the flame on.

If you do not have a gas stove, a broiler works fine. Place the peppers under the broiler and turn them as they blacken.

The flame turns the skin black. When the peppers are black all over, place them in a tightly closed brown paper bag or in a bowl covered with a plate for a few minutes. The steam loosens the skins for easy peeling.

Let the peppers cool until they can be handled. Pull off the burnt skin with your hands. If possible, avoid rinsing the peeled peppers with water. Rinsing removes the flavorful oils that enhance the pepper's taste.

Cut the stem and the seeds out. Now you are ready to slice, stuff, chop or purée.

# Tapenade

*1 cup black olives*
*1/2 cup green olives*
*1 shallot, chopped*
*1 tablespoon capers*
*2 anchovy fillets, chopped*
*1 clove garlic, chopped*
*5 to 6 fresh basil leaves*
*1 tablespoon parsley, chopped*
*dash of Tabasco*
*2 tablespoons olive oil*
*1 tablespoon red wine vinegar*

1. Pulse the olives and shallots in a food processor. Remove.

2. Put the remaining ingredients into the processor. Pulse until they are coarsely chopped.

3. In a bowl, combine the olive mixture and mix.

4. Set aside for 1 hour before using.

## Tasty Alternatives

This classic preparation can have many variations. Try adding:

- chopped winter savory
- puréed sun-dried tomatoes
- orange zest
- cooked tuna
- Dijon mustard
- cognac.

Also, try using tapenade in a wide variety of combinations. It works well on:

- stuffing for avocados or tomatoes
- a secret ingredient in tomato sauce
- leg of lamb stuffing
- stuffing for roasted duck.

## Wine Notes

 A crisp, dry Italian white wine, such as a Pinot Grigio or Orvieto, works nicely with these flavors.

# Asparagus Crespelle

*8 crêpes (opposite page)*
*Asparagus Filling (see page 74)*
*1 cup Truffle Butter Sauce (see page 74)*

1. Preheat the oven to 350°F.

2. Lay a crêpe on a cutting board.

3. Place a large spoonful of Asparagus Filling on the crêpe.

4. Fold the crêpe like a rectangular envelope. Repeat this process.

5. Bake the crêpes in the oven for 15 to 20 minutes.

6. Garnish with the warm asparagus tips that accompany the Asparagus Filling.

7. Ladle Truffle Butter Sauce over the crêpes.

**Makes 8 crêpes**

## Asparagus Tips

The best way to keep asparagus fresh is to wrap it in wet paper towels and store it in the refrigerator. This prevents it from drying out.

## Wine Notes

 A full-bodied Italian Chardonnay or a French white Burgundy works nicely with the rich flavors of the truffle.

# Crêpes

*2 cups all-purpose flour*
*4 tablespoons sweet butter*
*1 egg yolk*
*2 whole eggs*
*2 cups cold milk*
*1 tablespoon truffle oil*
*pinch of salt*

1. Mix all of the ingredients together.

2. Refrigerate for at least 1 hour to relax the batter.

3. Over medium heat, heat a non-stick skillet on the stove.

4. With a ladle, spread one-eighth of the batter out onto the pan.

5. Flip the crêpe over when the first side is lightly browned (approximately 1 minute). The second side usually browns more quickly.

6. As you add the 7 remaining crêpes to the stack, separate each with plastic wrap.

**Makes 8 crêpes**

# Asparagus Filling

*2 cups fresh asparagus*
*$1/2$ cup butter*
*2 tablespoons truffle oil*
*salt and freshly ground pepper, for seasoning*

1. Cut off the asparagus tips and reserve. Break off the tough bottom part of each spear. Cut the remaining spears into 1-inch pieces.

2. In a large pot of boiling water, cook the tips until they are al dente. Remove them from the water, chill and reserve.

3. Cook the remainder of the asparagus pieces in the boiling water. Remove them when they are al dente. Cool.

4. In a sauté pan, melt the butter over medium heat and cook until it turns medium brown. Remove. Cool to room temperature.

5. In a food processor, make a rough purée of the asparagus slices— but do not include the tips. Add the brown butter and truffle oil, and mix. Season with the salt and pepper, to taste.

# Truffle Butter Sauce

*2 tablespoons shallots, chopped*
*2 tablespoons white wine vinegar*
*$1/2$ cup white wine*
*1 cup cream*
*4 tablespoons butter, browned*
*1 tablespoon truffle oil*
*salt and freshly ground pepper, for seasoning*

1. Put the shallots, vinegar and wine in a small saucepan. Bring the mixture to a simmer and reduce until it is almost dry.

2. Lower the heat and swirl in the brown butter and truffle oil. Season with the salt and pepper.

3. Strain and discard the shallots. Serve.

**Makes approximately 1 cup**

## Another Butter Option

Like the other butter recipes presented throughout the book, Truffle Butter Sauce can be made ahead and stored in the refrigerator. You can make it into a log wrapped in parchment or wax paper, and keep it in the refrigerator for about 1 month.

## Asparagus Roots

Asparagus is actually an edible member of the lily family. A young stalk of asparagus is considered a luxury in many parts of the world. It can be served as a vegetable, with a soup, as an accompaniment or as an appetizer. Asparagus is delicious, either hot or cold. Avoid overcooking it, which may give it a strong, sometimes unpleasant, flavor.

## Wine Notes

 A light, crisp, dry Italian white wine is ideal. I suggest an Orvieto or Verdichhio.

# Grilled Asparagus Wrapped in Prosciutto

*24 asparagus spears, blanched al dente*
*12 large prosciutto slices, cut in half*
*8 tablespoons extra virgin olive oil*
*3 tablespoons balsamic vinegar*
*freshly ground pepper, for seasoning*
*5 cups fresh greens, such as spring mix*
*1 tablespoon lemon zest, chopped*

1. Tightly wrap each asparagus spear with prosciutto ham. (Make sure the wrapping is tight.)

2. Create a vinaigrette by mixing the oil and vinegar together. Season with fresh pepper.

3. Place the asparagus on the grill. Cook for 3 to 5 minutes, until the ham has nice grill marks. (Grill in 3 batches, so that you can watch the cooking carefully.)

4. Place the greens on 6 plates. Place the asparagus onto the greens.

5. Sprinkle with lemon zest and drizzle with the vinaigrette.

**Makes 6 appetizers**

# Goat Cheese Ravioli
## with Smoked Chicken, Fennel Purée and Tomato Coulis

*20 wonton skins*
*egg wash (1 egg beaten with 2 tablespoons water)*
*Goat Cheese Filling (opposite page)*
*Fennel Purée (opposite page)*
*Tomato Coulis (see page78)*
*10 ounces smoked chicken breast, sliced in 10-inch strips*
*1 tablespoon olive oil*
*fresh basil, chopped, for garnish*

## Ravioli Preparation:

1. Lay the wontons on a counter or pastry board.

2. Brush them around the edges with an egg wash.

3. Spoon a dollop of Goat Cheese Filling onto the center of half of the wontons.

4. Place a single wonton on top of each filled wonton, so that the edges with the egg wash face each other.

5. Use a fork or the back side of a cookie cutter to crimp the edges.

6. Make sure that the edges of the ravioli are sealed.

7. Keep a moist towel over the ravioli to prevent them from drying out.

8. When ready to serve, plunge the ravioli into a large pot of salted boiling water. Do not place too many ravioli into the pot at once.

9. Cook for approximately 3 minutes, until the ravioli rise to the top of the pot.

**Makes 10 ravioli**

## The Perfect Complement

This recipe has quite a few components. Each recipe is simple, with flavors that combine to make a wonderful dish.

## Wontons for Ravioli

If you don't have time to make your own ravioli pasta, wonton skins offer a great alternative. The flavor of the wonton is basically neutral, so make sure that your stuffing is well seasoned and flavorful. A nice sauce also helps.

You can cut them into 3¼-inch squares or 3½-inch rounds. The rounds work better for ravioli, as they are a bit thicker and hold up better when cooked in boiling water.

If you freeze your ravioli, wrap them airtight. Thaw them overnight in the refrigerator.

## Wine Notes

 Try this dish with a Sauvignon Blanc from Sancerre or Menetou Salon.

## Goat Cheese Filling

*2 tablespoons pancetta ham, chopped*
*2 tablespoons shallots, chopped*
*1/2 cup roasted red pepper, peeled, seeded and chopped (see page 70)*
*3 tablespoons fresh basil, chiffonade*
*2 tablespoons fresh parsley, chopped*
*1 tablespoon fresh rosemary, chopped*
*1 tablespoon fresh thyme, chopped*
*3/4 cup goat cheese, room temperature*
*1/4 cup cream cheese, room temperature*

1. In a pan, sauté the pancetta until brown.

2. Add the shallots. Cook until soft.

3. Add the pepper and herbs and cook for 1 minute. Cool.

4. Add the cheeses to the pepper mixture. Mix until well blended.

## Fennel Purée

*2 tablespoons olive oil*
*1 cup fennel bulb, chopped*
*1/2 teaspoon fresh garlic, chopped*
*1/2 cup chicken stock (see page 5)*
*salt and pepper, for seasoning*

1. Sauté the fennel bulb and garlic in the olive oil for 5 minutes.

2. Add the chicken stock. Simmer it until the fennel is tender and has absorbed the stock.

3. Place the fennel mixture into a food processor and purée.

4. Season with salt and pepper, to taste. Chill.

### Fennel

Fennel is a versatile ingredient. It can be used as a vegetable, herb or seed. Used since ancient times, it is essential to Italian cooking. Its flavor, of anise or licorice, can be bitter or sweet, depending on the variety. The plant is stalky with feathery leaves that often are confused with dill. The vegetable is the root or bulb, which resembles celery. The bulb can be part of a salad or stand on its own, braised or sautéed. The seeds are aromatic and can be used for flavoring biscotti, pickled vegetables and fish.

# Tomato Coulis

*3 cups tomato*
*1 tablespoon butter*
*¹/₂ cup onions, chopped*
*¹/₂ tablespoon fresh rosemary, chopped*
*3 tablespoons Cinzano white vermouth*
*salt and pepper, for seasoning*
*1 tablespoon extra virgin olive oil*

1. Cut the tomatoes in half and gently squeeze out the seeds. Chop.

2. Sauté the onions in the butter until they are soft.

3. Add the tomatoes, rosemary and vermouth. Cook for 3 minutes.

4. Place this mixture in a food processor and purée.

5. Strain through a sieve.

6. Reheat. Season with the salt and pepper, then whisk in the olive oil before serving.

**Makes 2 cups**

## To Assemble Goat Cheese Ravioli:

1. Sauté the chicken slices in olive oil for 2 minutes.

2. Spoon the Tomato Coulis evenly onto 5 plates.

3. Place 2 ravioli in the center of the coulis on each plate.

4. Arrange the chicken around the ravioli.

5. Top with a dollop of Fennel Purée.

6. Sprinkle with fresh basil.

**Makes 5 appetizers**

## Coulis

Coulis are fruit or vegetable purées that are made into sauces. They can be flavored with wine, brandy or any liqueur. They can be cooked or kept uncooked to make a fresher flavor. They also can be served either hot and cold.

## Creamy Cheese

Mimi loves this dish. She created it for one of our Italian wine dinners, and our guests loved it.

Taleggio cheese is a soft, ripe Brie-like cheese from Italy. Find it in Italian specialty markets or use Brie as a substitute.

# Soft Polenta
## *with Taleggio Cheese and Shiitakes*

*2 quarts water*
*1 teaspoon salt*
*3 cups polenta*
*4 tablespoons mascarpone cheese*
*1 cup heavy cream*
*fresh pepper, for seasoning*
*3 tablespoons olive oil*
*1¹/₂ cups button mushrooms, sliced*
*1 cup shiitake mushrooms, sliced*
*¹/₂ cup stock (any type), seasoned and reduced*
*4 slices Taleggio cheese*
*white truffle oil, for drizzling*

1.  Bring the water to a boil in a large thick-bottom pot. Add the salt.

2.  Over medium heat, add the polenta in a slow, steady stream. Use a pitcher to help you do this. Stir it with a whisk until it is completely blended.

3.  Turn the heat down to low and simmer for 45 minutes. Use a wooden spoon to stir. Polenta is done when it slides easily off the sides of the pot.

4.  Add the mascarpone cheese and heavy cream.

5.  Season it with the salt and pepper. Keep it covered and hot.

6.  Sauté the mushrooms in the oil and season with salt and pepper.

7.  Add the stock and reduce.

8.  Spoon the polenta into 4 bowls. Place a slice of Taleggio cheese on top of the polenta.

9.  Spoon the mushrooms, with their jus, on top of the polenta.

10. Drizzle the polenta with a tiny amount of truffle oil.

**Serves 4**

## Wine Notes

 Try this dish with a French Burgundy or an elegant Pinot Noir from Oregon. These wines pick up the earthy richness of this dish.

# Dickens Escargot

*1 stick butter (8 tablespoons)*
*4 tablespoons shallots*
*48 escargot pieces, drained and rinsed*
*¹/₂ cup white wine*
*8 puff pastry squares, each 5" x 5"*
*egg wash (1 egg beaten with 2 tablespoons water)*
*1 pound Brie Butter (opposite page)*

1.  In a sauté pan, melt the butter and sauté the shallots.

2.  Add the escargot and wine. Simmer until the wine evaporates. Cool.

3.  Preheat the oven to 450°F.

4.  Lay the pastry squares out on a cutting board. Put 6 snails and 3 tablespoons of Brie Butter on each pastry square.

5.  Brush the outer edges of the pastry with the egg wash.

6.  Bring the 4 corners of each dough square together, and pinch them to create a seal. Brush them again with the egg wash. Place the squares on a parchment-lined baking sheet.

7.  Bake for 15 minutes, until golden brown.

**Makes 8 appetizers**

**Celebrating Dickens**

This recipe comes from one of the Dickens extravaganza dinners that we host once a year in December. Guests dress in Victorian costumes and celebrate the works of Charles Dickens.

**Wine Notes**

The perfect match for this appetizer is a French Burgundy. The earthy flavors of the snails and the Brie create a wonderful synergy.

# Brie Butter

*$^1/_2$ pound butter, softened*
*$^1/_2$ pound ripe Brie cheese, skin removed and diced*
*1 tablespoon shallots, chopped*
*2 tablespoons fresh basil, chopped*
*$^1/_2$ cup toasted pine nuts, chopped*
*1 tablespoon Pernod*
*1 teaspoon salt*
*$^1/_4$ teaspoon white pepper*

1. Whip the butter in a mixing bowl or food processor.

2. Add the Brie and beat until blended.

3. Add the shallots, basil, pine nuts and Pernod.

4. Season with the salt and pepper.

**Makes 1 pound**

## The Best Brie

Make sure that the Brie you use is completely ripe in the center. It should not be dry and chalky. French Brie is usually the best quality.

Like the other butter recipes in this book, Brie Butter can be made ahead and refrigerated. It lasts in the refrigerator for about 1 month.

# Clams Galway

*24 topneck clams, opened*
*2 bags fresh spinach, sautéed lightly, seasoned with salt and pepper*
*1 pound Casino Butter (opposite page)*
*12 bacon slices, slightly cooked to render some of the fat, cut into*
*    thirds*

1.  Remove the clams from the shells.

2.  Place the spinach in the shells.

3.  Top each shell with a clam, slice of butter and slice of bacon.

4.  Bake at 375°F for approximately 10 to 15 minutes, until the bacon is crisp.

**Makes 6 appetizers**

**Clam Varieties**

The main type of raw clam that we use is the quahog. We use 3 sizes:

Little Necks are the smallest and most expensive of the legal-sized clams. We steam or sauté them.

Top Necks are medium-sized and produce a very tender clam. We use these when making clams on the half shell and baking clams casino or Galway style. Their price is often comparable to the little neck's.

Cherrystones are the largest and most commonly known clams that we use. They work well with soups, sauces and stuffed clams.

**Wine Notes**

 The nice salty sea flavor of the clams goes nicely with a French Muscadet or crisp Californian Pinot Blanc.

## A Dash of...

Like many recipes, this one calls for a "dash of" an ingredient. When suggesting that you use a dash, a recipe allows you to adjust the amount you use to your personal taste. In this case, you can choose for yourself what you consider to be a "dash of Tabasco." Since Tabasco is such a pungent condiment, made with assorted peppers of varying degrees of hotness, each person's tolerance may be quite different.

Remember to start by adding just a tiny amount of Tabasco sauce: You can always add more. But if you add too much at the start, there's nothing you can do to "cool it down."

# Casino Butter

*¹/₂ cup red onion, chopped*
*¹/₂ cup red pepper, chopped*
*¹/₂ cup green pepper, chopped*
*1 teaspoon garlic, chopped*
*3 tablespoons olive oil*
*1 pound butter, softened*
*¹/₄ cup scallions, chopped*
*2 tablespoons Worcestershire sauce*
*dash of Tabasco*
*juice of 1 lemon*
*salt and pepper, for seasoning*
*¹/₂ cup bread crumbs, fine*

1. Sauté the onions, peppers and garlic in the olive oil until the vegetables are soft. Cool completely.

2. Whip the butter with an electric mixer.

3. Add the cooled vegetables, scallions, Worcestershire sauce, Tabasco, lemon juice, salt, pepper and crumbs.

4. Combine all of the ingredients thoroughly.

5. Place the mixture on a sheet of parchment paper or plastic wrap. Roll it into a log. Chill for 1 hour.

6. The butter stays fresh for 1 week in the refrigerator and 6 weeks in the freezer.

**Makes 1 pound**

# Mussels Mariniere

*2 tablespoons butter*
*3 tablespoons shallots*
*1 cup dry white wine*
*2 tablespoons fresh parsley, chopped*
*3 pounds mussels, cleaned, debearded and brushed*
*freshly ground pepper, to taste*
*1 cup heavy cream (optional)*
*fresh parsley, for garnish*

1. In a large pot, melt the butter, then sauté the shallots.

2. Add the wine, parsley, mussels and pepper. If you want a richer dish, add the heavy cream.

3. Cover the pot and turn the heat up to high.

4. When the mussels are fully open, the dish is done. (This usually takes approximately 10 minutes.)

5. Spoon the mussels into bowls and pour in the broth.

6. Garnish with parsley.

**Makes 8 appetizers**

## Mussels

The best mussels are farm raised. They are usually larger, with good meat and consistent quality. Mussels should be kept alive until they are cooked. Often they are alive even when they are open. To test this, poke a knife in the meat; the shell closes up if the mussel is alive.

Three pounds of fresh mussels still in the shells provide one pound of mussel meat. For convenience, you can buy mussel meat without the shells from your seafood market. A good rule of thumb is to provide 12 mussels per person for an appetizer. Four ounces of meat is a proper portion per person.

## Debearding

When preparing mussels, pull off the seaweed hair on the inside part of the shell. If you do not, it shrinks into the meat during cooking. Keep uncooked mussels dry and refrigerated, with a moist towel covering them. Do not submerge them in water.

# Grilled Calamari
## with Arugula and Lemon Vinaigrette

*4 squid, medium size*
*4 cups arugula, soaked, rinsed and dried*
*Lemon Vinaigrette (below)*
*3 lemons, wedged and seeded*

1. Heat the grill. Leaving the bodies whole, clean the squid.

2. Cut each squid in half lengthwise. Lightly score the bodies, making a criss-cross pattern with a knife. Pat them dry

3. Place the squid and tentacles on the grill. Sear for 2 minutes on each side.

4. Toss the arugula in a small amount of the Lemon Vinaigrette.

5. Divide the flavored arugula among 4 plates. Put the calamari on top of each plate.

6. Drizzle with the remaining vinaigrette. Garnish with the lemons.

## Lemon Vinaigrette

*2 ounces fresh lemon juice*
*6 ounces extra virgin olive oil*
*salt and freshly ground pepper, for seasoning*

1. Mix the lemon juice and olive oil.

2. Season with the salt and pepper, to taste.

**Makes 4 appetizers**

# Crab Louis

*4 cups mixed salad greens*
*6-8 radicchio cups*
*1 pound crab meat, picked for shells*
*2 cups Louis Dressing (below)*
*2 tablespoons fresh chives, chopped*
*$^1/_8$ cup red peppers, diced*
*$^1/_8$ cup green peppers, diced*
*$^1/_8$ cup yellow peppers, diced*

1.  Arrange the greens on 6 to 8 salad plates. Place 1 radicchio cup in the center of each.

2.  Put 2 ounces ($^1/_4$ cup) of crab meat in each cup.

3.  Drizzle Louis Dressing over the crab meat.

4.  Sprinkle the chives and colored peppers over the plate as garnish.

**Serves 6 to 8 portions**

# Louis Dressing

*$^1/_2$ red onion, chopped*
*$^1/_2$ green bell pepper, chopped*
*$^1/_2$ cup chili sauce*
*$^1/_2$ cup heavy cream*
*$^1/_2$ cup mayonnaise, homemade or best store-bought quality*
*2 tablespoons Dijon mustard*
*1 tablespoon sun-dried tomato paste (optional)*
*salt and freshly ground pepper, for seasoning*
*4 tablespoons fresh dill, chopped*

1.  Put all of the ingredients—except the salt, pepper and dill—into a food processor and blend until smooth.

2.  Season with the salt, pepper and dill, to taste.

**Makes 2 cups**

## Nature-Made Cups

We use radicchio cups at the restaurant. They are simply the large leaves of radicchio, an Italian type of endive, that naturally take the shape of a cup. Any type of salad fits perfectly into these little cups. They can be used to serve many other foods, as well.

## Wine Notes

 This flavorful mayonnaise-based dressing goes well with a crisp Chardonnay from the Monterey area of California.

# Crab Meat Caponata

*3 large eggplants, skin on, cut into 3/4-inch cubes*
*salt, for coating*
*1/4 cup extra virgin olive oil*
*1 cup celery, diced*
*1 cup onions, diced*
*1 1/2 cups tomatoes, chopped*
*2 tablespoons fresh thyme, chopped*
*1 bay leaf*
*salt and pepper, to taste*
*1/4 pound black olives*
*3 tablespoons capers*
*4 tablespoons parsley, chopped*
*3 tablespoons sugar*
*2 tablespoons vinegar*
*1 pound jumbo lump crab meat, picked*
*3 tablespoons lemon rind, grated*

1. Salt the eggplant and let it drain in a colander.

2. In 2 tablespoons of oil, sauté the celery and onion until soft.

3. Add the tomatoes, thyme, bay leaf, salt and pepper. Cook over medium heat until nice and thick.

4. Rinse and then dry the eggplant. Fry it in the remaining oil.

5. Do not overcook. Remove the eggplant when it is just cooked.

6. Combine the tomato mixture and eggplant.

7. Add the olives, capers and parsley. Mix.

8. Dissolve the sugar into the vinegar, and stir this into the mixture.

9. Spoon the caponata onto 6 plates. Place 2 to 3 ounces of crab meat on top of each plate.

10. Garnish each with a lemon rind.

**Makes 6 appetizers**

# Crab Cakes
## with Roasted Red Pepper Cream Sauce

4 tablespoons butter
1/2 cup white onion, diced
1/2 cup green pepper, diced
1/2 cup red pepper, diced
4 slices soft white bread, crusts cut off and cubed
1/2 cup mayonnaise
1 tablespoon Dijon mustard
1 egg
1 tablespoon fresh horseradish
2 teaspoons Worcestershire sauce
1 pound jumbo lump crab meat
salt and pepper, for seasoning
1 cup unseasoned bread crumbs
3 cups Roasted Red Pepper Cream Sauce (opposite page)
6 sprigs of thyme, for garnish

1. Sauté the onions and peppers in 2 tablespoons of butter until al dente. Cool.

2. Place the bread cubes in a bowl, and add the mayonnaise, mustard, egg, horseradish and Worcestershire sauce. Stir to blend thoroughly.

3. Add the pepper and onion mixture.

4. Fold in the crab meat, being careful to avoid breaking up the lumps too much. Season with the salt and pepper.

5. Form into 6 cakes. Coat each cake with bread crumbs.

6. Melt the remaining butter (2 tablespoons) and sauté the cakes on both sides, until golden brown.

7. Place on a sheet pan. Bake in a preheated 350°F oven for 3 to 5 minutes.

8. Place approximately 1/4 cup of the Roasted Red Pepper Cream Sauce on each of 6 plates, then place a crab cake on top. Garnish with a sprig of thyme.

**Makes 6 appetizers**

## Homemade Horseradish

To make prepared horseradish, peel the root with a paring knife. Cut it into 2-inch pieces and process it in a food processor until it is finely minced. The horseradish releases burning fumes, so avoid breathing directly over the bowl. Store horseradish in a tightly sealed jar, as it loses its strong flavor if exposed to air.

## Wine Notes

These crab cakes are beautifully complemented by a fuller-bodied Chardonnay. The elegant style of many Sonoma Valley Chardonnays is perfect.

# Roasted Red Pepper Cream Sauce

*$^1/_2$ cup white wine*
*2 ounces shallots, chopped*
*1 teaspoon garlic, chopped*
*1 roasted red pepper, peeled and chopped (see page 70)*
*2 cups heavy cream*
*salt and pepper, for seasoning*

1. In a saucepan over medium heat, reduce the white wine, shallots, garlic and pepper until the pan is almost dry.

2. Add the heavy cream and reduce by half. (Watch that the pot does not overboil!)

3. Continue to reduce until the sauce coats the back of a spoon. Season with salt and pepper.

**Makes 1$^1/_2$ cups**

# Crab and Shrimp Cake

*1 pound lump crab meat*
*³/4 pound shrimp*
*1 whole egg*
*³/4 cup heavy cream*
*salt and pepper, for seasoning*
*¹/2 cup scallions, green part only, chopped*
*1 teaspoon Dijon mustard*
*1 teaspoon capers, chopped*
*2 tablespoons fresh parsley, chopped*
*1 teaspoon Worcestershire sauce*
*¹/4 teaspoon Tabasco*
*3 ounces clarified butter (see page 181)*

1.  Pick over the crab meat to remove any cartilage or shell. Leave the lumps as large as possible.

2.  Shell and devein the shrimp.

3.  Put the shrimp in a food processor. Add the egg, cream, salt and pepper. Blend as finely as possible.

4.  Place this mixture into a mixing bowl. Add the crab meat, scallions, mustard, capers, parsley, Worcestershire sauce and Tabasco. Blend gently, but thoroughly.

5.  Shape the mixture into 6 miniature cakes.

6.  Sauté the cakes in the butter until they are brown on both sides and firm to touch.

**Makes 6 appetizers**

## A Favorite Variation

This recipe is an adaptation from the crab cake served at Le Bec Fin. It receives rave reviews from guests.

## Wine Notes

 A rich California Chardonnay with toasty, vanilla flavors is delicious with these cakes.

# Doug's Barbecued Shrimp

*16 large shrimp, shelled and deveined*
*4 cups mixed field greens*

*Barbecue Sauce*
*$^1/_2$ cup ketchup*
*6 tablespoons lemon juice*
*1 tablespoon horseradish*
*2 tablespoons tomato juice*
*2 tablespoons Worcestershire sauce*
*$^1/_4$ cup olive oil*
*salt and pepper, for seasoning*

1. Combine all of the ingredients for the Barbecue Sauce in a small bowl.

2. Brush the shrimp with the sauce and place it on a hot grill. Continue basting the shrimp with the sauce.

3. Cook until just done (approximately 3 to 5 minutes).

4. Place the greens onto 4 plates. Place 4 shrimp on top of each bed of greens.

5. Drizzle the sauce onto the greens as a dressing.

**Makes 4 appetizers**

# Poached Oysters
## with Stilton Cream

*24 large oysters, freshly shucked*
*2 cups white wine or champagne*
*2 cups heavy cream*
*¹/₄ cup shallots, chopped*
*¹/₄ cup crumbled Stilton cheese*
*salt and freshly ground pepper, for seasoning*
*¹/₈ cup fresh parsley, chopped*

1. Shuck the oysters (or buy pre-shucked oysters).

2. In a saucepan, bring the wine and shallots to a boil. Cook them for a few minutes to soften the shallots and blend the flavors.

3. Reduce the heat to a simmer and add the oysters. Poach them just until the edges begin to curl (about 2 to 3 minutes).

4. Remove the oysters with a slotted spoon, and set them aside.

5. Add the heavy cream to the pan and simmer it until the cream is reduced by half. (The sauce should be thick enough to coat the back of a spoon.)

6. Whisk the Stilton cheese into the sauce. Season it to taste with the salt and pepper.

7. Return the oysters to the sauce to heat through. Finish the sauce by adding the chopped parsley.

8. Serve in shallow bowls.

**Makes 6 appetizers**

**A Dickens' Favorite**

This dish is another celebrated recipe that we serve during the annual Dickens extravaganza. Stilton cheese certainly evokes the best that England had to offer in Dickens' day.

**Wine Notes**

 A dry Graves, French Sancerre or crisp New Zealand Sauvignon Blanc all go nicely with the Stilton cheese.

## Bread Crumbs With a Bite

Japanese bread crumbs are larger and have a crunchier consistency than regular bread crumbs. This adds a crunchy character when baking a crust or breading before frying. You can find Japanese bread crumbs at Asian specialty stores.

# *Blue Point Oysters*
## *with Spinach and Crab Meat*

*2 tablespoons butter*
*$^1/_2$ cup onion, diced*
*3 tablespoons Pernod*
*8 cups spinach, washed and picked*
*$1^1/_2$ cups Béchamel Sauce, cooled (see page 10)*
*1 pound crab meat*
*$^1/_2$ cup Monterey Jack cheese, grated*
*20 Long Island oysters, washed and shucked*
*Japanese bread crumbs, as needed*

1.  In a large sauté pan over medium heat, sauté the onions in the butter until they are transparent.

2.  Add the Pernod and cook for 2 minutes. Season well with the salt and pepper.

3.  Add the spinach and heat until just cooked.

4.  Squeeze as much liquid out of the spinach as you can.

5.  Cut the spinach into $^1/_2$-inch strips.

6.  Combine the Béchamel Sauce, crab meat, cheese and spinach.

7.  Preheat the oven to 375°F.

8.  Top each oyster with the mixture, spreading it over the entire shell.

9.  Sprinkle the tops of the oysters with the bread crumbs.

10. Bake the oysters for 10 to 15 minutes, until golden brown.

**Makes 4 appetizers**

## Wine Notes

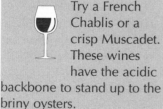

Try a French Chablis or a crisp Muscadet. These wines have the acidic backbone to stand up to the briny oysters.

# Star of Asia

3 tablespoons vegetable oil
1 pound tenderloin beef tips, cut into strips and seasoned with salt
   and pepper
1 cup carrots, cut julienne style
1 cup leeks, cut julienne style
6 radicchio cups
scallions, for garnish

## Tamari Ginger Sauce
2 teaspoons sesame oil
1 clove garlic, minced
1 tablespoon fresh ginger, grated
$^1/_2$ cup scallions, chopped
a few hot pepper flakes
$^1/_2$ cup tamari
3 ounces pineapple juice
2 tablespoons cornstarch
$^3/_4$ cup water

1.  Sauté the garlic, ginger and scallions in the sesame oil until soft.

2.  Add the hot pepper flakes, tamari and pineapple juice. Bring them to
    a boil, then reduce the heat to a simmer.

3.  In a bowl, mix the cornstarch and water.

4.  Whisk the cornstarch into the tamari sauce mixture. Bring it to a
    simmer and cook until it thickens. If the sauce is too thick or salty,
    add a touch more pineapple juice or water.

5.  Heat the vegetable oil in a sauté pan over medium-high heat. Add the
    beef tips, and sauté until the meat is seared. Add the carrots and
    leeks and cook for another minute.

6.  Add a ladle of the Tamari Ginger Sauce. Simmer for another minute.

7.  Place a radicchio cup on each plate and fill each to overflowing with
    the sautéed meat mixture. Ladle additional Tamari Ginger Sauce over
    the top and sprinkle with the scallions.

**Makes 6 appetizers**

## Eccentric Elephants

This dish is named after an elephant who once graced the shores of Cape May. Not just any elephant, Star of Asia was one of two wooden elephants built in south Jersey in the 1920s. Only one of these 70-foot-tall giants still stands: Lucy, in Margate, New Jersey. You can pay her a visit and walk around inside the structure.

## Wine Notes

 To match the dominant Asian flavors, try an Australian Shiraz or South African Pinotage.

*Soups & Salads*

Original Washington Inn Clam Chowder - 97
Cape May Clam Chowder, 1993 - 98
Lobster and Corn Chowder - 99
Lobster Bisque - 100
Rock Shrimp Bisque - 101
Scallop and Mushroom Bisque with Watercress - 102
Cream of Mustard Crab Soup - 103
Creamy Asparagus Soup - 104
Roasted Red Pepper Soup - 105
Beer and Cheddar Soup - 106
Tomato Gorgonzola Soup - 107
Mississippi Delta Seafood Soup - 108
Six Onion Soup - 110
Black Bean and Smoked Chicken Soup - 111
Duck and Wild Rice Soup - 112
Chilled Two-Melon Soup - 113
Watercress and Beet Salad with Raspberry Vinaigrette - 114
Jersey Tomatoes with Pesto Vinaigrette - 115
Jicama Salad - 116
Shaved Fennel Salad with Black Olives and Oranges - 117
Caesar Salad - 118
Mushroom Salad - 119
Spinach and Mushroom Salad with Hot Bacon Dressing - 120
Shrimp, Arugula and Roasted Pepper Salad with Garlic Aioli - 121
Marandino's Seafood Salad - 122
Smoked Trout Salad with Fresh Greens - 123
*Horseradish Vinaigrette - 123*
Pecan Crusted Goat Cheese - 124
*Mimosa Vinaigrette - 124*
Thai Peanut Salad - 125
Austrian Potato Salad - 126
Irma's Bean Salad with Walnut Dill Dressing - 127
Farmer Frank's Cucumber Relish - 128

## Wine Notes

 An Alsatian Pinot Blanc, Sylvaner or dry Riesling works nicely with this soup.

# Original Washington Inn Clam Chowder

*3 large potatoes, peeled and diced large*
*$1/2$ cup cornstarch*
*2 quarts milk*
*5 cups canned chopped clams with juice*
*chicken bouillon cubes*
*$1/2$ cup Clams Casino mix (see page 42)*
*8 steamed clams*
*paprika, as needed*

1.  Boil the potatoes until they are cooked al dente. Cool and reserve.

2.  Mix the cornstarch with 1 cup of cold milk and reserve.

3.  Heat the remaining milk, juice from the clams and chicken bouillon cubes to boiling.

4.  Turn down the heat and slowly add the cornstarch mixture.

5.  Whisk until the mixture is smooth and thick.

6.  Add the Clams Casino mix, canned clams and potatoes.

7.  Cook for 5 minutes.

8.  Place a steamed clam in the bottom of each bowl. Pour the soup into the bowls, and sprinkle with paprika.

**Serves 8**

# Cape May Clam Chowder, 1993

*4 slices of bacon*
*2 cups onions, diced*
*$^1/_4$ cup green pepper, diced*
*$^1/_2$ cup celery, diced*
*$^1/_2$ cup carrots, diced*
*1 clove garlic, chopped*
*1 bay leaf*
*3 medium potatoes, peeled and diced*
*1 teaspoon salt (for boiling potatoes)*
*1 teaspoon Worcestershire sauce*
*6 drops Tabasco*
*3 cups half-and-half or light cream*
*1 tablespoon fresh parsley, chopped*
*1 tablespoon dried thyme*
*salt and pepper, to taste*
*2 cups clam juice*
*2 cups clams, chopped*
*fresh parsley sprigs, for garnish*

1. Boil the potatoes in salted water until cooked. Discard the water.

2. In a preheated 350°F oven, bake the bacon until crisp. Drain and save the fat. Crumble the bacon and set aside.

3. In the bacon fat, slowly sauté the potatoes, onions, green pepper, celery, carrots, garlic and bay leaf until tender.

4. Add the sautéed vegetables, Worcestershire sauce, Tabasco, parsley, thyme, salt and pepper. Beat with a mixer or a sturdy whisk until creamy: The longer you beat, the smoother and thicker it becomes.

5. In a separate pan, cook the clams in the clam juice at just under boiling for 3 minutes.

6. Add the clams, juice and bacon to the vegetable mixture. Stir in the half-and-half and cook for 10 minutes. Garnish with parsley.

**Serves 4 to 6**

**Seafood Festival Winner 1993**

This recipe, from chef Richard Allen, won Cape May's first Seafood Festival Clam Chowder Contest, in 1993.

This recipe uses the potato as the thickener—a non-traditional technique, but it works well.

**Wine Notes**

Enjoy an Alsatian Pinot Blanc with this regional favorite recipe.

**Wine Notes**

Try a dry Riesling or a lighter French Burgundy with this soup.

# Lobster and Corn Chowder

*3 tablespoons butter*
*1/2 cup onions, diced*
*1/4 cup celery, diced*
*1/2 tablespoon fresh garlic, chopped*
*1 large potato, diced*
*2 cups corn kernels, fresh or frozen*
*1 1/2 cups chicken stock (see page 5)*
*1 12-ounce can of creamed corn*
*1 cup lobster meat, chopped*
*salt and freshly ground pepper, for seasoning*
*1 1/2 cups heavy cream*

1. In a large pot, sauté the onions, celery and garlic in the butter until they are soft. Do not brown them.

2. In a large pot, boil the potato in water until al dente.

3. Purée 1 cup of corn in a food processor. Add it to the sautéed vegetables.

4. Add the stock, creamed corn and remaining corn. Simmer for 5 minutes.

5. Add the lobster and potato. Season with salt and pepper.

6. Add the cream and simmer for 20 minutes.

**Serves 4**

# *Lobster Bisque*

¹/₂ cup butter
2 cups onions, diced
1 cup celery, diced
1 cup carrots, diced
1 bunch fresh thyme, chopped
1 teaspoon fresh garlic, chopped
1 bay leaf
¹/₂ cup flour
¹/₂ cup brandy
6 cups lobster stock or lobster base (see sidebar)
1 tablespoon tomato paste
pinch of cayenne pepper
1 teaspoon Worcestershire sauce
2 cups heavy cream
¹/₂ - 1 pound lobster meat
salt and white pepper, for seasoning

1. Sauté the onions, celery, carrots, thyme, garlic and bay leaf in the butter until golden brown.

2. Add the flour and stir well. Cook for a few minutes, until a nice paste forms.

3. Add the brandy, lobster stock, tomato paste, cayenne pepper and Worcestershire sauce.

4. Whisk until thick and smooth. Simmer for 30 minutes.

5. Strain the thickened broth.

6. Add the cream and lobster meat.

7. Season with salt and white pepper, to taste.

**Serves 8**

## Lobster Stock

The more shells that you use in this stock, the better.

Use 7 pounds of lobster shells. In ¹/₄ cup of hot clarified butter, add the shells and sear. Crush the shells in the pot with a mallet.

Melt 3 tablespoons of butter or vegetable oil in a large stockpot over medium heat. Add 3 chopped onions, 1 chopped celery stalk and 2 chopped leeks, and sauté until soft. Add 2 cups of white wine and 18 cups of water and bring to a boil. Simmer for 1 hour, reducing the broth by one-third. The yield is about 1 gallon. Reduce it further for a more concentrated flavor. Strain, then freeze or refrigerate.

Lobster base is a reduced, concentrated version of lobster stock. You can buy it in most gourmet specialty stores.

## Wine Notes

 Try a full, elegant French Burgundy, such as Puligny-Montrachet or Chassagne-Montrachet. A fuller style Mâcon Village also matches up nicely.

# Rock Shrimp Bisque

*$^1/_2$ cup butter*
*2 cups onions, diced*
*1 cup celery, diced*
*1 cup carrots, diced*
*1 bunch fresh thyme, chopped*
*1 teaspoon garlic, chopped*
*1 bay leaf*
*$^1/_2$ cup flour*
*$^1/_2$ cup brandy*
*6 cups strong shrimp stock (see page7)*
*1 tablespoon tomato paste*
*pinch of cayenne pepper*
*1 teaspoon Worcestershire sauce*
*2 cups heavy cream*
*2 pounds rock shrimp, cooked*
*salt and white pepper, for seasoning*

1. Sauté the onions, celery, carrots, thyme, garlic and bay leaf in the butter until golden brown.

2. Add the flour and stir well. Cook for a few minutes until a nice paste forms.

3. Add the brandy, shrimp stock, tomato paste, cayenne and Worcestershire sauce.

4. Whisk the mixture until it is thick and smooth. Simmer for 30 minutes.

5. Strain the thickened broth.

6. Add the cream and shrimp.

7. Season with salt and pepper, to taste.

**Serves 8**

# Scallop and Mushroom Bisque
## with Watercress

11 tablespoons butter
1 teaspoon garlic, chopped
3 cups mushrooms, sliced
2 pounds fresh scallops
1/2 cup onions, diced
1/2 cup flour
1 cup white wine
4 cups seafood stock or clam juice (see sidebar)
1 cup cream
salt and pepper, for seasoning
1 cup fresh watercress, chopped

1. Over medium heat, sauté the garlic, mushrooms and scallops in 3 tablespoons of butter. Cook for 10 minutes.

2. Strain out the scallops and mushrooms and set aside. Set the broth aside separately.

3. In the same pan, add the onions and the remaining butter (8 tablespoons). Sauté for 5 minutes. Add the flour and stir well. Cook for a few minutes until a nice paste forms.

4. Add the white wine, stock and strained broth.

5. Whisk this mixture until it is thick and smooth. Let it simmer for 30 minutes.

6. Strain this thickened broth.

7. Add the mushrooms and scallops back into the thickened broth.

8. Add the cream. Season with salt and pepper.

9. Add the watercress and serve.

**Serves 8**

### Seafood Stock and a Substitute

To make your own seafood stock, in a large stockpot bring 3 tablespoons vegetable oil, 4 cups rinsed and drained seafood shells (shrimp shells are fine), 3 onions, 3 carrots, 3 celery stalks and 8 cups cold water to a boil. Reduce the heat and simmer it, partially covered, for 20 minutes. Pour it through a strainer, pressing the shells to extract any remaining liquid. Let the stock cool, then refrigerate it until ready to use.

For this recipe, you can use clam juice as a substitute for seafood stock. To enhance its flavor, cut it in half with water and add some dry white wine or vermouth, then let it simmer with some chopped onion and a bay leaf for a few minutes. Remove the vegetables before using it.

### Wine Notes

 Try a medium-bodied Chardonnay from California.

# Cream of Mustard Crab Soup

$^1/_4$ pound bacon, diced
2 tablespoons butter
1 $^1/_2$ cups onion, diced
1 cup celery, chopped
1 teaspoon fresh garlic, chopped
1 bay leaf
4 tablespoons flour
2 cups chicken stock (see page 5)
1 cup clam broth or fish stock, if available (see page 7)
$^1/_2$ cup white wine
1 teaspoon Worcestershire sauce
1 teaspoon dry mustard
2 cups heavy cream
1 pound crab meat
3 tablespoons Dijon mustard
salt and pepper, for seasoning

1. Sauté and brown the bacon in a large stockpot.

2. Add the butter, onion, celery, garlic and bay leaf. Simmer for 5 minutes.

3. Add the flour and stir well. Cook for a few minutes until a nice paste forms.

4. Slowly add the chicken stock, clam broth, white wine, Worcestershire sauce and dry mustard.

5. Reduce the heat and simmer for 15 to 20 minutes.

6. Temper the cream and add it to the thickened broth.

7. Strain the soup. (Discard the strained ingredients.)

8. Add the crab meat and Dijon mustard.

9. Season with salt and pepper.

**Serves 6**

# Creamy Asparagus Soup

*3 pounds fresh asparagus*
*2 tablespoons butter*
*1 cup onions, diced*
*1/2 quart chicken stock (see page 5)*
*2 cups cream*
*3 tablespoons Dijon mustard*
*salt and pepper, to taste*

1. Break off the tough part of the asparagus spears. Cut off the tips, and reserve. Cut the rest of the asparagus into 2-inch pieces.

2. Blanch the asparagus tips in boiling water. Remove and chill.

3. Melt the butter in a heavy soup pot.

4. Sauté the onions and asparagus over medium heat for 5 minutes.

5. Add the chicken stock and simmer for 15 to 20 minutes. Skim off any scum that may accumulate on top of the stock.

6. Strain out the vegetables, carefully putting them into a food processor or blender. Purée them until smooth.

7. Add the purée back into the broth.

8. Add the cream and mustard. Simmer for a few minutes, then add the tips.

9. Season with the salt and pepper.

**Serves 6**

---

**Perfect Asparagus**

To buy the most tender asparagus, look for firm, straight spears that are apple green in color with tight, purple-tinged tips. While you'll see both thick and thin asparagus spears, size is not related to quality. You should look for stalks that measure at least 1/2-inch in diameter. At gourmet shops you can sometimes find white asparagus, a variety that is popular in Europe and has a slightly bitter flavor. Asparagus is best cooked the same day of purchase, but you can store it tightly wrapped in a plastic bag for 3 to 4 days.

**Wine Notes**

 A grassy Sauvignon Blanc goes quite well with the pronounced flavor of the asparagus.

**Wine Notes**

 An Italian Sauvignon Blanc or Pinot Grigio complements this soup nicely.

# Roasted Red Pepper Soup

$^1/_2$ cup butter
$1^1/_2$ cups potatoes, diced and cooked
1 cup celery, diced
1 cup onions, diced
$^1/_2$ cup leeks, cut julienne style
1 tablespoon garlic, chopped
$^1/_2$ cup flour
2 quarts chicken stock (see page 5)
1 cup cheddar cheese, grated
1 cup heavy cream
2 cups roasted red pepper, skinned, seeded and chopped (see page 70)
dash of Tabasco
salt and pepper, to taste
3 tablespoons parsley, chopped, for garnish

1.  Over medium heat, sauté the potatoes, celery, onion, leeks and garlic in the butter for 5 minutes.

2.  Add the flour and stir well. Cook for a few minutes, until a nice paste forms.

3.  Add the chicken stock and whisk until thick and smooth.

4.  Simmer for 30 minutes.

5.  Strain the thickened broth. (Discard the vegetables.)

6.  Add the cheese, cream and peppers.

7.  Season with the Tabasco, salt and pepper.

8.  Garnish with parsley.

**Serves 8**

# Beer and Cheddar Soup

*1 stick butter (8 tablespoons)*
*2 cups onions, chopped*
*1 teaspoon fresh garlic, chopped*
*1 cup carrots, chopped*
*1 cup celery, chopped*
*1/2 cup flour*
*12 ounces of tasty beer*
*3 cups chicken stock (see page 5)*
*3 cups heavy cream*
*1 pound sharp cheddar, grated*
*salt and pepper, for seasoning*

1. In a soup pot, sauté the onions, garlic, carrots and celery in butter for 10 minutes.

2. Sprinkle the mixture with flour and cook for a few minutes.

3. Add the beer and stock and whisk well until thickened. Simmer for 15 minutes.

4. Place the mixture into a food processor and purée.

5. Place it back into the pot and add the cream and cheese.

6. Stir until the cheese is melted and the cream is thoroughly mixed.

**Serves 6**

## Not Just for Drinking

Beer can appear in many recipes. Combine it with mustard, ginger and honey as a marinade before broiling or grilling meats. You also can use it as a coating with foods such as beer-batter shrimp. Also match it with cheddar in breads and fondues. For this recipe, any beer you have on hand will do, but you'll probably enjoy the soup more if you choose a beer you like to drink— whether that be a strong ale or mild lager.

## Wine Notes

The richness of this soup is cut nicely by a dry French Côtes du Rhône or an Italian Pinot Bianco.

## Simple Substitutions

This is a great year-round soup. Use frozen fresh basil in the winter. To make this a vegetarian soup, omit the bacon and use vegetable stock. For a richer soup, add light or heavy cream at the finish.

## Slurry

Slurry can refer to a paste made of cornstarch and water, or flour and water, that is used to thicken soups or sauces. The trick to mixing a smooth slurry is using cold water. Mix it slowly, using a whisk to gradually add the flour to the water. Remember: No lumps!

The cornstarch just needs to be dissolved in a little liquid (but mix this first, rather than adding dry cornstarch directly to the soup). One tablespoon of cornstarch can thicken approximately 1$^1$/$_2$ to 2 cups of liquid. For the flour paste, the ratio is 2 parts water to 1 part flour.

## Wine Notes

 Try a Sauvignon from Italy or a Sauvignon Blanc from California.

# Tomato Gorgonzola Soup

$^1$/$_2$ pound bacon, chopped
1 cup onion, diced
$^1$/$_2$ cup celery, diced
1 tablespoon butter
2$^1$/$_2$ cups plum tomatoes, canned and chopped
2 cups chicken stock (see page 5)
$^1$/$_4$ cup white wine
1 cup V-8 juice
$^1$/$_2$ cup tomato paste
$^1$/$_4$ teaspoon cayenne pepper
1 tablespoon Worcestershire sauce
1 tablespoon thyme
1 bay leaf
salt and pepper, for seasoning
$^1$/$_2$ cup Gorgonzola cheese, crumbled
$^1$/$_4$ cup fresh basil
light cream (optional)

*Slurry*
$^1$/$_4$ cup flour
$^1$/$_2$ cup cold water

1. In a large pot, sauté the bacon, onions and celery in the butter until they are tender.

2. Add all of the ingredients, except for the slurry (flour and water), Gorgonzola and basil. Simmer for approximately 45 minutes.

3. Make a slurry with the flour and cold water, whisking the flour slowly into the water. Be sure the slurry has no lumps.

4. Add the slurry to the soup, and use a whisk to mix it as it thickens.

5. Simmer for 15 more minutes, until the flour taste is gone.

6. Add the crumbled Gorgonzola cheese, fresh basil and light cream, to your liking.

**Serves 6**

# Mississippi Delta Seafood Soup

2 quarts chicken broth
$^1/_2$ cup brandy
2 cups white wine
2 tablespoons butter
3 cups mushrooms, sliced
1 cup green pepper, chopped
1 cup red pepper, chopped
3 cups green onions, sliced
1 pound shrimp, medium, peeled and chopped
1 pound scallops
salt and pepper, for seasoning

### Roux
$1^1/_4$ cup butter
$^1/_2$ pound shrimp shells
2 cups onions, chopped
1 cup celery, chopped
$1^1/_4$ cups flour

### Seasoning Mix
$^3/_4$ teaspoon salt
$^1/_2$ teaspoon granulated garlic
$^1/_2$ teaspoon cayenne pepper
$^1/_4$ teaspoon white pepper
$^1/_4$ teaspoon black pepper
$^1/_4$ teaspoon sweet basil, dried
$^1/_2$ teaspoon thyme, dried
$^1/_4$ teaspoon oregano, dried
$^1/_2$ cup fresh parsley, chopped

**Stock Versus Broth**

Richard Allen, one of our chefs, came up with this soup. It was an instant hit.

Chicken broth is made by simmering a whole chicken in water with onions, carrots, celery and a bouquet garni. The chicken is then taken out and used in some manner in a soup, casserole or salad.

Chicken stock is made from simmering the chicken bones to extract the nutrients, flavor and protein. Roasting the bones gives stock a different flavor.

Both flavors are different from each other, but can easily substitute for each other.

**Wine Notes**

Try a dry French Gewürztraminer or a dry German Riesling.

## Roux

A roux is a mixture of flour and oil (or butter) used to thicken liquids. The mixture is 50% flour and 50% oil by weight (meaning, for example, $1/2$ pound flour and $1/2$ pound butter). Roux can be made ahead or while you are preparing a dish. A rule of thumb for using roux is: Always add a cold liquid to a hot roux or a cold roux to a hot liquid. This activates the starches correctly for maximum thickening power.

## To Prepare Roux

Heat the oil to very hot. Add the flour and stir well so the flour is absorbed by the oil. Lower the heat and cook until the roux turns a light brown color. Be careful, as this mixture is extremely hot.

# Mississippi Delta Seafood Soup

1. Over medium heat, sauté the shrimp shells, onions and celery in $1^1/_4$ cups butter until the shells turn bright orange.

2. Add the flour and seasoning mix and stir well. Cook for a few minutes until a nice paste forms. This is called a roux.

3. Add the chicken broth, brandy and white wine. Whisk it until it becomes smooth and thick. Simmer for 30 minutes.

4. In another pan, sauté all of the vegetables in 2 tablespoons butter until they are tender.

5  Add the shrimp and scallops.

6. Strain the thickened chicken broth.

7. Add the seafood and vegetable mixture to the thickened broth.

8. Cook for 10 minutes. Adjust the seasoning.

**Serves 8**

# Six Onion Soup

*4 tablespoons butter*
*4 cups onions, chopped*
*4 large leeks, white parts only, sliced*
*1/2 cup shallots, chopped*
*6 medium garlic cloves, chopped*
*4 cups chicken stock (see page 5)*
*1 teaspoon thyme*
*1 bay leaf*
*1 teaspoon fresh pepper*
*1 cup heavy cream*
*1/4 cup green onions, cut on a bias*
*salt, to taste*
*homemade croutons, for garnish (see page 3)*
*fresh chives, for garnish*

1. Sauté the onions, leeks, shallots and garlic in the butter. Cover, but keep stirring occasionally. Lower the heat and cook for 25 minutes, until all of the ingredients are softened.

2. Add the stock, thyme, bay leaf and pepper. Bring to a simmer, and cook for another 20 minutes.

3. Strain the soup. Reserve the liquid.

4. Purée the cooked vegetables in a food processor. Add a little stock if needed.

5. Return the purée to the liquid. Stir in the cream and green onions.

6. Garnish with homemade croutons and fresh chives.

**Serves 4 to 6**

## Lovely Leeks

Leeks are related to the onion family, but are superior to their relatives when it comes to nutrition, offering more vitamins and minerals than onions or scallions. Leeks also have a milder, sweeter flavor and crunchy texture, which makes them tasty served on their own as a side dish.

The most popular method of cooking leeks is braising, but they're also famous in vichyssoise, a cold potato and leek soup. Take extra care when cleaning leeks, as dirt and grit can collect between overlapping leaves. Chopping them into pieces first, then submerging them in a pot of water makes them easier to clean.

## Wine Notes

Try a dry Vouvray or a Savennières with this soup. The steely flavors of the Chenin Blanc grape work well.

# Black Bean and Smoked Chicken Soup

*1 pound chicken breast, boneless and skinless*
*olive oil, for seasoning*
*salt and pepper, for seasoning*
*hickory, apple or other hardwood chips*
*8 strips bacon, diced*
*1 large Spanish onion, diced*
*3 large celery ribs, diced*
*2 cloves fresh garlic, finely chopped*
*3 bay leaves*
*1 teaspoon dried thyme*
*1 teaspoon cumin*
*1 teaspoon ground coriander*
*$^1/_2$ teaspoon oregano*
*1 teaspoon basil leaves*
*$^1/_2$ teaspoon dry mustard*
*1 pound black beans, soaked overnight in water*
*$1^1/_2$ quarts chicken stock (see page 5)*

1.  Season the chicken with the olive oil, salt and pepper. Place on a rack or wire insert.

2.  Place the hardwood chips in a heavy skillet. Place this on the stove top over high heat. When the chips start to smoke, place the chicken in the skillet and cover it tightly with aluminum foil. Place the pan in a preheated, 450°F oven for 10 minutes.

3.  Remove and cool. Cut the chicken into strips julienne style.

4.  Heat the bacon in a soup pot. When it turns brown and fat is rendered, add the onions, celery, garlic and bay leaves. Cook until the onions turn translucent.

5.  Add the spices, then the black beans and stock. Simmer until the beans are tender.

6.  Remove one-fourth of the beans. Purée them in a food processor until they are smooth. Return them to the soup and add the chicken.

**Serves 8**

# Duck and Wild Rice Soup

*¹/₂ cup butter*
*¹/₂ cup flour*
*2¹/₂ cups water*
*1 cup wild rice blend*
*4 pounds duck legs and thighs; meat, bones and fat separated*
  *(see Duck Confit on page 196)*
*2 tablespoons garlic*
*1 cup onions, chopped*
*2 tablespoons thyme, chopped*
*1 bay leaf*
*2 cups white wine*
*2 quarts chicken stock (see page 5)*
*1 cup shiitake mushrooms, sliced*
*1 cup button mushrooms, sliced*
*4 tablespoons parsley, chopped*
*3 cups heavy cream*
*salt and pepper, for seasoning*

1.  Melt the butter in a saucepan. Add the flour and stir well. Cook for a few minutes, until a nice paste forms to create a roux. Cool.

2.  In a separate pot, mix the water and rice. Cover with a lid and slowly simmer until cooked (approximately 45 minutes).

3.  In a separate pan, sear the duck bones in the duck fat. Add the garlic, onions, thyme and bay leaf. Cook for 10 minutes.

4.  Add the wine and stock to deglaze the pan. Boil and reduce the mixture by half (takes approximately 20 minutes). Strain.

5.  Crumble in the roux. Whisk until thickened. Cook for 15 minutes.

6.  Cut the duck meat into bite-size pieces.

7.  Sauté the mushrooms with the duck meat in its natural fat for 5 minutes. Add this to the thickened soup.

8.  Add the rice and parsley. Finish by adding the cream. Season with salt and pepper.

**Serves 6**

## Bouquet Garni

This flavor enhancer is easy to make and wonderful when added to simmering broths, soups, sauces or stews. Just wrap dried herbs in cheesecloth or use fresh herbs tied together in a "bouquet." Make several bouquet garnis and put them in the freezer in zip-lock bags until you are ready to use them.

Standard ingredients in a bouquet are bay leaves, celery, leeks, parsley, thyme, garlic and sometimes rosemary.

## Wine Notes

 An Oregon Pinot Noir or a fruity Zinfandel from California works well with the rich duck flavor in this soup.

### Wine Notes

 Try an off-dry Riesling or a Muscat from California.

# Chilled Two-Melon Soup

*1 large ripe cantaloupe, halved, seeded, peeled and coarsely chopped*
*2 tablespoons fresh lemon juice*
*4 tablespoons honey*
*1 medium-size ripe honeydew melon, halved, seeded, peeled and coursely chopped*
*2 tablespoons fresh lime juice*
*mint sprigs, for garnish*

1. Purée the cantaloupe and lemon juice in a blender or food processor until smooth.

2. Stir in 2 tablespoons of the honey. Pour into a bowl and set aside. Rinse the food processor.

3. Place the honeydew with the lime juice and chopped mint in the food processor and purée until smooth.

4. Stir in the remaining honey and pour into a separate bowl.

5. Cover both bowls and chill for at least 1 hour, or overnight.

6. At serving time, spoon about $1/2$ cup of each purée into well-chilled soup bowls, allowing the colors to mix in the middle.

7. Garnish with mint sprigs.

**Serves 4**

# Watercress and Beet Salad
## with Raspberry Vinaigrette

*5 medium-size beets*
*¹/₂ cup Raspberry Vinaigrette (see page 21)*
*1 head green leaf lettuce, cleaned and cut into bite-size pieces*
*3 bunches watercress, tough stems removed*
*3 tablespoons orange zest, chopped*
*1 red onion, sliced thin*
*1 cup Washington Inn Croutons (see page 3)*

1. In a medium saucepan, heat the beets with enough water to cover them. Bring them to a rolling boil. Lower the heat and simmer for 30 minutes, or until the beets are tender.

2. Cool the beets. Peel them and cut them into julienned slices.

3. Place the beets in a bowl and ladle some vinaigrette over them to marinate.

4. In a bowl, mix the lettuce, watercress and orange zest with the Raspberry Vinaigrette.

5. Divide the lettuce mix among 6 plates. Sprinkle the beets around the plate. Top with the onion and croutons.

**Makes 6 salads**

### Wonderful Watercress

Watercress gets its name from the way it grows: This plant grows in cool running water near streams and brooks. With its crisp leaves and peppery taste, it adds zest to any salad. When selecting watercress, look for bunches with leaves that are deep green in color and have no yellow spots or wilting. Wash and shake watercress dry before using it in dishes. Watercress can last up to 5 days in the refrigerator in a plastic bag. In addition to livening up salads, watercress stands in for parsley as an attractive and flavorful garnish for soups and cooked dishes.

## Pesto, Presto!

Pesto, an uncooked sauce traditionally made with a mortar and pestle, originates from Genoa, Italy. Made with fresh basil, garlic, pine nuts, Parmesan cheese and oil, it has a fresh distinctive taste. Pesto can also be made with other herbs such as cilantro, mint or sage. In a pinch, walnuts also can stand in for pricey pine nuts.

### Wine Notes

 Try this dish with a grassy Sauvignon Blanc from the Monterey area of California.

# *Jersey Tomatoes*
## *with Pesto Vinaigrette*

*2 cups fresh basil leaves*
*4 garlic cloves, peeled and chopped*
*1 cup pine nuts*
*1 cup olive oil*
*1/4 cup white wine vinegar*
*salt and freshly ground pepper, for seasoning*
*1 cup Parmesan cheese*
*1/4 cup Romano cheese*
*4 pounds of ripe Jersey tomatoes*
*fresh basil, for garnish*

1. In a food processor, combine the basil, garlic and nuts.

2. While the processor is still running, slowly pour the olive oil into the mixture.

3. Place this mixture into a bowl, and season with the vinegar, salt and freshly ground pepper.

4. Fold in the cheeses—and your Pesto Vinaigrette is ready!

5. Cut each tomato into nice, thick slices. Arrange them on a platter, and pour the pesto vinaigrette over the tomatoes.

6. Garnish with fresh basil and serve.

**Makes 2 cups**

# Jicama Salad

4 large jicama, peeled and diced into ³/₄-inch cubes
3 jalapeño peppers, seeds removed and chopped
1 bunch cilantro, chopped
1 cup freshly roasted corn kernels
¹/₂ cup red pepper, diced
¹/₂ cup green pepper, diced
¹/₂ cup black beans, cooked
¹/₂ cup olive oil
¹/₈ cup cider vinegar
1 tablespoon sugar
1 teaspoon garlic, chopped
zest of 1 lemon
juice of 1 lime
salt and fresh pepper, for seasoning

1.  Mix all of the ingredients together.

2.  Marinate for 2 to 4 hours.

**Makes 1 bowl**

**Jicama (Pronounced Hicama)**

Jicama, referred to as the Mexican apple, is a crunchy vegetable with the texture of a crisp apple. It is neutral in flavor, so you can jazz it up however you see fit.

This vegetable is a tuber of a pea-producing plant that is native to Mexico. Its ivory-white flesh does not react with oxygen to become discolored.

The jicama must be peeled before its use. Cut it in half, then peel it with a paring knife to make it easier to handle. Jicama is delicious raw, but also can be cooked. You can boil or bake it like a potato.

Serve raw slices of jicama sprinkled with lime or lemon and your favorite seasoning blend. Cut into chips, jicama is a wonderful, guilt-free snack. It also stands in well for water chestnuts in recipes, especially stir fries. To store cut jicama, place pieces in cold water in a sealed container.

## On Olives...

Although olives do not offer the typical sweetness of a fruit—that's exactly what they are. Both green and black olives come from the same type of evergreen trees, which originated in the Mediterranean. Green olives are picked unripe, while black ones are fully ripe. When buying olives, remember that size is not always the best sign of quality. Large, woody, dull green olives are not as tasty and succulent as the smaller yellowish Manzanilla variety.

## Wine Notes

 With this salad, try a crisp wine like a young Chablis or Sauvignon Blanc from the Loire Valley of France.

# Shaved Fennel Salad
## with Black Olives and Oranges

*4 cups greens, spring mix*
*3/4 cup fresh black olives, pitted and sliced (not canned)*
*orange segments from 2 oranges, peeled*
*1 large bulb of fennel, cored and sliced thin*
*1 medium red onion, sliced very thin*

*Dressing*
*1 tablespoon shallots, chopped*
*juice of 1 orange*
*1 tablespoon chives, chopped*
*3/4 cup olive oil*
*salt and freshly ground pepper, for seasoning*

1   Whisk together the shallots, orange juice and chives.

2.  Slowly add the olive oil to make an emulsion (having a consistency like mayonnaise).

3.  Season with the salt and pepper.

4.  With half of this dressing, toss the greens. Divide them among 4 plates.

5.  Sprinkle the olives and orange segments onto each plate.

6.  Add the fennel and onion slices, then drizzle the remainder of the dressing over the top.

**Serves 4**

# Caesar Salad

*1 clove garlic*
*2 anchovy fillets*
*$^1/_4$ teaspoon salt*
*1 large egg, cooked for 1 minute in boiling water*
*10 grinds freshly ground black pepper*
*1 teaspoon Worcestershire sauce*
*1 tablespoon Dijon mustard*
*$^1/_4$ cup olive oil*
*juice of half a lemon*
*1 head romaine lettuce, chopped into 1-inch pieces*
*$^1/_2$ cup Parmesan cheese*
*2 cups of garlic croutons (see page 32)*

1. In a large salad bowl, rub and crush the garlic and anchovies into the salt. Rub this mixture along the edges of the bowl as well.

2. Add the egg and whisk well.

3. Add the freshly ground pepper, Worcestershire sauce and mustard.

4. In a steady stream, slowly whisk in the olive oil.

5. Add the lemon juice. Then add the romaine lettuce and Parmesan cheese.

6. Toss the romaine gently, until the leaves are coated evenly.

7. Toss in the garlic croutons before serving.

**Serves 4**

## The Original Caesar

Caesar Salad was originally conceived in Tijuana, Mexico, by Caesar Cardini. The original recipe was prepared tableside. Romaine lettuce leaves were lightly dressed with olive oil, salt, freshly ground pepper, lemon juice and Worcestershire sauce. The egg had already been coddled (cooked for 1 minute) and was then cracked directly into the bowl.

## Wine Notes

 Try this salad with a dry crisp Chardonnay from Sonoma.

## Nonreactive Pots

Nonreactive cookware are pots and pans that are not affected by the acids found in citrus juice, vinegar or wine. Anodized aluminum cookware is nonreactive and safe to use with these foods, as is glass, enamel, stainless steel and most non-stick cookware. Copper, unlined aluminum or cast iron can react with these foods and may cause an off flavor or discoloration.

## Wine Notes

 A dry rosé from Provence or a light Oregon Pinot Noir blends nicely with the seasoning in this mushroom dish.

# Mushroom Salad

*2 pounds button mushrooms*
*juice of 1 lemon*
*2 tablespoons parsley, chopped, for garnish*

*Marinade*
*3 tablespoons white vinegar*
*2 tablespoons mustard*
*1 cup olive oil*
*$^1/_4$ cup white wine*
*juice of 1 lemon*
*1 tablespoon oregano*
*salt and freshly ground pepper, for seasoning*

1. Mix all of the marinade ingredients together in a nonreactive pot.

2. Bring to a simmer.

3. Immediately pour the marinade over the mushrooms. Let this sit for at least 1 hour.

4. Squeeze the lemon juice onto the marinated mushrooms.

5. Season with salt and freshly ground pepper.

6. Garnish with chopped parsley.

**Serves 4**

# Spinach and Mushroom Salad
## with Hot Bacon Dressing

*8 cups fresh spinach, washed and picked*
*2 cups mushrooms, sliced*
*salt and freshly ground pepper, for seasoning*
*1 cup Washington Inn Croutons (see page 3)*

*Hot Bacon Dressing*
*4 strips of bacon, diced*
*¼ cup onion, diced*
*⅓ cup chicken stock (see page 5)*
*⅓ cup vinegar*
*1½ tablespoons sugar*
*¼ cup kirschwasser*
*1 tablespoon cornstarch*
*2 tablespoons white wine*

1.  In a thick-bottom pan, sauté the bacon until it is brown.

2.  Add the onions, and sauté until translucent. Remove this mixture from the pan and set it aside.

3.  Deglaze the pan by adding the stock, vinegar, sugar and kirsch.

4.  Simmer this mixture for 5 minutes.

5.  In a separate bowl, dissolve the cornstarch into the white wine.

6.  Add this mixture to the dressing in the pan. Whisk to avoid lumps.

7.  Return the onions and bacon to the mixture. Simmer for 5 minutes.

8.  Divide the spinach among 4 plates.

9.  Place the mushrooms on top of the spinach.

10. Ladle the Hot Bacon Dressing onto the salads.

11. Season with salt and pepper. Top with the homemade croutons.

**Serves 4**

---

**A Touch of Cherry**

Kirschwasser—also referred to as kirsch (the German word for "cherry")—is a brandy made from cherries. Popularly used in cheese fondues, it is renowned for its distinctive flavor.

**Wine Notes**

A dry Pinot Blanc or German Riesling works well with this salad.

### Arugula (a.k.a. Rocket)

A staple in many Italian vegetable gardens, arugula, also called rocket, is a wonderful green. Its leaf is shaped like a baby oak leaf or dandelion. It can be hot like a radish and has a peanut-like taste. This green can get quite sandy, so make sure that you soak the leaves in cold water to remove any soil.

### Wine Notes

 This dish is delicious with a Pinot Blanc from Alsace or Oregon. Their crisp fruit balances the light vinaigrette.

# Shrimp, Arugula and Roasted Pepper Salad with Garlic Aioli

16 large shrimp
1 tablespoon fresh lemon juice
1 tablespoon champagne vinegar
1 teaspoon black pepper
3 ounces extra virgin olive oil
salt and freshly ground pepper, for seasoning
4 cups arugula, soaked and cleaned
$^{1}/_{2}$ cup roasted yellow peppers, cut julienne style (see page 70)
$^{1}/_{2}$ cup roasted red peppers, cut julienne style (see page 70)
3 tablespoons Roasted Garlic Aioli (see page 155)
12 Baby Pear or cherry tomatoes, cut in half
4 sprigs of oregano

1. Fill a large pot with water and bring it to a boil.

2. Drop the shrimp into the water and cook for approximately 4 minutes, or until just done. Do not overcook.

3. Remove the shrimp and plunge them into ice water. When cool, peel the shrimp completely. Devein the shrimp and keep them refrigerated.

4. In a bowl, make a vinaigrette by whisking together the lemon, vinegar, pepper and olive oil. Taste and season with salt and pepper if necessary.

5. In a salad bowl, toss the arugula and peppers with enough vinaigrette to coat the leaves. Divide equally onto 4 salad plates.

6. Place 4 shrimp on top of the greens on each plate.

7. Drizzle the garlic aioli over each salad.

8. Garnish with tomatoes and oregano.

**Serves 4**

# Marandino's Seafood Salad

*2 tablespoons salt*
*1 pound calamari tubes, sliced*
*¹/₂ pound octopus, large chunks*
*1 pound monkfish fillet, diced large*
*4 pounds mussels, cleaned, steamed and meat removed*
*1 red pepper, diced medium*
*1 green pepper, diced medium*
*1 small red onion, diced medium*

## Vinaigrette
*¹/₄ cup fresh basil, cut chiffonade*
*¹/₈ cup Italian parsley, chopped*
*1 cup virgin olive oil*
*¹/₃ cup balsamic vinegar*
*1 tablespoon fresh lemon juice*
*1 teaspoon white pepper*
*salt, to taste*

1.  With a whisk or in a food processor, mix together all of the ingredients for the vinaigrette.

2.  Fill a large pot with water. Add the salt and bring to a boil.

3.  Quickly blanch the calamari and octopus. Remove and chill them.

4.  Add the monkfish to the water and poach it until fully cooked (approximately 5 minutes).

5.  Mix the monkfish with the vinaigrette. Season well with additional salt and pepper, if necessary.

6.  Combine the calamari, octopus, mussels, peppers and onion, then add the monkfish and vinaigrette. Toss.

7.  Marinate for 2 hours. Adjust the seasoning before serving.

**Serves 4 appetizer salads**

## Viva Italia!

Doug Marandino is the restaurant's sous chef. He first prepared this dish for one of our Italian wine dinners. Twice a year, in the spring and fall, we offer a special menu featuring authentic Italian dishes matched with their ideal Italian wines.

## Wine Notes

 A dry Vernaccia or Cortese di Gavi from Italy brings out the freshness of this seafood salad.

## Wine Notes

 A Beaujolais or a Dolcetto from Italy holds up to the strong flavors of the trout and horseradish.

# Smoked Trout Salad
## with Fresh Greens and Horseradish Vinaigrette

*8 ounces smoked trout fillets, broken into pieces*
*6 cups greens, spring mix*
*Horseradish Vinaigrette (below)*
*2 fresh beets, peeled and cut julienne style*
*12 pumpernickel croutons (see page 3)*

1. Place the trout and greens in a large mixing bowl.

2. Add enough vinaigrette to coat the greens and trout. Be careful to just lightly coat the greens, without adding too much vinaigrette.

3. Divide the salad among 4 plates. Sprinkle with the julienned beets.

4. Use pumpernickel croutons as a good accompaniment.

## Horseradish Vinaigrette

*1 cup sour cream*
*1/2 cup mayonnaise*
*1/2 cup horseradish, drained*
*2 tablespoons champagne vinegar*
*juice of 1 lemon*
*dash of Worcestershire sauce*
*salt and freshly ground pepper, for seasoning*

1. Using a wire whisk, mix together all of the ingredients.

2. Let this rest in the refrigerator for 1 hour while the flavors blend.

**Serves 4**

# Pecan Crusted Goat Cheese
## with Mimosa Vinaigrette

*2 logs goat cheese, 3¹/₂ ounces each*
*1¹/₂ cups pecans, finely chopped*
*3 tablespoons olive oil*
*3 cups greens, spring mix*
*Mimosa Vinaigrette (below)*
*1 cup orange segments, peeled and diced large*
*1 tablespoon orange zest, chopped*
*freshly ground pepper, for seasoning*

1.  Cut each cheese log into 4 slices, taking care not to break them.

2.  Put the cheese slices in the pecans, pressing the pecans into the cheese to make a crust. Sauté in 3 tablespoons olive oil, a few minutes on each side.

3.  Place the greens in a large mixing bowl. Add enough vinaigrette to lightly coat the greens, but do not add too much.

4.  Divide the greens among 4 plates, and sprinkle each with the orange segments and zest.

5.  Place 2 slices of goat cheese on top of the greens on each plate. Season with the pepper.

## Mimosa Vinaigrette

*3 tablespoons orange juice*
*3 tablespoons sparkling wine*
*1 tablespoon champagne vinegar*
*6 ounces extra virgin olive oil*
*salt and freshly ground pepper, for seasoning*

1.  Mix all of the liquid ingredients together.

2.  Taste, then season with the salt and pepper.

**Serves 4**

**A New Kind of Knife**

Try using dental floss to cut the goat cheese. This method works well in the restaurant for cheesecakes as well as goat cheese.

With this recipe, which calls for sautéing the cheese, the trick is to use cold cheese— the colder, the better!

**Wine Notes**

A Sancerre, Pouilly Fumé or minerally dry Vouvray matches the sharp flavors of the goat cheese.

## The Three C's

Cumin is an herb that is often associated with international foods, such as curry, chili, beans and rice dishes.

Coriander is another herb that is commonly used in curry, but can also appear in foods ranging from apple pie to pickles. Although these foods use the seeds of the coriander plant, many other dishes contain the leaves.

When the leaves of the coriander plant are the featured spice, they are frequently referred to as cilantro or Chinese parsley. It may sound confusing, but bear in mind that they are simply different forms of the same plant—named in different languages.

## Wine Notes

Try a Gewürztraminer or a dry Riesling from Alsace. The pronounced Asian flavors of this salad blend nicely with the racy flavors of these wines.

# Thai Peanut Salad

1 pound spaghetti or linguine, cooked al dente
4 ounces snow peas, blanched al dente and cut julienne style
1 red pepper, cut julienne style
1 cucumber, peeled, seeded and sliced into half moons

### Dressing

$1^1/_4$ teaspoons fresh garlic, chopped
1 teaspoon ginger, dry
$^1/_2$ teaspoon cumin
$^1/_2$ teaspoon coriander
1 teaspoon black pepper
$^1/_2$ teaspoon salt
$^1/_2$ teaspoon cayenne pepper
$^2/_3$ cup peanut butter
2 tablespoons sesame oil
$^1/_2$ tablespoon cilantro, finely chopped
$^1/_2$ tablespoon basil, finely chopped
$^1/_4$ cup rice vinegar
$^1/_4$ cup green onions, sliced
$^3/_8$ cup pineapple juice
$^1/_2$ tablespoon fish sauce (optional)
    (if not using, add 1 extra teaspoon salt)
2 limes, zested and juiced
6-ounce can coconut milk
$^1/_2$ tablespoon hot sauce
$^1/_2$ cup soy oil

1. In a food processor, mix all of the dressing ingredients—except the soy oil.

2. Slowly blend in the soy oil.

3. Combine the noodles, snow peas, peppers and cucumbers. Toss with the dressing.

4. Marinate for at least 45 minutes before serving.

**Makes 1 large bowl**

# Austrian Potato Salad

*1 pound bacon*
*3 pounds Red Skin potatoes, diced*
*1 cup red onion, chopped*
*1/2 cup green onions, green part only, chopped*
*6 tablespoons Dijon mustard*
*1/8 cup red wine vinegar*
*1/4 cup olive oil*
*1/8 cup parsley, chopped*
*salt and freshly ground pepper, for seasoning*

1. In a preheated 350°F oven, cook the bacon until it is crisp. Set aside the bacon fat. Chop the bacon.

2. Fill a large pot with salted water. Bring the water to a boil.

3. Add the potatoes and cook until they are just done (approximately 10 minutes).

4. Strain and cool the potatoes with running water.

5. Mix all of the remaining ingredients together (including the bacon fat). Toss in the potatoes. Season with salt and freshly ground pepper.

6. Serve immediately, or refrigerate and serve later.

**Makes 1 medium bowl**

### Serving Suggestions

This salad is always good, but it is best when it's served just after tossing.

This dish offers a wonderful alternative to traditional mayonnaise-based potato salads because it will keep better in the cooler. It is also perfect served on a luncheon buffet, placed on a platter lined with crisp lettuce greens such as romaine. It is delicious served warm, at room temperature or slightly chilled, and can be made ahead of time.

# Irma's Bean Salad
## with Walnut Dill Dressing

*1 pound green beans, trimmed*

*Dressing*
*$^1/_2$ cup red onions, chopped*
*$^1/_4$ cup Italian parsley, chopped*
*$^1/_3$ cup fresh dill, chopped*
*3 tablespoons white wine vinegar*
*$^1/_4$ cup toasted walnuts, chopped*
*2 tablespoons plain lowfat yogurt*
*2 tablespoons sour cream*
*salt and freshly ground pepper, to taste*

1. Cook the beans in a pot of salted water until they are tender but still crisp (approximately 10 minutes).

2. In a food processor, blend all of the dressing ingredients until smooth.

3. Spoon the dressing over the beans.

**Serves 4**

# Farmer Frank's Cucumber Relish

*6 fresh cucumbers, scored with a fork and sliced thin*
*1 onion, cut in half and sliced*

*Marinade*
*3 cups white vinegar*
*¹/₄ cup sugar*
*2 tablespoons fresh dill, chopped*
*3 tablespoons olive oil*
*salt and freshly ground pepper, to taste*

1.  Mix all of the ingredients together.

2.  Allow the flavors to blend for at least 2 hours before serving.

**Makes 1 small bowl**

**Fresh is Best**

Farmer Frank Matiera has provided us with local produce for many years. Cucumbers, corn, tomatoes, melons and peppers are his yearly staples. We served this salad for years as a complementary relish. We still have customers who request it.

**Scoring**

Scoring is the practice of making shallow or deep cuts in a decorative pattern with a sharp knife. While scoring is usually done with vegetables, it also can be used on the thicker parts of fish so they can cook as quickly as thinner areas. With meat, scoring is done to tenderize, assist flavor absorption during marinating or promote the draining of excess fat while cooking.

*Seafood*

## Carefree Crabs

This preparation, developed by Douglas Gomersall, is a great way to prepare crabs ahead with easy cooking. Use your imagination and stuff them with different fillings.

## Grades of Crab Meat

Jumbo lump meat is the most expensive, with mostly the largest lumps of meat. It has very few shells, and takes the least amount of time to pick.

Lump meat has both large lumps and small pieces of crab. It is mostly free of shells, but has more than jumbo lump crab meat. It is also less expensive.

Backfin meat has small pieces of crab meat with a good amount of shells.

Special meat has small pieces of crab meat and a lot of shells. It is the least expensive.

Claw meat is a brown, very flavorful meat. It has very few shells and is great for soups, stews and even crab cakes. You just need to adjust to the color. The price of this meat is well under half that of jumbo lump.

# Stuffed Soft Shell Crabs

12 soft shell crabs, cleaned
2 tablespoons clarified butter (see page 181)
1 pound jumbo lump crab meat, picked
1 pound spinach, cleaned, cooked and chopped
1 clove fresh garlic, chopped
1/2 onion, chopped
1 cup fresh Parmesan cheese, grated
2 roasted red peppers, peeled and diced (see page 70)
salt and freshly ground pepper, for seasoning
4 ounces melted butter
Classic Beurre Blanc (see page 11) or extra virgin olive oil (optional)

1. Sauté the onion and garlic in 2 tablespoons clarified butter until translucent. Cool.

2. Mix all of the ingredients together—except the melted butter and crabs. Season with salt and pepper.

3. Pull up the tips of each crab's shell and stuff each side with the mixture. (Crabs will have puffed out shoulders.)

4. Place the crabs on the baking sheets. Brush amply with the melted butter.

5. Bake in a preheated 400°F oven for 15 to 20 minutes.

6. Serve with Beurre Blanc, or simply drizzled with extra virgin olive oil.

**Serves 6**

# *Jewel of Provence*

*2 cups Jewel Broth (opposite page)*
*16 large shrimp, peeled and deveined*
*1 pound scallops*
*1/2 cup tomatoes, chopped*
*1 cup Herb Butter (opposite page)*
*4 tablespoons fresh basil, chiffonade*
*1 pound fettucine, cooked*

1.  In a large saucepan, bring the Jewel Broth to a simmer. Add the shrimp, scallops and tomatoes and poach for 3 minutes.

2.  Remove the seafood and tomatoes and keep warm.

3.  Reduce the broth by half.

4.  Add the seafood and tomatoes back in.

5.  Add 1 cup of Herb Butter. Shake the pan to incorporate it and make a sauce.

6.  Add the basil.

7.  Reheat the pasta in hot water.

8.  Serve the seafood over the pasta on 4 separate plates. Pour the sauce over all.

**Makes 4 entrées or 6 appetizers**

**Chiffonade**

This is a type of cut that pertains to finely cut leafy greens and herbs. It tends to look like a long thin strand or sliver. Basil is an herb that is often cut this way. The leaves do not bruise when cut this way: They are stacked and then rolled tightly, like a cigarette. The cut is made finely across the roll. This cut is good for both garnishing and making a bed on a plate.

**Wine Notes**

 A crisp Sauvignon Blanc with grassy undertones complements the seafood and herb broth.

We named this dish Jewel of
Provence in celebration of all
its ingredients. The scallops
and shrimp seem to sparkle
like jewels, and highlight its
presentation. Many of the
ingredients—basil, fresh
herbs, garlic, and olive oil—
are frequently used in
Provence.

Jewel Broth itself is quite
versatile. It is blended before
we cook the dish so that we
always keep the right
proportions. You can use this
broth for cooking fish or any
other type of seafood, tossing
with pasta or preparing
escargot. It also makes a
great marinade for chicken or
fish.

# Jewel Broth

*1¹/₂ cups white wine*
*¹/₂ cup olive oil*
*4 tablespoons shallots, chopped*
*4 tablespoons garlic, chopped*
*juice of 3 lemons*
*salt and pepper, for seasoning*

1.  Mix all of the ingredients together. Season with salt and pepper.

**Yields 2¹/₂ cups**

# Herb Butter

*1 pound butter, softened*
*4 tablespoons fresh basil, chopped*
*4 tablespoons fresh parsley, chopped*
*3 tablespoons shallots, chopped*
*1 tablespoon fresh rosemary, chopped*
*1 tablespoon fresh thyme, chopped*
*2 teaspoons garlic, chopped*
*1 teaspoon salt*
*1 teaspoon freshly ground pepper*

1.  In a mixer, blend all of the ingredients together.

2.  Roll the butter in plastic wrap or parchment paper. Refrigerate or
    freeze it until ready for use.

**Makes 1 pound**

# Seared Scallops
## with Tomato-Mushroom Risotto

6 tablespoons butter
1 medium onion, peeled and diced
2 teaspoons garlic, chopped
2 cups arborio rice
1/2 cup white wine
4 1/2 cups chicken stock
2 cups water
2 pounds scallops
1/2 cup tomatoes, chopped
1 cup mushrooms, sliced
1/2 cup heavy cream
1/2 cup Parmesan cheese
salt and freshly ground pepper, for seasoning

1.  Over medium heat, melt 1 tablespoon butter in a heavy sauce pan. Add the onions and garlic. Sauté them until the onions are translucent. Do not brown the garlic.

2.  Add the rice, and sauté it for 1 or 2 minutes, until it is opaque and starts to make a clicking sound.

3.  Slowly add the white wine. Stir constantly until the rice absorbs it.

4.  Continue to add the remaining liquids slowly, stirring frequently and adding only enough for the rice to absorb. Continue this process until the rice is cooked al dente.

5.  Meanwhile, season the scallops with salt and pepper. In a hot pan with 3 tablespoons butter, sear the scallops for 3 minutes on each side. Reserve and keep warm.

6.  In the same pan, add 2 tablespoons butter and sauté the mushrooms, tomatoes and spinach until al dente.

7.  Add the sautéed vegetables, cream and cheese into the rice. Mix well.

8.  Place the risotto on the center of each of 4 plates. Place the scallops on top of each. Serve immediately.

**Serves 4**

**Scallops**

Scallops are a staple and always available fresh in Cape May. Scallops are not stationary creatures like clams. They can swim from place to place by opening and closing their shells. This is the reason that they have such a large abductor muscle. This is the only part of the scallop that most Americans eat.

At the restaurant we specify dry scallops and always get clam boat scallops. These scallops, caught on clam boats, are less than 24 hours old and are usually larger than other commercial scallops. The taste is sweet and delicious and the same quality as diver scallops. These scallops pan sear and sauté beautifully.

**Wine Notes**

 Try a rich toasty Meursault for a complementary flavor or a light crisp Gavi for a contrasting taste.

## Capers: Animal or Vegetable?

These small green buds are actually from the flowers of a caper plant, a low prickly shrub of Mediterranean origin. The buds are pulled and used in various ways. For example, we use them in sauces for meats and fish and in salads to add that extra piquant character.

## Wine Notes

We like this dish with a smooth Merlot or a spicy Châteauneuf-du-Pape.

# *Pan-Seared Salmon*
## *with Tomatoes, Capers and Red Onions*

*4 skinless salmon fillets, 6 ounces each*
*1/4 cup cracked black pepper (more or less, depending on your taste)*
*1/4 cup olive oil*
*1 large red onion, sliced*
*3 cups tomato, diced*
*3 tablespoons capers*
*2 tablespoons fresh lemon juice*
*1/4 cup white wine*
*4 tablespoons butter (optional)*
*salt and pepper, to taste*

1. Sprinkle the salmon fillets with black pepper and press it gently to make a crust.

2. In a large sauté pan, heat the olive oil over medium-high heat.

3. Sear the salmon, for about 4 minutes on each side. Remove it from the sauté pan and place on a baking sheet.

4. Place it in a preheated 350°F oven for about 5 minutes.

5. In the sauté pan, combine the onions, tomatoes and capers. Sauté for about 2 minutes.

6. Add the lemon juice and white wine. (Also add butter if you would like a richer preparation.) Cook for 3 minutes.

7. Season with salt and pepper.

8. Place 1 salmon fillet on each plate and top with the tomato mixture.

**Serves 4**

# Mako Shark Mousseline

*4 mako shark steaks, 8 ounces each*
*3 tablespoons butter*
*salt and pepper, for seasoning*

*Mousseline*
*3 eggs*
*2 cups mayonnaise*
*4 tablespoons capers and brine, chopped*
*¹/₄ cup Dijon mustard*
*¹/₄ cup red onions, diced*
*4 tablespoons green onions, chopped*
*1 teaspoon lemon juice*
*dash of Tabasco*

1. Whisk the eggs and set aside.

2. In a large bowl, combine all of the other mousseline ingredients.

3. Add the eggs and whisk well.

4. Season with salt and pepper.

5. Sauté the steaks in the butter for 1 minute on each side.

6. Remove and place in a sheet pan.

7. Spoon the mousseline on top of the fish, covering it completely.

8. Bake in a preheated 375°F oven for 15 minutes until the mousseline is cooked and golden.

9. Use a spatula to carefully lift each steak off of the pan. Gently place 1 steak on each plate. Serve.

**Serves 4**

## Making a Mousseline

Mousseline is a French word meaning muslin. The name is given to different styles of preparations that are as feather-light as the delicate fabric. Mousselines of fish, poultry, or meat often include the main ingredient combined with beaten egg whites and cream and then cooked in a water bath.

Mayonnaise and other sauces that have been lightened by the addition of eggs or whipped cream also are descibed as mousseline, as in this recipe. This dish has a nice creamy imperial topping. It is delicious plain or with a light butter sauce.

## Wine Notes

 A rich Australian Chardonnay or any barrel-fermented Chardonnay stands up to this rich mousseline.

# Seafood Sauté

*3 tablespoons butter, for sautéing*
*12 ounces scallops*
*12 jumbo shrimp (16-20 count)*
*8 ounces lobster meat*
*8 ounces crab meat*
*1 shallot, minced*
*6 ounces champagne*
*1 cup lobster stock (see page 100)*
*1 quart heavy cream*
*2 tablespoons beurre manie (see page 173)*
*salt and pepper, to taste*
*dash of Tabasco sauce*
*1 pound spinach pasta, freshly cooked*
*fresh parsley, chopped, for garnish*

1.  Melt the butter in a large sauté pan. Add the scallops, shrimp and lobster. Cook for approximately 7 minutes. Add the crab meat and cook until it is heated all the way through.

2.  Remove the seafood with a slotted spoon and reserve.

3.  Add the shallots, champagne and lobster stock to the sauté pan. Simmer until the liquid has reduced by two-thirds. Do not allow it to boil over.

4.  Add the heavy cream and reduce again by one-third. Add the beurre manie and whisk it as it thickens to a sauce-like consistency.

5.  Season with salt, pepper and Tabasco.

6.  Put the seafood back into the sauce and heat gently.

7.  Place the pasta in 4 bowls or on 6 appetizer plates. Spoon the seafood and sauce on top and serve. Garnish with chopped parsley.

**Makes 4 generous servings or 6 appetizers**

---

## What's the Number?

The number on shrimp indicates the number of shrimp per pound.

## Take That Strap Off!

Scallops have a small tough strap that is attached to the muscle. It should be removed. Save and freeze them because they are great for shellfish stock.

## Wine Notes

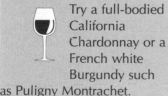
Try a full-bodied California Chardonnay or a French white Burgundy such as Puligny Montrachet.

# Flounder Anna

4 fluke or flounder fillets, 7 ounces each
1 teaspoon Seafood Seasoning, plus enough for coating (opposite page)
juice from half a lemon
$^1/_4$ cup wine
1 tablespoon butter
1/2 cup green onions, sliced
1 tablespoon Worcestershire sauce
$^1/_4$-pound unsalted butter, cut into small pieces
1 pound crab meat

1. Preheat the oven to 350°F.

2. Sprinkle the flounder with Seafood Seasoning on both sides.

3. Place in a baking pan with the lemon, wine and water to cover the bottom of the pan.

4. Bake for 12 minutes. Be careful not to overcook.

5. Melt the tablespoon of butter in a sauté pan.

6. Add the green onions, 1 teaspoon of Seafood Seasoning and the Worcestershire sauce.

7. Whisk in the unsalted butter. Fold in the crab meat.

8. Keep this sauce warm. (We call it Anna Sauce.)

9. Place 1 baked fillet on each plate. Top with Anna Sauce and serve.

**Serves 4**

## Flounder Family

Fluke is actually part of the flounder family, along with turbot and sole. Flounder, with its mild taste and light texture, is perfect for pairing with seafood such as crab meat. It is also sturdy enough to be stuffed, broiled or baked.

## Wine Notes

 Try a rosé from Tavel or the Loire Valley to complement the Cajun spices.

**True Paprika**

Sometimes mistakenly considered an herb in its own right, paprika is actually a blend of peppers that creates this unique condiment. When prepared correctly, paprika is a highly prized spice, the best of which is imported from Hungary. Although many supermarkets sell it, the best paprika is usually found in specialty food stores and Hungarian grocery stores.

# Seafood Seasoning

*1/3 cup paprika*
*1/3 cup salt*
*1/4 cup ground black pepper*
*3 tablespoons onion powder*
*2 tablespoons cayenne pepper*
*2 tablespoons thyme*
*2 tablespoons oregano*

1. Combine all of the ingredients and mix thoroughly.

2. Store the mix in an airtight container and use it as you do other spices.

**Makes 2 cups**

# Flounder Jefferson

6 tablespoons butter
$^1/_4$ cup onion, finely chopped
1 egg
$^1/_4$ cup mayonnaise
1 tablespoon fresh lemon juice
$^1/_2$ teaspoon Worcestershire sauce
dash of Tabasco
$^1/_4$ cup green onions, chopped
3 ounces Monterey Jack cheese, grated
1 pound crab meat, picked and cleaned
salt and pepper, for seasoning
$1^1/_2$ pounds flounder or fluke fillets (6 medium-size fillets)
$^1/_2$ cup white wine
Brandy Cream Sauce (opposite page)
4 cups cooked rice, for serving

1.  Sauté the onions in 2 tablespoons of butter until translucent. Set them aside to cool.

2.  In a bowl, combine the egg and mayonnaise. Add the lemon juice, Worcestershire and Tabasco sauces. Mix in the cooled onions, green onions and cheese. Blend well.

3.  Fold in the crab meat. Season with salt and pepper.

4.  Cut the fish fillets lengthwise along their seams to create 12 long half-pieces.

5.  Place 2 heaping tablespoons of crab stuffing on each fillet, and then roll it up. Place the roulades upright on a cookie sheet.

6.  Mix together approximately 4 tablespoons of butter, the salt, pepper and white wine. Put a dot of this on top of each roulade.

7.  Bake the roulades in a preheated 400°F oven for 15 minutes.

8.  Place some rice in the center of 4 plates and add 3 roulades to each. Ladle Brandy Cream Sauce over the roulades.

**Serves 4**

## Is It Flounder or Fluke?

This crab-meat-stuffed flounder is one of our most popular dishes. This presentation is different, using stuffed roulades (small rolls) of flounder.

At the restaurant we specify fluke because of its superior quality and taste. Other species of flounder that are available and of good quality include yellowtail flounder, American plaice and blackback.

## Wine Notes

 This rich brandy cream sauce needs a nice Chardonnay from the Central Coast of California with oaky, tropical fruit flavors.

## Sweet Brandy

Brandy is a distilled spirit made from the fermented juice of grapes, apples, peaches, plums or other fruit. Because it comes from fruit juice, brandy offers a subtle sweetness when added to dishes.

# Brandy Cream Sauce

*1 tablespoon shallots*
*¹/₂ cup white wine*
*¹/₄ cup brandy*
*1 cup reduced shrimp stock (see page 7) or lobster stock (see page 100)*
*³/₄ cup heavy cream*
*1 tablespoon beurre manie (see page 173)*
*salt and pepper, for seasoning*

1. In a saucepan, combine the shallots, wine, brandy and stock. Bring to a boil and reduce by half.

2. Add the heavy cream and cook until it begins to thicken. Add small amounts of the beurre manie, and whisk until the sauce thickens.

3. Add more shrimp or lobster base if you want to intensify the flavors. Add salt and pepper, to taste.

**Makes 1¹/₂ cups**

# Maple-Mustard Glazed Salmon
## with Pecan and Thyme Beurre Blanc

*4 slamon fillets, 6 ounces each, skinless*
*1¹/₂ teaspoons mustard seeds*
*2 tablespoons maple syrup*
*salt and pepper, for seasoning*
*Pecan and Thyme Beurre Blanc (opposite page)*

1. Preheat the oven to 375°F.

2. Rub the salmon with mustard seeds and coat lightly with maple syrup.

3. Season with salt and pepper.

4. Place the fillets on a cookie sheet.

5. Bake in the oven for 15 minutes.

6. Place 1 fillet on each plate. Lace each with Pecan and Thyme Beurre Blanc.

**Serves 4**

---

**Pure Maple**

Use pure maple syrup, not pancake syrup for this recipe. Maple syrup is rated by color. The darker the color, the more intense the flavor. Pure maple syrup can be expensive, but a little goes a long way. Storing it in the refrigerator or freezer helps retain its flavor.

**Wine Notes**

 A ripe Merlot with rich berry fruit nicely matches the salmon and the sweet crust. For a different taste, try a fruity Gamay Beaujolais from California.

## Toasting or Roasting Nuts

In a dry heavy sauté pan, large or small, depending upon the amount of nuts, heat the pan and add the nuts. When the nuts begin to smell, or just begin to turn brown, remove the pan from the heat. Shake the pan so the nuts toast all over. Remove the nuts from the pan.

You may want to oven roast the nuts. To do this, place them on a baking sheet and bake them at 350°F or until golden brown (approximately 5 to 10 minutes).

# Pecan and Thyme Beurre Blanc

*3 tablespoons plus 2 sticks (1/2 pound) butter*
*3 whole shallots, chopped*
*3/4 cup white wine*
*1/4 cup sherry vinegar*
*1 teaspoon black peppercorns, crushed*
*1 tablespoon fresh thyme, chopped*
*3/4 cup pecans, toasted and chopped*
*1/2 cup heavy cream*
*juice of half a lemon*
*salt and freshly ground pepper, for seasoning*

1. Melt 3 tablespoons of butter in a small saucepan. Add the shallots, white wine, vinegar, peppercorns and thyme.

2. Reduce over a medium flame to two-thirds.

3. Add the nuts and cream and reduce by half.

4. Remove from the heat. Cut the sticks of butter in small pieces and whisk them into the reduction.

5. Season with lemon juice, salt and pepper, to taste.

**Makes 1 cup**

# Monkfish with a Horseradish Crust and Mustard Sauce

*1/2 pound butter, softened*
*1 cup Dijon mustard*
*6 tablespoons horseradish, fresh or jarred*
*pinch of salt*
*2 cups fresh bread crumbs*
*2 1/2 pounds fresh monkfish fillets, 4 ounces each*
*1 cup all-purpose flour seasoned with salt and pepper*
*1/4 cup olive oil*
*3 cups spinach, cleaned*
*salt and pepper, for seasoning*
*Mustard Sauce (opposite page)*
*parsley, chopped, for garnish*
*1 lemon, sliced*

1.  Mix the butter, mustard, horseradish, pinch of salt and bread crumbs in a small mixing bowl. Use your fingers to blend well but do not over-mix.

2.  Cut the monkfish into 2-inch medallions. Lightly dust them in the flour.

3.  Put half of the oil in a sauté pan. Sear the monkfish on both sides, and place them on a baking sheet.

4.  Evenly cover the tops of the monkfish medallions with the crumb mixture. Place them in a preheated 350°F oven for approximately 12 minutes.

5.  Sauté the spinach in 3 tablespoons of olive oil. Season with salt and pepper.

6.  Place a layer of Mustard Sauce on each serving plate. Arrange the spinach and monkfish beside each other on top of the sauce.

7.  Garnish with chopped parsley and lemon.

**Serves 4**

**Poor Man's Lobster**

Monkfish are always plentiful in Southern New Jersey, as scallop fisherman often catch them in their dredges. This fish has a delicate, sweet taste because it feeds on shell fish. It is often referred to as "poor man's lobster."

The underlaying sauce highlights the color and texture of the food, without sacrificing any flavor.

**Wine Notes**

Oregon Pinot Gris or a crisp Alsatian Pinot Blanc work well with the horseradish and mustard flavors.

# Mustard Sauce

*2 tablespoons shallots, finely chopped*
*1 cup white wine*
*1/4 cup whole grain mustard*
*1 tablespoon champagne vinegar*
*3 sticks (3/4 pound) whole butter*
*salt and white pepper, for seasoning*

1. Place the shallots, white wine, mustard and vinegar in a small saucepan.

2. Over a medium flame, reduce this mixture until the wine has almost evaporated.

3. Cut the butter into small pieces. Whisk into the mustard mixture.

4. Season with salt and pepper, to taste.

**Makes 1$^{1}/_{2}$ cups**

# Berber Rubbed Mahi Mahi
## with White Bean and Arugula Salad

*4 mahi mahi fillets, 8 ounces each*
*White Bean and Arugula Salad (opposite page)*

*Dry Spices*
*1 teaspoon cardamom seeds*
*pinch of ground cloves*
*1 teaspoon cinnamon*
*1 teaspoon nutmeg*
*2 teaspoons fennel*
*1 teaspoon cumin*
*2 teaspoons coriander*
*¹/₈ cup paprika*
*2 teaspoons cayenne*
*2 teaspoons kosher salt*
*2 teaspoons black pepper*

*Wet Ingredients*
*2 teaspoons olive oil*
*2 teaspoons ginger, minced*
*2 teaspoons fresh garlic, chopped*
*¹/₂ cup red wine*
*¹/₄ cup orange juice*

1. In a 350°F oven, toast all of the dry spices for 5 to 10 minutes. Set aside.

2. Combine all of the wet ingredients in a saucepan and cook over medium heat. Reduce by half.

3. Stir the toasted spice mix into the wet ingredients to make the berber rub. Cool.

4. Marinate the fish in the berber rub mix for 30 minutes.

5. Sear the fish in a sauté pan over medium heat for 4 minutes on each side, or until cooked.

6. Place the fish on 4 plates. Partially cover the fish with the salad.

**Serves 4**

**Berber Rub**

This is a wet rub with North African origins. The rub can be piquant or mild, depending on how much cayenne you add. It is a flavorful marinade, and also can be used with beef or chicken.

**Wine Notes**

Either a German Spätlese or an Alsatian Sylvaner works nicely with the North African spices.

# White Bean and Arugula Salad

*1 pound white beans, Great Northern, soaked and cooked until tender*
*1 clove fresh garlic, minced*
*$^1/_2$ cup red onion, chopped*
*$^1/_2$ bunch cilantro, chopped*
*$^1/_2$ cup parsley, chopped*
*juice from 1 lemon*
*salt and freshly ground pepper, for seasoning*
*bunch of arugula leaves, soaked, cleaned and chopped*

1. Mix all of the ingredients—except the arugula—together.

2. Let sit for 2 hours before serving.

3. Toss in the arugula just before serving.

**Serves 4**

## Preparing Dried Beans

Whether for soups, salads or sauces, the traditional way to clean beans is the best. Minimally processed beans tend to have stones, soil and moldy beans, so this debris must be sorted out.

Pour the beans into a shallow baking pan, spread the beans out and go over them to pick out any visible undesirables. After sorting them, remove the dust and dirt by rinsing or soaking them in water.

Cooking time for beans can be sped up by soaking them in water. With quick cooking beans such as lentils, you can shorten the cooking time by 15 minutes. You can shorten the cooking time of longer cooking beans, such as black beans, by as much as a half hour.

## How Much Water?

Make sure that you use plenty of water when cooking beans. A good rule of thumb is 2$^1/_2$ cups of water to 1 cup of beans.

## Salt?

Add salt at the end of the cooking process. Since salt slows down the cooking process, beans toughen up if you add salt at the start.

# Crusted Swordfish
## with a Light Dill Sauce

*1/2 cup Dijon mustard*
*1/4 cup white wine*
*1 cup bread crumbs*
*3 tablespoons parsley, chopped*
*salt and pepper, for seasoning*
*4 swordfish steaks, 6 ounces each*
*1/4 cup olive oil*
*2 capers, chopped (optional)*

1.  Mix the mustard and wine together in a bowl.

2.  In a separate dish, season the bread crumbs with the parsley, salt and pepper.

3.  For a tasty variation, add a few chopped capers to the crumb mix.

4.  Preheat the oven to 350°F.

5.  Dip the fish into the wine mixture, and then into the crumbs. Make sure the fish is completely coated.

6.  Sauté the steaks in the oil until they are golden brown (approximately 5 minutes on each side). Finish by baking them in the oven for 12 minutes.

**Serves 4**

---

**Fish Cuts: Fillets and Steaks**

A fillet is cut from the side of the fish, from its head to its tail. A fillet may be boneless or may have pin bones that should be removed before cooking. Salmon often has these bones, which are most easily removed with needle nose pliers.

A steak is a cut made across the width of the fish. It may have a piece of the backbone or it may be boneless. Salmon steaks usually contain the back bone, whereas tuna steaks do not.

Steaks are usually cut from firmer fleshed fish. They are better for grilling, as they do not break up on the grill as smaller flaked fish do. These firmer fish grill better if they are kept whole, with their skin on to keep the flesh intact.

**Wine Notes**

 A crisp, minerally French Chablis or a steely Sancerre highlights the fish and dill flavors.

## Light Dill Sauce

1 tablespoon butter
1 red onion, chopped
$^1/_2$ cup white wine
$3^1/_4$ cups chicken stock (see page 5)
$^1/_4$ cup champagne vinegar
2 tablespoons slurry (cornstarch and water mix, see page 107)
1 bunch fresh dill, chopped
$^1/_2$ cup parsley, chopped
1 bunch green onions, green part only, chopped
salt and pepper, to taste

1. In a saucepan, sauté the red onions in the butter for 2 minutes. Add the white wine, chicken stock and champagne vinegar. (If champagne vinegar is not available, you can substitute with cider or rice vinegar.) Bring to a simmer.

2. Add the slurry mixture and whisk until it thickens.

3. Cook for 10 minutes over medium heat

4. Add the dill, parsley and green onions. Cook for another 5 minutes.

5. Season with salt and pepper.

# Roasted Red Snapper
## with a Crust of Herbs and Tomato Fondue

*4 fresh red snapper fillets, 6 ounces each*
*1¹/₄ cups softened Herb Butter (see page 135)*
*1 tablespoon shallots, chopped*
*1 teaspoon garlic, finely chopped*
*1 cup Italian parsley, chopped*
*1 cup chervil, chopped*
*¹/₂ cup fresh basil leaves, chopped*
*3 tablespoons fresh thyme, chopped*
*2 cups fresh bread, chopped fine (or Japanese bread crumbs)*
*¹/₂ cup white wine*
*salt and pepper, for seasoning*
*2 cups Tomato Fondue (opposite page)*

1.  Sauté the shallots and garlic in a teaspoon of the butter until soft. Cool.

2.  Add the parsley, chervil, basil, thyme, remaining butter and bread crumbs. Combine well.

3.  Spread the Herb Butter generously over each fillet. Place them on a baking sheet and refrigerate them for 1 hour or longer.

4.  Preheat the oven to 400°F.

5.  Pour white wine in the bottom of the baking sheet and bake the fillets for 8 to 12 minutes.

6.  Brown the fish under the broiler. Make sure the fish is not too close to the broiler or the topping will burn.

**Serves 4**

## Lean or Fatty Fish?

There are two fish categories that determine the best method of cooking.

Lean fish are best fried, sautéed, poached or steamed. Some lean fish include swordfish, flounder, cod, monkfish, red snapper, and croaker.

Fatty fish are best cooked with dry heat, like broiled, grilled or baked. Some fatty fish include bluefish, salmon, striped bass, some tuna, mackerel, and shad.

Some fish are great either way: broiled, grilled or sautéed. These include swordfish, tuna and mahi mahi. Salmon or cod are delicious both poached and broiled.

## Wine Notes

 This dish goes well with white wine since the tomato butter sauce is quite soft. Try a full-bodied California Chardonnay or a full-bodied French Burgundy such as Puligny Montrachet.

# Tomato Fondue

*¹/₂ cup mushrooms, diced*
*2 tablespoons shallots, chopped*
*¹/₈ teaspoon garlic powder*
*1 tablespoon butter*
*1¹/₂ sticks (12 tablespoons) butter, softened*
*1 cup tomato, seeded and chopped (about 3 large plum tomatoes)*
*2 tablespoons brandy*
*1 cup white wine*
*1 tablespoon lemon juice*
*1 tablespoon parsley, chopped*
*salt and pepper, for seasoning*
*fresh herbs, for garnish*

1. Sauté the mushrooms, shallots, and garlic powder in 1 tablespoon butter until soft.

2. Add the tomatoes, brandy, wine and lemon juice.

3. Cook over medium heat for 5 to 8 minutes until reduced by half.

4. Lower the heat and gradually add the remaining butter. Stir continuously until you get a sauce-like consistency.

5. Add the parsley. Season with salt and pepper, to taste.

6. Spoon and spread about ¹/₄ cup fondue on each plate. Lay the fish over the fondue.

7. Garnish with fresh herbs.

**Makes 2 cups**

## Fondue

Cheese fondue is not alone in the world of fondues. This classic French culinary technique has another meaning.

When a chopped vegetable is cooked for a long period of time in butter or oil until it is reduced to a purée, it becomes a fondue. This type of sauce is a wonderful component of many dishes.

# Sesame Coated Bass
## with a Mirin Butter Sauce and
## Shiitake Mushroom Salad

*4 sea bass fillets, 8 ounces each*
*1 cup sesame seeds*
*¹/₄ cup oil or clarified butter*
*¹/₂ cup Mirin Butter Sauce (opposite page)*
*pickled ginger, for garnish*
*Shiitake Mushroom Salad (opposite page)*

1. Coat the fillets with sesame seeds. Press the seeds into the fish with your hand.

2. In a sauté pan over medium heat, sauté the fish in oil for 4 minutes on each side. Be careful not to burn the coating.

3. Place the fillets on 4 plates and ladle Mirin Butter Sauce over them. Spoon the mushroom salad onto each plate.

4. Garnish with pickled ginger.

**Serves 4**

**Kudos**

Mimi perfected the use of sesame crusting for this fish. It is one of our most popular dishes.

**Ginger**

Originating in southeast Asia, the use of ginger dates back more than 3,000 years. It is an integral ingredient in Asian cooking. The root has a strong taste that can be overpowering. Used subtly, the flavor can add depth of flavor to chutneys, marinades and sauces.

**Wine Notes**

Try a full-bodied Alsatian Gewürztraminer. It stands up to the complex Asian flavors of this dish.

## Mirin Butter Sauce

*3 tablespoons shallots, chopped*
*1 teaspoon garlic, chopped*
*1 teaspoon ginger, grated*
*2 tablespoons rice wine vinegar or cider vinegar*
*3/4 cup white wine*
*4 tablespoons mirin*
*1/2 cup heavy cream*
*2 sticks (1/2 pound) butter*
*1 tablespoon fermented black beans, soaked in 2 tablespoons water*
*salt and freshly ground pepper, for seasoning*

1. Put the shallots, garlic, ginger, vinegar and wines in a small saucepan. Bring them to a simmer and reduce until almost dry.

2. Add the cream. Simmer and reduce to a sauce-like consistency.

3. Lower the heat and swirl in the butter. Season with fermented black beans, salt and pepper.

**Makes 1 cup**

# Shiitake Mushroom Salad

*2 cups shiitake mushrooms, sliced*
*1/4 cup sesame oil*
*1 cup green onions, green part only, sliced*
*1 tablespoon sesame seeds*
*1 teaspoon Thai chili paste*
*salt, for seasoning*

1. Sauté the mushrooms in sesame oil until soft. Cool to room temperature.

2. Toss with the green onions, sesame seeds and chili paste. Season with salt. Add more oil if necessary.

3. Marinate for 30 minutes. Serve chilled or at room temperature.

**Serves 4**

# Sautéed Black Sea Bass
## with White Wine Cioppino Broth and Roasted Garlic Aioli

*White Wine Cioppino Broth (opposite page)*
*Roasted Garlic Aioli (opposite page)*
*4 black bass fillets, 8 ounces each*
*1 cup flour, seasoned with salt and pepper*
*2 tablespoons olive oil*
*2 tablespoons parsley, chopped*

1.  Prepare White Wine Cioppino Broth and Roasted Garlic Aioli.

2.  Dredge the bass in flour.

3.  In a hot pan with olive oil, sauté the fillets for 3 minutes on each side.

4.  Ladle the cioppino into 4 shallow bowls and place the fish on top.

5.  Dollop each with 2 tablespoons of Roasted Garlic Aioli.

6.  Sprinkle with parsley.

**Serves 4**

## Complementary Components

Cioppino is a tomato-based seafood stew that originated in California.

Aioli comes from the Provence region of southern France. It refers to a mayonnaise made with olive oil and prodigious amounts of crushed fresh garlic. The mayonnaise, made of egg yolks, vinegar and olive oil, creates a creamy sauce, which is often served with poached fish.

This version of the classic San Francisco Cioppino has a lighter style, so the broth does not overpower the sea bass. The sweetness of the roasted garlic brings all the components together.

## Wine Notes

 Enjoy a dry white Graves from France or a dry Sylvaner from Alsace.

**To Use Roasted Garlic**

Break off a clove of garlic and slip out the roasted insides. Purée or mash it.

# White Wine Cioppino Broth

*1/4 cup olive oil*
*1 cup mushrooms, sliced*
*1/2 cup onions, diced*
*1 tablespoon garlic, chopped*
*2 cups tomatoes, diced*
*1 tablespoon tomato paste*
*1 cup white wine*
*1 cup fish stock (see page 7)*
*salt and pepper, for seasoning*
*2 tablespoons fresh basil, chopped*

1. In a large pot, heat the olive oil. Add the mushrooms, onions and garlic. Cook for a few minutes

2. Add the tomatoes and paste. Cook for 5 minutes.

3. Add the wine and fish stock. Simmer for approximately 20 minutes.

4. Season with salt and pepper. Add the fresh basil.

**Serves 4**

# Roasted Garlic Aioli

*1 tablespoon roasted garlic (see page 4)*
*1 egg yolk*
*3/4 cup olive oil*
*1/2 teaspoon lemon juice or vinegar*
*salt and pepper, for seasoning*

1. Mix the garlic and egg yolk in a food processor while slowly pouring in a steady stream of olive oil.

2. When the mixture has a mayonnaise-like consistency, add the lemon juice or vinegar. Season with salt and pepper.

**Makes 3/4 cup**

# Chilean Sea Bass
## with Curry Dust and Grilled Pineapple Salsa

*4 Chilean sea bass fillets, 8 ounces each*
*³/4 cup Curry Dust (below) or curry powder*
*4 tablespoons butter*
*4 cups Grilled Pineapple Salsa (opposite page)*

1.  Dredge the fillets in the curry powder.

2.  In a pan, melt the butter. Sauté the fillets for 4 minutes on each side.

3.  Place the fillets in a preheated, 350°F oven for 12 to 15 minutes.

4.  Place them on plates. Spoon the pineapple salsa on top.

**Serves 4**

# Curry Dust

*¹/4 cup turmeric*
*3 tablespoons coriander*
*2 tablespoons cumin*
*1 tablespoon white peppercorns*
*1 tablespoon ginger, ground*
*1 tablespoon cloves, whole*
*1 tablespoon cardamom*
*1 tablespoon mace, ground*
*2 teaspoons cayenne*

1.  Place all of the ingredients into a blender and grind.

2.  Seal the mixture in an airtight container.

**Makes approximately ³/4 cup**

---

**Chilean Sea Bass**

Technically this fish is not a member of the bass family. It is an ugly-looking deep water fish with large visible pointed teeth. The meat is moderately oily, with firm, white, large flaky flesh.

**Curry: Homemade or Store-Bought?**

What we call Curry Dust is actually a recipe for making your own curry powder—it's easier than you thought! If you don't want to make your own curry powder, you can buy it already prepared in the spice section of any supermarket. We believe the best kind is the Madras-style curry powder.

**Wine Notes**

 A flinty Californian Chenin Blanc or a French Vouvray complements these complex curry and sweet pineapple flavors.

## Ripe Pineapples

Test to see if your pineapple is ripe. Smell the base: It should be sweet. Pull out a leaf of the pineapple: If it comes out easily, it is ripe and ready to use.

Skin color is not a good indication of ripeness because some pineapples are green or range from green to golden when ripe. Pineapples, unlike tomatoes or pears, must be picked when they are already ripe because they don't ripen off the vine or tree. The pineapple should be fresh looking with a dark green crown.

Avoid pineapples with bruised areas, discolored soft spots, traces of mold or an unpleasant odor.

# Grilled Pineapple Salsa

*1 ripe pineapple, peeled, cored and sliced*
*1 red pepper, diced*
*1/2 green pepper, diced*
*1 small red onion, diced*
*1/2 bunch scallions, chopped*
*1/4 bunch cilantro, chopped*
*1/2 teaspoon cumin*
*1/4 cup white wine*
*juice of 3 limes*
*salt and pepper, to taste*

1. Place the pineapple on a hot grill. Grill for 2 minutes on each side. Cool and dice the pineapple.

2. Combine the pineapple with all of the ingredients and let the flavors meld for 30 minutes.

**Makes approximately 4 cups**

# Grilled Yellowfin Tuna
## with Red Onion-Mango Salsa

*4 yellowfin tuna steaks, 8 ounces each*
*1 teaspoon olive oil*
*salt and pepper, for seasoning*

*Salsa*
*2 ripe mangoes, diced*
*1/2 cup red onions, diced*
*1 tablespoon jalapeño peppers, chopped*
*juice of 2 fresh limes*
*dash of Tabasco*
*2 teaspoons honey*
*salt and pepper, for seasoning*

1. Mix all of the salsa ingredients together. Let them sit for 1 hour.

2. Heat the grill until the grates are hot.

3. Season the tuna with the olive oil, salt and pepper.

4. Place on the grill and cook the steaks for 3 to 6 minutes on each side, until you reach your desired doneness.

5. Place each tuna steak on a plate, and spoon the salsa on top of each.

**Serves 4**

## How Long to Cook Fish

The best rule of thumb is that used by the Canadian fisheries. This method cooks the fish 10 minutes for every inch of thickness. Follow this rule and your fish will always be moist and delicious.

## Wine Notes

 Try a semi-sparkling Muscato d'Asti or Conundrum from Caymus of Napa Valley.

# Fresh Grilled Tuna
## with Red Onion Confit

*4 fresh yellowfin tuna steaks, 1-inch thick, 7 ounces each*
*salt and pepper, for seasoning*
*2 tablespoons olive oil*
*Red Onion Confit (below)*

1. Season the tuna steaks with the salt, pepper and olive oil.

2. Grill for approximately 4 minutes on each side (more or less, depending on their thickness and how you like them cooked).

3. Cook until they are still pink in the center. Tuna tends to dry out if it is overcooked, so be careful.

4. Place each steak on a plate. Spoon the onion confit over the top.

## Red Onion Confit

*6 cups red onions, sliced*
*4 tablespoons butter*
*2 tablespoons red wine vinegar*
*¼ cup white wine*
*1 teaspoon fresh lemon juice*
*4 teaspoons honey*
*2 teaspoons whole grain mustard*
*salt and pepper, for seasoning*

1. Over medium heat, sauté the onions in 2 tablespoons of butter. Stir constantly for 10 to 15 minutes until the onions begin to caramelize.

2. Add the vinegar, white wine and lemon juice. Cook until all of the liquid evaporates.

3. Stir in the honey and mustard. Cook for 5 minutes.

4. Whisk in 2 tablespoons of butter. Reserve and keep warm.

**Serves 4**

# Grilled Mahi Mahi
## with Jersey Tomato Salsa and Avocado Butter

*4 mahi mahi fillets, 6 ounces each*
*salt and pepper, for seasoning*
*olive oil, for brushing*
*Jersey Tomato Salsa (opposite page)*
*Avocado Butter (opposite page)*
*fresh cilantro, for garnish*

1. Season the fillets and brush them with oil.

2. Grill the fish for 5 minutes on each side.

3. Place it on a plate, and spoon salsa over half of the fillet.

4. Place a large slice of butter on top.

5. Garnish with fresh cilantro.

**Serves 4**

## Mahi Mahi

This delicious fish is caught in waters off of Cape May in the summer.

## How Much Fish to Buy?

Here are some rules of thumb to follow.

For fish fillets, buy 6 ounces per person. For fish steaks, buy 8 ounces per person.

For whole fish, buy 1 pound per person.

For mussels, 3 pounds of fresh mussels in the shell provide 1 pound of mussel meat. You can buy just the meat from your seafood market. Four ounces of meat is a proper portion per person, which serves about 12 mussels per person for an appetizer.

## Wine Notes

 Match with a dry Chenin Blanc or a medium-bodied Italian Vernaccia. For a red wine, try a light Beaujolais or Dolcetto.

## Jersey Tomatoes

**Jersey Tomatoes**

The Jersey beefsteak tomato is a true pleasure of summer. Tomatoes are actually a fruit, and Jersey's variety offer the perfect balance of flavor, acidity and sweetness. The vine-ripened tomatoes are always the best; we have a farmer bring us these during the season. They are perfect in a coulis, with fresh mozzarella or with crab meat.

Do not refrigerate tomatoes! Keep them at room temperature. Chilling them causes all the delicate flavors to deteriorate.

# Jersey Tomato Salsa

*3 large Jersey tomatoes, chopped*
*4 tablespoons red onion, chopped*
*4 tablespoons yellow pepper, chopped*
*2 teaspoons jalapeño peppers, chopped*
*2 tablespoons fresh cilantro, chopped*
*salt and fresh pepper, to taste*

1. Mix all the ingredients together, season with salt and pepper.

2. Let the flavors blend for at least 30 minutes.

**Makes 3 cups**

# Avocado Butter

*2 ripe avocados, skinned and mashed*
*3 tablespoons lemon juice*
*1 pound butter, softened*
*2 tablespoons red pepper, chopped*
*salt and pepper, for seasoning*

1. Combine all the ingredients and blend well. Season with salt and pepper

2. Spoon onto parchment paper and make a roll.

3. Refrigerate until needed.

**Makes 1¹/₂ pounds**

# Crab Casanova

*5 tablespoons butter*
*2 pounds jumbo lump crab meat*
*4 tablespoons brandy*
*$^1/_2$ cup dry white wine*
*3 tablespoons fresh lemon juice*
*1 tablespoon parsley, chopped*
*salt and white pepper, to taste*
*12 French bread croutons, toasted (see page 32)*
*3 tablespoons carrots, cut to curl*

1.  In a sauté pan, melt 3 tablespoons butter. Add the crab meat. Shake the pan to avoid sticking, but be careful to avoid breaking up the lumps.

2.  Carefully add the brandy and wine to the pan. This mixture may flame a bit at first, but the alcohol will cook out.

3.  Add the lemon juice, parsley, salt and pepper, and toss.

4.  Add 2 tablespoons of softened butter and toss again to make a nice smooth sauce.

5.  Spoon the crab meat over the croutons and garnish with the carrot curls.

**Serves 6**

**Combining Classics**

This dish highlights the delicious flavor of the crab meat. The flavors of the brandy and lemon combine for a unique taste.

**Buying Crab Meat**

The two basic ways to buy crab meat are fresh or pasteurized.

The best fresh crab meat is bought in season from late April through September. During the winter, fresh crab meat is available, but it usually comes from dredged crabs, which have less meat. The shelf life of fresh crab meat is usually 2 to 3 days.

Pasteurized crab meat, available year-round, is shelf-stable if refrigerated. Pasteurized meat can be of excellent quality. To maintain the best quality, do not freeze the crab meat, as it can become stringy.

**Wine Notes**

 This dish is perfect with a French Chablis or a white Marsanne. Both wines are light, but flavorful enough to hold up to the crab meat.

*Poultry*

Madison Chicken - 165
Chicken Tuscany - 166
*Tomato Butter Sauce - 167*
Chicken Champignon - 168
Chicken Bella - 169
Summer Grilled Chicken with Fresh Pepper Confit - 170
Chicken and Shrimp Picante - 171
Chicken Albertina - 172
*Shrimp Cream Sauce - 173*
Chicken Cordon Rouge - 174
*Mornay Sauce - 175*
Pommery Chicken - 176
*Mustard Cream Sauce - 177*
Chicken Sonoma with Brunoise of Vegetables - 178
*Roasted Soft Garlic Cream - 179*
Chicken Sarah - 180
*Sarah Sauce - 181*
Sandcastle Chicken - 182
*Lemon Beurre Blanc - 183*
Chicken Victoria - 184
Lemon-Thyme Roasted Chicken - 185
Chicken Chalmers - 186
Chicken Pecan - 187
Chicken in Balsamic Vinegar - 188
Raspberry Chicken - 189
Cornish Game Hens with Fresh Cherries and Sour Cream - 190
Roasted Duck with Garlic and Turnips - 191
Duck Breast - 192
*Sweet Potatoes - 193 • Ginger-Port Cream Sauce - 193*
Duck and Portabella Mushrooms - 194
Banfi Duck - 196

**Wine Notes**

 Try a dry and
fruity rosé from
California or
from France.

# Madison Chicken

*4 boneless chicken breasts, 8 ounces each*
*2 cups buttermilk*
*1 tablespoon rosemary, chopped*
*2 tablespoons chives, chopped*
*1 teaspoon white pepper*
*2 tablespoons thyme, chopped*
*2 tablespoons basil, chopped*
*2 teaspoons salt*
*1 cup cornmeal*
*2 ounces clarified butter (see page 181)*
*1½ cups red onions, sliced and grilled*
*1 teaspoon garlic, chopped*
*1½ cups roasted peppers, sliced (see page 70)*
*8 slices of Pepper Jack cheese*
*salt and pepper, for seasoning*

1. Cut the chicken breasts in half. Pound them to make them even, if you desire.

2. Soak the chicken in the buttermilk for 30 minutes to 1 hour.

3. Mix all of the herbs, salt and cornmeal. Dredge the chicken in this mixture and tap off any excess.

4. In a sauté pan with the butter, sauté the chicken until it is golden brown, approximately 2 to 3 minutes on each side. Reserve the chicken breasts in an oven-safe dish.

5. In a sauté pan add the onions, garlic and pepper. Toss this mixture and sauté it for 5 minutes. Season with salt and pepper, to taste.

6. Top the chicken with the onions and peppers. Place the cheese on top.

7. Place the chicken in a 375°F oven to nicely melt the cheese, for approximately 8 minutes.

8. Place 2 pieces of chicken on each of 4 serving plates.

**Serves 4**

# Chicken Tuscany
## with Tomato Butter Sauce

*4 chicken breasts, 8 ounces each, boneless, skinless and cut into
quarters (totalling 16 pieces)*
*salt and pepper*
*¹/₂ cup flour*
*¹/₂ cup olive oil*
*³/₄ cup red onions, cut julienne style*
*1 tablespoon garlic, chopped*
*¹/₂ pound hot Italian sausage, cooked and sliced on the bias*
*4 cups spinach, picked and cleaned*
*1 head radicchio, cut julienne style*
*1¹/₂ cups roasted red peppers, sliced (see page 70)*
*¹/₂ pound fusilli pasta, cooked al dente*
*1¹/₂ cups Tomato Butter Sauce (opposite page)*
*1 cup Romano cheese, grated*

1.  Season the chicken with salt and pepper; dredge in flour.

2.  In a sauté pan with ¹/₄ cup of olive oil, brown the chicken on both
    sides. Sauté it until it is cooked through, then remove it and place it
    in a warm oven (250°F).

3.  In another sauté pan, sauté the red onions, garlic and sausage in the
    remaining ¹/₄ cup of olive oil.

4.  Add the spinach, radicchio and roasted peppers. Stir enough to heat
    through the vegetables and slightly wilt them.

5.  Heat the cooked pasta in boiling water. Drain it well and add it to the
    vegetables. Season with salt and pepper.

6.  Spoon the pasta mixture into 4 bowls. Place the chicken on top.

7.  Ladle the Tomato Butter Sauce on top and sprinkle it with freshly
    grated Romano cheese.

**Serves 4**

---

**Sheep Cheese**

Parmesan cheese is made from cow's milk. Romano cheese is made from sheep's milk, which gives it a much sharper flavor. At the restaurant, we buy 80-pound wheels of Pecorino Romano, then cut off smaller pieces to grate.

Keep these dry cheeses covered or in an airtight container. They lose their flavor when exposed to the air; both are best when used right after grating.

**Wine Notes**

 The Italian style ingredients work well with a dry crisp Gavi or Pinot Grigio. A California Sauvignon Blanc with crisp citrus fruit also works well.

# Tomato Butter Sauce

*2 tablespoons shallots, chopped*
*¹/₂ cup white wine*
*¹/₄ teaspoon garlic, chopped*
*1 tablespoon tomato paste*
*1 ounce white wine vinegar*
*1 sprig of thyme*
*1 cup heavy cream*
*2 sticks (1 cup) softened butter*
*salt and pepper, for seasoning*

1. In a small saucepan, add the shallots, white wine, garlic, tomato paste, white wine vinegar and thyme.

2. Bring to a simmer, then lower the heat and cook until the mixture is reduced to a few tablespoons of syrupy liquid. Be careful not to scorch the pan.

3. Add the heavy cream, and simmer until it is reduced by half.

4. Take the pan off of the heat. Whisk in the softened butter, 1 tablespoon at a time.

5. Season with salt and pepper.

**Makes 1 cup**

## Important to Note

It is important to maintain a constant temperature for this sauce. Moving the pan on and off a burner with a low flame is the best way to do this. The sauce must be kept warm. If it overheats, the butter melts and the sauce breaks. If it gets too cool, it congeals.

# Chicken Champignon

*4 chicken breasts, 8 ounces each, boneless and skinless*
*1 cup flour, seasoned with salt and pepper*
*4 tablespoons olive oil*
*2 cups button mushrooms, sliced*
*2 cups shiitake mushrooms, stemmed and sliced*
*³/₄ cup white wine*
*1¹/₂ cups chicken stock (see page 5)*
*¹/₄ cup shallots, chopped*
*4 tablespoons butter, softened*
*salt and pepper, for seasoning*
*4 tablespoons parsley, chopped, for garnish*

1. Cut the chicken breasts in half. Pound them to make them even, if you desire.

2. Dredge the chicken in the flour and tap off any excess.

3. In a sauté pan with the oil, sauté the chicken until it is golden brown, approximately 2 to 3 minutes on each side. Reserve the breasts in a hot oven.

4. Add the mushrooms and shallots. Toss. Sauté for 5 minutes.

5. Add the white wine and stock, and shake the pan to mix. Reduce this sauce by two-thirds.

6. Lower the heat. Add the butter, and mix until the sauce thickens.

7. Adjust the seasoning with salt and pepper.

8. Place the chicken on 4 plates. Spoon the mushrooms and then the sauce over the top.

9. Garnish with the chopped parsley.

**Serves 4**

## More on Mushrooms

Mushrooms contain 90% water. During cooking, they can lose half of their liquid and up to 40% of their volume. The liquid that is lost provides great flavor that enhances both sauces and soups.

If you have to wash the mushrooms, do not wash them until you are ready to use them. Otherwise, the water starts to break them down.

## Wine Notes

Try an earthy Pinot Noir from Oregon or a Côte de Beaune Village from Burgundy. The earthy cherry fruit of the Pinot matches nicely with similar flavors in the mushrooms.

## Sun-dried Tomatoes

This recipe came from Pauline Stewart, who managed our Love the Cook store in Haddonfield, New Jersey.

The sun-dried tomatoes add distinctive flavor to many dishes. You can buy them marinated in olive oil or simply dried. Be careful, as some brands of tomatoes are salted heavily. Dried tomatoes that are not marinated in oil should have a bright red color. They should not be dark brown or brittle, which is an indication that they may be old. When using dried tomatoes, you may need to moisten them with wine or water to soften them up. Tomatoes marinated in oil do not usually have a bright red color.

## Wine Notes

 A crisp refreshing lemony Pinot Grigio or a Sauvignon Blanc can cut through the richness of the sauce.

# Chicken Bella

*4 chicken breasts, 8 ounces each, boneless and skinless*
*1 cup flour seasoned with salt and pepper, for dredging*
*4 tablespoons olive oil*
*1 tablespoon garlic, chopped*
*2 cups marinated artichokes*
*1/2 cup sun-dried tomatoes*
*1 cup chicken broth*
*1/2 cup white wine*
*1 cup black olives*
*salt and pepper, for seasoning*
*fresh parsley, for garnish*

1. Cut the chicken breasts in half. Pound them to make them even, if you desire.

2. Dredge the chicken in the flour and tap off any excess.

3. In a sauté pan with the oil, sauté the chicken and garlic until the breasts are golden brown, approximately 2 to 3 minutes on each side.

4. Add the artichokes, their marinade and the sun-dried tomatoes.

5. Add the broth and wine, and bring to a simmer.

6. Lower the heat and cover. Cook for a total of 5 to 8 minutes, turning the chicken 2 or 3 times during the process.

7. Add the olives and adjust the seasoning.

8. Garnish with the parsley.

**Serves 4**

# Summer Grilled Chicken
## with Fresh Pepper Confit

*4 chicken breasts, 8 ounces each, boneless and skinless*
*1 red onion, sliced*
*salt and pepper, for seasoning*
*2 tablespoons olive oil*
*2 yellow peppers, roasted, peeled and sliced (see page 70)*
*2 red peppers, roasted, peeled and sliced*
*2 green peppers, roasted, peeled and sliced*
*3 tablespoons capers*
*1 cup fresh basil, chiffonade*
*¼ cup balsamic vinegar*
*¼ cup extra virgin olive oil*
*olive oil, for coating*
*freshly ground pepper, for seasoning*

1. Season the onion slices with salt and pepper and toss them with 2 tablespoons olive oil. Roast them in a 350°F oven until they are soft but still al dente.

2. Mix the onions, peppers, capers and basil together.

3. In a separate bowl, mix the vinegar and ¼ cup extra virgin olive oil together. Pour the vinegar mixture over the vegetables and season with fresh pepper and salt.

4. Brush the chicken breasts lightly with some olive oil and season with salt and pepper.

5. Grill the breasts on both sides (totalling approximately 10 to 15 minutes) until done, but juicy.

6. Place 1 chicken breast on each of 4 plates and garnish with the pepper mixture. Serve immediately.

**Serves 4**

## Sweet Peppers

All three types of peppers used in this recipe—yellow, red and green—are considered sweet peppers. They are called that because they are not hot, like many other types of peppers. Also unlike many other peppers, these three types can usually be found in supermarkets year-round. Their availability and bright blend of fresh colors allows you to serve up a taste of summer at any time of year!

## Wine Notes

 A chilled glass of Beaujolais or a fruity Zinfandel from California is wonderful.

## Reducing

With the modern emphasis on lighter style cooking, many recipes require reduction, the process of cooking liquids out of sauces in order to intensify their flavors. Doing this is simple. Just boil liquids, uncovered, until their volume is reduced to the desired amount. Reduced liquids have a rich, concentrated flavor and a syrupy consistency that makes an instant sauce or gravy, without the need for thickening agents.

## Wine Notes

 Try a crisp Sauvignon Blanc from Sancerre or a Pouilly Fumé. The lemony flavor of the sauce nicely complements the crispness of these wines.

# Chicken and Shrimp Picante

*4 chicken breasts, 8 ounces each, boneless and skinless*
*1/2 cup Wondra (instant) flour*
*1/4 cup olive oil*
*1 teaspoon garlic*
*8 large shrimp, peeled and deveined*
*1/2 cup white wine*
*1/2 cup chicken stock (see page 5)*
*12 slices of lemon, cut very thin*
*6 ounces Lemon Butter (see page 186), softened*
*2 teaspoons black peppercorns, cracked*
*salt, to taste*
*3 tablespoons parsley, chopped*

1. Cut the chicken breasts in half. Pound them to make them even, if you desire.

2. Dredge the chicken in the flour and tap off any excess.

3. In a sauté pan with the oil, sauté the chicken and garlic until they are golden brown, approximately 2 to 3 minutes on each side. Remove them and place them in a 300°F oven.

4. In the sauté pan, add the shrimp, toss and sear. Remove this and place it in the oven.

5. In the sauté pan, add the white wine and chicken stock. Bring it to a simmer and reduce by two-thirds.

6. Add the lemon slices and softened lemon butter. Shake the pan to make a sauce. Be careful not to bring it to a boil.

7. Season with the peppercorns and salt. Sprinkle in the parsley.

8. Place the chicken on 4 plates. Put 3 lemon slices on top of each, then add the shrimp. Spoon the sauce over the top.

**Serves 4**

# Chicken Albertina
## with Shrimp Cream Sauce

*1 pound angel hair pasta*
*Shrimp Cream Sauce (opposite page)*
*3 chicken breasts, boneless, cut into quarters and pounded (totalling*
    *12 pieces)*
*salt and pepper, for seasoning*
*3 eggs*
*³⁄₄ cup milk*
*1 cup flour*
*3 cups bread crumbs, seasoned with salt and pepper*
*¹⁄₄ cup vegetable oil*
*12 shrimp, peeled and deveined*
*fresh parsley, chopped, for garnish*

1.  Make the Shrimp Cream Sauce before you prepare the chicken and
    shrimp.

2.  Season the chicken with salt and pepper.

3.  Beat together the eggs and milk.

4.  Dredge the chicken pieces in flour. Dip them in the egg mixture, and
    then cover them with the bread crumbs.

5.  In a sauté pan with the oil (minus 1 tablespoon), brown the chicken
    breasts on both sides. Remove them to a baking pan and finish
    cooking them in a preheated 300°F oven for 10 minutes.

6.  Sauté the shrimp in 1 tablespoon of oil until it is just cooked,
    approximately 5 minutes. Reserve and keep warm.

7.  Cook the angel hair pasta in boiling water. Drain well. Divide the
    pasta among 4 plates and place 3 pieces of chicken on top of each.

8.  Spoon the Shrimp Cream Sauce over the chicken and pasta.

9.  Place 3 shrimp on top of each serving.

10. Garnish with chopped parsley and serve.

**Serves 4**

---

**A Tasty Tribute**

This dish has enjoyed immense popularity, and we still make it for special requests. It is named after my grandmother.

**Breading: The 3-Step Method**

When breading, try the two-hand method. Use one hand for dipping only in the flour and eggs. Use the other hand for dipping the crumbs. This technique keeps your hands from "gumming up."

**Wine Notes**

 Try a buttery Chardonnay from Napa Valley or Australia. A white Burgundy such as Meursault or Chassagne-Montrachet also is nice.

## Beurre Manié

A beurre manié is a butter and flour mixture that is used to thicken sauces. The ratio of flour to butter is the same as that for a roux (equal parts of each by weight). When adding these butter-pats to a stock, cream or reduction, thickening occurs in minutes. They can be wrapped into small balls and stored in the refrigerator for a few weeks, or frozen for months.

## To Make a Beurre Manie

1/4 cup flour
1/4 cup butter, softened

1. Knead the butter into the flour until they are thoroughly mixed.

2. Form this mixture into little balls. If you do not plan to use them right away, cover them and refrigerate or freeze.

3. When adding the balls to a liquid, whisk them to help incorporate and thicken.

# Shrimp Cream Sauce

1 tablespoon shallots, chopped
1/2 cup white wine
3 tablespoons brandy
1 cup shrimp stock (see page 7)
3/4 cup heavy cream
1 teaspoon beurre manié (see sidebar)
shrimp bisque base, as needed to enhance flavor (found in specialty food stores)
salt and pepper, for seasoning
parsley, chopped, for garnish

1. In a saucepan, combine the shallots, wine, brandy and stock. Bring them to a boil, and reduce by half.

2. Add the heavy cream and cook until it begins to thicken. Add small pieces of the beurre manié, and whisk until thickened. Simmer for 10 minutes. Strain this sauce.

3. Add the shrimp base if you need to intensify the flavors. Season with salt and pepper, to taste.

# Chicken Cordon Rouge
## with Mornay Sauce

*4 chicken breasts, 8 ounces each, boneless and skinless*
*1/2 cup Wondra (instant) flour*
*1/4 cup olive oil*
*2 shallots, chopped*
*2 cups button mushrooms, sliced*
*8 slices of Capicola ham, diced*
*1/4 cup white wine*
*3 cups fresh tomatoes, diced*
*salt and white pepper, for seasoning*
*Mornay Sauce (opposite page)*
*3 tablespoons parsley, chopped, for garnish*

1. Cut the chicken breasts in half. Pound them to make them even, if you desire.

2. Dredge the chicken in the flour and tap off any excess.

3. In a sauté pan with the olive oil, sauté the chicken until it is golden brown, approximately 2 to 3 minutes on each side. Remove the breasts to a baking sheet and put them in a 300°F oven.

4. In the sauté pan, add the shallots, mushrooms and ham. Sauté this for a few minutes, until the shallots and mushrooms begin to soften.

5. Add the wine and tomatoes to the pan. Cook for about 10 minutes.

6. Season with the salt and pepper.

7. Arrange the chicken on a platter, and top it with the tomato mixture. Pour the Mornay Sauce over the chicken and tomatoes.

8. Garnish with the chopped parsley.

**Serves 4**

**Chicken Skins**

Chicken does not absorb much fat from the skin while cooking, so you can leave the skin on to hold goodies next to the meat and infuse flavor while they cook. The infused flavor is great. Try veggies, herbs, spices, butters and any other taste sensations you can imagine.

**Wine Notes**

 Spicy, cheesy, creamy, this dish has many different flavors happening. Try a Gewürztraminer from Alsace. Pick one that is not too spicy.

# Mornay Sauce

*3 tablespoons butter*
*2 tablespoons shallots, chopped*
*3 tablespoons flour*
*2 cups light cream or half-and-half*
*³/4 cup rich chicken stock (see page 5)*
*¹/2 teaspoon Worcestershire sauce*
*1 teaspoon salt*
*¹/4 teaspoon white pepper*
*pinch of cayenne pepper*
*¹/4 cup Swiss cheese, grated*
*3 tablespoons Parmesan cheese, grated*

1. Melt the butter in a small saucepan. Add the shallots and cook them over medium heat until they are softened but not brown.

2. Turn down the heat and sprinkle in the flour. Stir over a low heat for 2 to 3 minutes to cook the flour. Do not brown the flour.

3. Pour in the cream and chicken stock. Thicken the sauce and bring it to a simmer, stirring it often with a whisk.

4. Add the Worcestershire sauce, salt, pepper and cayenne. Simmer the sauce for 15 minutes.

5. At this point, check the consistency of the sauce. You may want to thin it with a bit more chicken stock or cream.

6. Strain the sauce into another saucepan using a medium-textured sieve. Discard the contents of the sieve.

7. Place the new saucepan back on the burner on low heat. Add the cheeses, stirring as they melt and mix.

**Makes 2¹/2 cups**

## More on Mornay

Mornay sauce is béchamel sauce with the addition of cheese, such as Parmesan or Swiss. It can be varied by the addition of fish or chicken stock or, for added richness, cream or egg yolks. Mornay sauce is usually served with fish, eggs, vegetables or chicken.

# Pommery Chicken
## with Mustard Cream Sauce

*4 chicken breasts, skin on, 8 ounces each*
*salt and pepper, for seasoning*
*¼ cup olive oil*
*¼ cup white wine*
*1 cup Pommery mustard or a whole grain mustard*
*Mustard Cream Sauce (opposite page)*
*1 bunch watercress, chopped, for garnish*

1. Preheat the oven to 425°F.

2. Season both sides of the chicken breasts with salt and pepper, then brush them with olive oil.

3. In a baking pan, roast the chicken for 10 minutes.

4. Remove the chicken and brush it with the mustard. Be generous with the mustard.

5. Put the breasts back into the oven for another 5 to 10 minutes, until they are done.

6. Remove the breasts and slice them crossways. Arrange the chicken slices like shingles, and drizzle the Mustard Cream Sauce over the chicken.

7. Garnish with the chopped watercress.

**Serves 4**

---

**Whole Grain Mustard**

For this recipe, Pommery or any whole grain mustard works best. A whole grain mustard is made by keeping the mustard seeds mostly intact rather than grinding them to a powder. (In the case of smooth-style mustards, prepared mustard powder is used.) You can substitute any coarsely ground mustard that looks grainy to the eye.

**Wine Notes**

 With this dish, we enjoy a lighter Chardonnay, such as a Mâcon Village or even a crisp Chablis from France. A light, dry Sauvignon Blanc from Napa Valley also works.

## Lotsa Shallots

Shallots look more like garlic, because of their multiple cloves, than the onion family to which they belong. Look for dry-skinned, plump and firm shallots with no sign of wrinkles or sprouts. Shallots can be refrigerated for up to a week or stored in a cool, dry, well-ventilated spot for up to a month. They have a mild flavor and are often paired with cream and wine in sauces. They can be used interchangeably with other onions in most recipes.

# Mustard Cream Sauce

*3 tablespoons butter*
*2 tablespoons shallots, chopped*
*3 tablespoons flour*
*1/4 cup white wine*
*2 tablespoons Dijon mustard*
*1/2 cup chicken stock (see page 5)*
*2 cups heavy cream*
*salt and pepper, for seasoning*

1. Melt the butter in a small saucepan. Add the shallots and cook over medium heat until they are softened but not brown.

2. Turn down the heat and sprinkle in the flour. Stir in the flour, cooking it over low heat for 2 to 3 minutes. Do not brown the flour.

3. Add the white wine, mustard, chicken stock and heavy cream.

4. Raise the heat and bring the sauce to a simmer, stirring often.

5. Season with salt and pepper, to taste.

**Makes 3 cups**

# Chicken Sonoma
## with Brunoise of Vegetables
## and Roasted Soft Garlic Cream

*6 chicken breasts, 8 ounces each, boneless and cut in half*
*6 tablespoons olive oil, for sautéeing*
*1¼ cup zucchini, diced small*
*1¼ cup red onion, diced small*
*1¼ cup eggplant, diced small*
*1 cup tomato, peeled and diced small*
*salt and pepper, for seasoning*
*Roasted Soft Garlic Cream (opposite page)*

1. Add 1½ teaspoons olive oil to a hot sauté pan. Add each type of vegetable individually. Cook them quickly for 2 minutes, then place them in a shallow container to cool. The vegetables should still have some crunch left. Repeat this process for all of the vegetables, except the tomatoes.

2. Mix all of the vegetables together, except the tomatoes.

3. Sauté the chicken breasts in 4 tablespoons olive oil, browning them on both sides. Remove them to a baking pan and bake at 300°F for 10 minutes.

4. Combine and reheat the vegetables in a wok or sauté pan while the breasts are cooking. When the vegetables are hot, add the tomatoes. Season the vegetables well with salt and pepper.

5. Place the chicken on a serving platter. Spoon the vegetables on top of the chicken.

6. Ladle the Roasted Soft Garlic Cream over the chicken and vegetables.

**Serves 6**

**Sear Separately**

All of the vegetables should be seared separately and cooled, then added together. The pan must be hot, so that the vegetables cook quickly. A wok is a great pan for cooking the vegetables because it works so fast. This process can be done a few hours in advance, and then the vegetables can be refrigerated.

**Wine Notes**

 Try a full flavored, floral white wine like an off-dry Riesling from Germany or a flinty Chenin Blanc from California. Lighter, fruity reds also go well with this dish.

# Roasted Soft Garlic Cream

*6 bulbs fresh garlic*
*2 tablespoons olive oil*
*$^1/_2$ teaspoon salt*
*freshly ground black pepper, for seasoning*
*2 tablespoons shallots, chopped*
*$^1/_2$ cup white wine*
*2 tablespoons champagne vinegar*
*1 cup heavy cream*
*$^1/_2$ pound (2 sticks) whole butter, softened*

You can roast the garlic a day ahead.

1. Preheat the oven to 350°F. Season the garlic bulbs with the olive oil, $^1/_2$ teaspoon salt and a few grinds of pepper. Put them in a small casserole dish, tightly covered with aluminum foil. Bake for 45 minutes. The garlic should be very soft. Let it cool, then squeeze out the pulp.

2. Combine the garlic, shallots, wine and vinegar in a saucepan. Simmer this wine mixture over medium heat until the liquid nearly evaporates. Be careful not to burn the pan.

3. Add the cream and simmer until it is reduced by half and has the consistency of a sauce.

4. Turn the heat to low. Whip in the butter, 1 tablespoon at a time, stirring constantly until all the butter is incorporated. Season with salt and pepper, to taste.

5. Strain the sauce through a medium sieve to give it a silky consistency. For a more rustic sauce, leave in the garlic and shallots.

---

**Best Way to Peel a Tomato**

To peel a tomato, cut an X on the smooth bottom, then submerge the tomato in boiling water for 15 seconds. Remove and cool under cold water for a few seconds. Then using a paring knife, cut out the stem end of the tomato. The skin will then slip off easily. To seed, cut the tomato in half across its width. Hold it over a sink or bowl and squeeze out the seeds and watery pulp.

# Chicken Sarah

*4 chicken breasts, 8 ounces each, boneless*
*1 cup flour, seasoned with salt and pepper*
*8 slices mozzarella cheese*
*¼ cup olive oil*
*salt and pepper, for seasoning*
*Sarah Sauce (opposite page)*

1.  Cut the chicken breasts in half. Pound them to make them even, if you desire.

2.  Dredge the chicken in the flour and tap off any excess.

3.  Preheat the oven to 350°F.

4.  In a sauté pan with the olive oil, sauté the chicken until it is golden brown, approximately 2 to 3 minutes on each side.

5.  Place the chicken on a platter, and put it in the oven. Bake it for 5 to 8 minutes.

6.  Place 2 slices of cheese over each breast and continue cooking for 5 more minutes. The cheese should be barely melted, not browned.

7.  Place the chicken on a platter and ladle the Sarah Sauce over the top.

**Serves 4**

**Simple Substitutions**

For this dish, veal can be substituted for chicken and it becomes our Veal Betsy. The veal can simply be floured or breaded before cooking.

**Wine Notes**

 A crisp Muscadet or a Pinot Gris from Oregon matches nicely. A Dolcetto or Beaujolais also goes well with this dish.

## Clarified Butter

Whole butter contains 16% water and milk solids. Clarified butter is the fat that has been separated from the water and the milk solids. This raises the smoking temperature of the fat, since the milk solids burn at a much lower temperature than the oil.

To make clarified butter, melt butter over low heat without stirring. Then pour off the clear liquid on the surface, leaving behind the milk solids. The clear liquid is the clarified butter, which is also an important ingredient in Indian cooking, called *ghee*.

# Sarah Sauce

*1 tablespoon shallots, chopped*
*2 tablespoons butter*
*1 cup beef stock (see page 8)*
*1 cup rich chicken stock (see page 5)*
*3 ounces dry Sherry*
*1 tablespoon Sherry*
*1¹/₂ tablespoons cornstarch*
*salt and pepper, for seasoning*

1.  Sauté the shallots in the butter until they are translucent.

2.  Add the beef and chicken stocks and 3 ounces dry Sherry. Bring them to a boil.

3.  Dissolve 1¹/₂ tablespoons cornstarch in 1 tablespoon Sherry.

4.  Whisk in the cornstarch mixture and stir until the sauce thickens. Simmer for 10 minutes, until the taste is smooth.

5.  Season with the salt and pepper.

6.  If you desire a silkier consistency, strain the sauce.

**Makes 2¹/₄ cups**

# Sandcastle Chicken

*4 chicken breasts, 8 ounces each, boneless and skinless*
*1 cup Wondra (instant) flour*
*¼ cup olive oil*
*1 cup red onions, cut julienne style*
*1 tablespoon garlic, chopped*
*1 cup mushrooms, sliced*
*1 cup leeks, cut julienne style*
*3 tablespoons fresh thyme, chopped*
*3 tablespoons fresh marjoram, chopped*
*3 cups spinach, picked, washed and dried*
*salt and pepper, for seasoning*
*Lemon Beurre Blanc (opposite page)*
*parsley, chopped, for garnish*

1. Cut the chicken breasts in half. Pound them to make them even, if you desire.

2. Dredge the chicken in the flour and tap off any excess.

3. Preheat the oven to 250°F.

4. In a sauté pan with the oil, sauté the chicken until it is golden brown, approximately 2 to 3 minutes on each side. Reserve the breasts, covered, in the oven.

5. In the same sauté pan, add the onions, garlic, mushrooms and leeks. Toss and sauté for 5 minutes.

6. Add the herbs and spinach, and cook for 2 minutes. Season with salt and pepper, to taste.

7. Place the chicken on 4 plates. Spoon the vegetables and then the Lemon Beurre Blanc over the top.

8. Garnish with the chopped parsley.

**Serves 4**

**Julienne Strips**

To cut julienne or match-stick-sized strips, cut food into 2-inch lengths first. Then cut each length into ¼-inch-thick slices. Stack several slices and cut them into ¼-inch-thick strips.

**Wine Notes**

Try an off-dry Riesling or a Chenin Blanc from Vouvray.

## About Beurre Blanc

This French sauce of reduced wine, vinegar and shallots involves whisking chunks of cold butter into the reduced sauce until smooth. It is said to have originated by accident in the 1900s, when a cook making a béarnaise sauce forgot to add egg yolks. It became so popular, that it changed from a mistake to a classic recipe. For more on beurre blanc and its variations, see page 11.

# Lemon Beurre Blanc

*3 tablespoons shallots, chopped*
*2 tablespoons white wine vinegar*
*¹/₄ cup white wine*
*juice of 2 lemons*
*1 cup heavy cream*
*¹/₂ pound (2 sticks) butter*
*2 tablespoons lemon zest, chopped*
*2 tablespoons parsley, chopped*
*salt and freshly ground pepper, for seasoning*

1. Put the shallots, vinegar, wine and lemon juice in a small saucepan. Bring to a simmer and reduce by two-thirds.

2. Add the cream. Reduce it until the sauce thickens.

3. Lower the heat and swirl in the butter. Add the lemon zest and parsley. Season with the salt and pepper.

**Makes 1 cup**

# Chicken Victoria

*4 chicken breasts, 8 ounces each, boneless, skinless and pounded flat*
*4 tablespoons olive oil*
*2 tablespoons shallots, chopped*
*6 cups spinach, picked and cleaned*
*salt and pepper, for seasoning*
*1 11-ounce can of frozen lobster meat*
*3 eggs*
*³/4 cup milk*
*1 cup flour*
*3 cups Japanese bread crumbs, seasoned with salt, pepper and parsley*
*4 tablespoons parsley, chopped*
*spray can of vegetable oil*
*Mornay Sauce (see page 174) or Mustard Cream Sauce (see page 177)*

*butcher's twine*

1.  In a large sauté pan, cook the shallots in olive oil for 4 minutes. Add the spinach and heat it for approximately 3 minutes, until just cooked. When the spinach is cool enough, squeeze it dry in a strainer. Season with salt and pepper.

2.  Season the pounded, chicken fillets with salt and pepper. Place ¹/4 of the spinach in the center of each breast, spreading it to within a half-inch of the edge. Divide the lobster evenly, placing it in the center of each breast.

3.  Carefully roll each chicken fillet into a log, tucking in the corners. Tie them securely with butcher's string, and place them in the freezer for 30 minutes.

4.  Beat together the eggs and milk. Using the 3-step method (see page 172), dredge the chicken rolls in flour, dip them in the egg mixture and then dip them in the bread crumbs.

5.  Preheat the oven to 350°F. Place the breasts in a baking pan and spray each with the vegetable oil. Bake for 30 minutes.

6.  Carefully slice each roll in half before placing it on a plate. Serve with Mornay Sauce or Mustard Cream Sauce.

**Serves 4**

## Rolled Fillets

To create extra thin fillets from basic chicken breasts, we recommend this procedure: Spread the chicken breasts onto a cutting board covered with plastic wrap. Place another layer of wrap on top of the chicken. With a mallet, pound the breasts to make them a half-inch thick. It's best to pound from the center outward to the edges.

## Wine Notes

Try a barrel-fermented Chardonnay from California for this rich and majestic dish. A butter-flavored Chardonnay holds up well to the richness of this dish.

## Adding Zest

Adding a zest does just that! Fresh citrus zest creates a much livelier flavor than simply adding an extract. To get the best flavor, use a hand grater to scrape zest from only the colored parts of the citrus skin (as the white portion tastes bitter). The zest is so intense because it contains an oil that has a strong, fresh flavor.

## Wine Notes

 This classic dish is wonderful with a crisp dry Sauvignon Blanc. The wine's citrus flavors work together with the dish's lemon zest. Try one from California or the Loire Valley.

# Lemon-Thyme Roasted Chicken

4 chicken breasts, bone-in
2 tablespoons fresh thyme, finely chopped
2 tablespoons lemon zest, finely chopped
1 teaspoon salt
salt and freshly ground pepper, for seasoning
1 onion, sliced
2 stalks celery, sliced
1 carrot, peeled and sliced
1 1/2 teaspoons garlic, chopped
1 cup chicken stock (see page 5)
4 tablespoons Herb Butter (see page 135)
Mashed Potatoes (see page 289)

1. Mix together the thyme, lemon zest and teaspoon of salt.

2. Gently pull the skin of each chicken breast up and rub the herb mixture under the skin. Make sure to keep the skin attached at the edges.

3. Season the breasts with the salt and pepper.

4. Preheat the oven to 350°F.

5. Place the vegetables and garlic in a roasting pan and place the breasts on top. (Do not cover the pan.)

6. Roast the breasts for 30 to 40 minutes until done.

7. Remove the breasts from the pan. Add the chicken stock to deglaze.

8. Cook the stock and reduce it by one-half. Strain it into a gravy boat.

9. Top each breast with a dollop of Herb Butter.

10. Serve with mashed potatoes and the jus on the side.

**Serves 4**

# Chicken Chalmers

*4 chicken breasts, 10 ounces each, boneless and skinless*
*salt and white pepper*
*¹/₂ cup flour*
*¹/₄ cup vegetable oil*
*1 cup white wine*
*2 ounces shallots, chopped*

*Lemon Butter*
*juice of 1 lemon*
*zest of 1 lemon, chopped*
*¹/₄ cup fresh parsley, chopped*
*pinch of granulated garlic*
*pinch of salt and pepper*
*2 sticks butter (1 cup), softened*

1.  Mix all of the Lemon Butter ingredients together.

2.  Sprinkle the chicken breasts with salt and white pepper. Dredge in the flour.

3.  Preheat the oven to 300°F.

4.  In a sauté pan with the oil, sauté the chicken until golden, approximately 2 to 3 minutes on each side. Put it on a baking sheet and place it in the oven for 15 minutes.

5.  In the sauté pan, add the white wine and shallots and reduce it until almost dry.

6.  With the dash of white wine left in the pan, slowly whip in the Lemon Butter.

7.  Do not bring this mixture to a boil. Whip it until it develops the consistency of a sauce.

8.  Put each chicken breast on a plate. Pour the sauce over the top.

**Serves 4**

## A Chicken Dish Devotee

This dish is named for Douglas Chalmers, who orders only chicken when he dines here. We consider him part of our quality-control family.

## Wine Notes

Light and crisp wines, like an Oregon Pinot Gris or a Washington State Fumé Blanc, are nice choices. Also try a Sauvignon Blanc from Dry Creek Valley in Sonoma.

## Egg Wash

An egg wash can be made by combining either egg yolks or whites with water or milk. It is often brushed on bread, pastry and rolls before baking to add color and shine.

To make a smaller amount, combine 1 egg with 2 tablespoons of milk or water.

## Wine Notes

Lighter whites or dry rosés work well with this dish. A California Chardonnay or Mâcon Village from France complement the nutty flavors.

# Chicken Pecan

*4 chicken breasts, 8 ounces each, boneless, skinless and pounded flat*
*salt and pepper, for seasoning*
*1 cup Wondra (instant) flour*
*egg wash (3 eggs and ¹/₂ cup milk)*
*1 cup pecans, chopped rough*
*¹/₄ cup clarified butter (see page 181)*
*¹/₄ cup white wine*
*1 cup reduced chicken stock (see page 5)*
*4 tablespoons bourbon*

*Pecan Butter*
*1 stick butter (¹/₂ cup)*
*2 tablespoons shallots, chopped*
*4 tablespoons parsley, chopped*
*3 tablespoons pecans, chopped*
*1 tablespoon honey*

1. Mix all of the Pecan Butter ingredients together in a food processor until they are well blended. Wrap it in wax paper and refrigerate.

2. Season the chicken breasts with salt and pepper.

3. Dredge them in the flour, then through the egg wash and then the pecans. Press the pecans into the chicken with your hands. Place the chicken in the refrigerator for 1 hour.

4. In a hot pan with the clarified butter, sauté the chicken until it is brown on both sides.

5. Remove it from the pan, drain the fat and place it in a preheated 300°F oven for 10 minutes.

6. In the pan, add the white wine, stock and bourbon. Shake the pan to stir. Reduce the liquid to the consistency of a sauce.

7. Add the Pecan Butter, shaking the pan to incorporate it into the original sauce. Add salt and pepper, to taste.

8. Place the chicken on 4 plates. Spoon the sauce over the top.

**Serves 4**

# Chicken in Balsamic Vinegar

*2 garlic cloves, chopped*
*¹/₄ cup red wine vinegar*
*¹/₄ cup balsamic vinegar*
*1 tablespoon rosemary leaves, chopped*
*2 tablespoons salt*
*1 tablespoon paprika*
*1 teaspoon white pepper*
*1 teaspoon onion powder*
*¹/₄ teaspoon cayenne pepper*
*6 chicken breasts, 8 ounces each, skin on, cut in half*
*¹/₂ cup olive oil*
*¹/₂ cup chicken stock (see page 5)*
*watercress, chopped, for garnish*

1.  Combine the garlic, vinegars and rosemary. Let sit for at least 1 hour.

2.  Mix all of the remaining seasonings together. Liberally season both sides of the chicken breasts with this mix.

3.  In a heavy sauté pan, heat the oil. When it is hot, add the chicken breasts and sauté them for 2 minutes on each side, until they are brown all over.

4.  At the same time, bring the chicken stock to a boil.

5.  Add the broth to the chicken. Lower the heat and simmer until cooked (approximately 10 minutes).

6.  Preheat the oven to 350°F.

7.  Pour the vinegar mixture over the breasts and raise the heat to high.

8.  Put the breasts into the oven for 5 to 10 minutes, until they are done.

9.  Remove the breasts and slice them crossways. Shingle the slices, then drizzle the sauce over them.

10. Garnish with chopped watercress.

**Serves 6**

## Serving Shingled

To give this dish an added appeal, I suggest shingling the sliced chicken. Shingling means to lay the edge of each slice over the edge of the slice beneath it, like shingles on a roof. You can use this arrangement for many types of sliced foods.

## Wine Notes

Try a Zinfandel from California or a spicy Côtes du Rhône from France.

# Raspberry Chicken

*4 chicken breasts, 8 ounces each, boneless and skinless*
*¹/₄ cup Wondra (instant) flour*
*6 tablespoons clarified butter (see page 181)*
*2 shallots, chopped*
*¹/₂ cup white wine*
*2 ounces raspberry liqueur*
*4 tablespoons raspberry vinegar*
*¹/₂ cup chicken stock (see page 5)*
*¹/₄ cup heavy cream*
*3 tablespoons butter, softened*
*¹/₂ pint fresh raspberries*
*salt and pepper, for seasoning*

1. Cut the chicken breasts in half. Pound them to make them even, if you desire.

2. Dredge the chicken in the flour; tap off any excess.

3. In a skillet with the clarified butter, sauté the chicken and shallots until golden brown, approximately 2 to 3 minutes on each side. Remove the chicken, drain off the fat and keep it warm in a 300°F oven.

4. In the same pan, add the white wine and raspberry liqueur and bring it to a boil.

5. Add the vinegar and stock and simmer. Reduce for 5 minutes.

6. Add the cream and reduce for 5 minutes, or until it has the consistency of a sauce.

7. Swirl in the softened butter. Shake the pan until you have a nice smooth sauce. Set aside several raspberries for a garnish, and add the rest to the sauce.

8. Divide the chicken among 4 plates; pour the sauce on top. Garnish with fresh berries and thyme.

**Serves 4**

# Cornish Game Hens
## with Fresh Cherries and Sour Cream

*4 Cornish game hens*
*salt and pepper, for seasoning*
*1¹/₂ teaspoons paprika*
*2¹/₂ teaspoons cinnamon*
*3 tablespoons butter*
*1¹/₂ large onions, diced*
*1 cup chicken stock (see page 5)*
*³/₄ cup Madeira wine*
*1¹/₂ cups fresh cherries, pitted*
*3 tablespoons sour cream*

1.  Preheat the oven to 425°F. Season the hens with salt, pepper, ¹/₂ teaspoon cinnamon and ¹/₂ teaspoon paprika. Place them in a roasting pan and cook for 45 minutes.

2.  Combine the cherries and Madiera wine. Let sit for 45 minutes.

3.  Remove the hens from the oven and let them cool enough to handle. Cut the hens into quarters and remove their back bones. Return them to the baking pan and warm them in the oven on low heat (250°F).

4.  In a braising pan, sauté the onions in the butter, until soft (approximately 10 minutes). Add the remaining cinnamon and paprika. Cook for 5 minutes.

5.  Drain the Madiera wine off of the cherries and set them aside. Add the stock and Madiera wine to the braising pan. Cook over high heat and reduce until thickened.

6.  Add the cherries and cook until heated. Season with salt and pepper.

7.  Add the hens back into the sauce and reheat them. Swirl in the sour cream and heat.

8.  Place the hens on a platter. Spoon the sauce over the top and serve.

**Serves 4**

### A Cherry Jubilee

This recipe is from Square One Restaurant in San Francisco. It is a celebration of the fresh cherries that we get every June. The cinnamon and paprika help thicken the sauce and have a synergistic effect in this dish. It is one of my favorites and is best served with Washington Inn Rice.

### Wine Notes

What better wine than a dry Pinot Noir from Oregon or California? The soft cherry fruit of these wines matches nicely with the cherry and cinnamon flavors of this dish.

## Brown Chicken Stock

Brown chicken stock is made by roasting the chicken bones first. To do that, place the bones in a 400°F oven until they turn brown (approximately 45 minutes). When browned, these bones can be used in the recipe for chicken stock on page 5 to create brown chicken stock.

## Wine Notes

 Try a nice Sangiovese from Italy. A Chianti or Brunello di Montalcino is also delicious.

# Roasted Duck
## with Garlic and Turnips

*1 5- to 6-pound duck*
*1 teaspoon kosher salt*
*1/8 teaspoon white pepper*
*3 tablespoons peanut oil*
*2/3 cup fresh garlic cloves, peeled*
*1 bouquet garni (4 parsley stems, 1 bay leaf, 1/2 bunch fresh thyme)*
*2 pounds white turnips, peeled*
*1 1/2 cups brown chicken stock (see sidebar)*
*1/4 cup white wine*
*1/2 tablespoon beurre manié (see page 173)*
*1/4 cup parsley, chopped*

1. Season the duck inside and out, with salt and pepper. Pat it dry.

2. Add the oil to a large cast iron casserole-baking dish. Over medium heat, slowly brown the duck on all sides. Remove the duck, drain off and reserve the fat and season the duck with more salt.

3. Toss the garlic in the drained fat and place it in the casserole dish. Return the duck to the covered casserole. Add the bouquet garni. Roast them in a preheated 350°F oven for 50 to 60 minutes.

4. Cut the turnips into large dice. Boil in salted water for 5 minutes. Drain.

5. After 1 hour, add the turnips to the duck. Toss with the fat and garlic. Continue cooking for another 20 to 40 minutes. Baste the garlic and turnips with the fat.

6. The duck is done when its juices are clear. Remove and keep it warm. With a slotted spoon, remove the garlic, turnips and herbs.

7. Drain the fat and place the casserole on the stove. Deglaze it with the chicken stock and reduce by half. Whisk in the beurre manié until the stock is thickened. Season with salt and pepper. Toss in the garlic and turnips and bring to a simmer.

8. Slice the duck and place it on a warm platter. Spoon the sauce with the turnips and garlic over the duck. Sprinkle with parsley.

**Serves 4**

# Duck Breast
## with Sweet Potatoes
## and Ginger-Port Cream Sauce

*4 duck breasts, 10 ounces each, fat trimmed off*
*salt and pepper, for seasoning*
*¹/₄ cup green onions, sliced on bias*
*¹/₄ cup shiitake mushrooms, sliced*
*1 tablespoon butter*
*Sweet Potatoes (opposite page)*
*Ginger Port Cream Sauce (opposite page)*
*green onions, for garnish*
*shiitake mushrooms, for garnish*

1.  Season the duck breasts with salt and pepper.

2.  Preheat the oven to 350°F.

3.  In a sauté pan, place the duck skin-side down. Keep the heat on medium. Cook it for 10 minutes, until the skin is crisp and the fat is rendered. Turn the breast over and quickly sear the other side.

4.  Remove them from the pan and place them in a baking pan in the oven for 10 minutes.

5.  In the sauté pan with the butter, quickly sauté the scallions and shiitake mushrooms.

6.  Pull the duck from the oven, let it sit for 5 minutes so that the juices set, then slice it into ¹/₄-inch slices.

7.  Place a large spoonful of sweet potatoes in the center of each of 4 plates.

8.  Arrange the slices on top of the sweet potatoes, to look like a fan.

9.  Drizzle the Ginger-Port Cream Sauce over the duck.

10. Garnish with green onions and mushrooms.

**Serves 4**

## Roasting Duck

The breast of a duck is best served rare, as its flesh is tender and has less fat. The legs and thighs are tougher, so they need to be cooked longer to make them tender. The legs hold their moisture better with a longer cooking time. How do you keep the breast rare but the legs tender?

When roasting a duck, French chefs have found a technique that keeps the breast medium rare. Roast the duck in the normal way, but take it out of the oven when the breast reaches 135°F. Cut off the legs and the thighs and put them back in the oven for 30 to 40 more minutes.

Serve the breasts and legs together, or serve the legs after the breasts. You can even save the leg meat for a later use.

## Wine Notes

 An Italian Dolcetto or a lighter style Merlot are both good choices. Try a Merlot from northern Italy or the French country side.

# Sweet Potatoes

*1¹/₂ pounds sweet potatoes, peeled and cut into 1-inch chunks*
*¹/₂ stick butter, softened*
*2 ounces heavy cream*
*salt and pepper, for seasoning*
*pinch of cinnamon*

1. In a pot of boiling water, cook the sweet potatoes until they are nice and soft. Strain off the water.

2. Place the potatoes in a food mill or food processor, and purée them. If using a food processor, do not over process them.

3. Place the potatoes in a bowl. Stir in the butter and cream.

4. Season with salt, pepper and cinnamon.

5. Serve immediately.

**Serves 4**

# Ginger-Port Cream Sauce

*4 tablespoons shallots, thinly sliced*
*1 tablespoon balsamic vinegar*
*1 teaspoon soy sauce*
*2 tablespoons ginger, peeled and thinly sliced*
*¹/₂ cup Port wine*
*¹/₂ cup vermouth*
*2 cups heavy cream*
*salt and pepper, to taste*

1. In a saucepan, combine the shallots, vinegar, soy sauce, ginger, Port wine and vermouth. Reduce until they are almost dry.

2. Add the cream. Simmer until it has the consistency of a sauce.

3. Strain. (Discard the strained ingredients.) Season with salt and pepper.

**Makes 1¹/₂ cups**

# Duck and Portabella Mushrooms

1 duck breast, 16 ounces, trimmed
2 cups oil
2 cups leeks, cleaned, dried and cut julienne style
2 tablespoons shallots
1 cup veal stock, reduced (see page 9)
1 tablespoon honey
1/4 pint blackberries, crushed
1/4 pint blackberries, whole
1 teaspoon peppercorns, cracked
4 portabella mushrooms, stems off and reserved
salt and pepper, for seasoning
1/2 cup portabella mushroom stems, sliced thin

## Marinade
3 tablespoons oil
3 tablespoons thyme, chopped
1 bay leaf
1/4 cup balsamic vinegar
2 tablespoons shallots
1 teaspoon Tabasco

**Bay Leaf Basics**

This highly aromatic herb should be used carefully. Less than half of a single leaf can season a quart of stew. The French use bay leaf frequently in cooking, and often as a complement to thyme. A key ingredient in a bouquet garni, bay leaf also can be used to flavor broiled vegetables, stuffing, stocks and—as in this recipe—marinades. One word of advice: Always remove the leaf before serving.

**Wine Notes**

This dish goes well with a fuller bodied wine. Try a Napa Valley Cabernet Sauvignon or a fuller bodied Merlot from the same area.

## Portabella Mushrooms

This large dark brown mushroom can easily measure six inches across. It gets its dense, meaty texture and flavor from exposed gills that reduce its moisture content and enrich its flavor. Portabella mushrooms are a perfect substitute for hamburgers at a barbecue—they're delicious marinated in balsamic vinegar and oil and then grilled. Serve them with mozzarella cheese and roasted peppers, either in sandwiches or sliced over salad greens.

# Duck and Portabella Mushrooms

1. Make the marinade and marinate the duck breast for 4 hours.

2. Remove the breast and pat it dry.

3. Preheat the oven to 400°F.

4. In an uncovered baking pan, roast the duck breast for 20 minutes in the oven.

5. Heat the oil in a pot. When it is hot (approximately 450°F) drop half of the leeks in. Fry them until they are crisp and golden brown. Remove them and repeat this with the other half of the leeks.

6. Remove the duck and let it cool. Pull off the skin and slice the breast into $1/4$-inch slices. Set aside.

7. In a little duck fat, sauté the shallots.

8. Add the veal stock and reduce it down to a sauce-like consistency.

9. Add the honey, crushed blackberries and cracked pepper. Cook for 10 minutes. Strain.

10. Season the portabellas with salt and pepper and place them on a hot grill until they are fully cooked.

11. Sauté the mushroom stems and duck slices. Add the sauce and whole blackberries. Cook for 2 minutes.

12. Place the portabella mushrooms on 4 plates. Spoon the mixture over them. Top with the fried leeks.

**Serves 4**

# Banfi Duck

*3 pounds duck legs and thighs*
*salt and freshly ground pepper, for seasoning*
*fresh thyme, for seasoning*
*¹/₄ pound pancetta ham or bacon*
*¹/₄ cup olive oil*
*¹/₂ cup red onions, sliced*
*¹/₂ tablespoon garlic*
*6 cups spinach, stems removed, cleaned and dried*
*1 cup radicchio, chopped*
*4 cups penne pasta, cooked al dente*
*¹/₂ cup Parmesan cheese*

1. Season the duck legs and thighs with salt, pepper and thyme. In a thick-bottom pan, sear and brown the duck.

2. Place it in a baking dish and put it in a preheated 400°F oven. Roast, uncovered, for 1¹/₂ hours, until the meat is fork tender. Remove and cool.

3. Place the duck in a container and pour the fat over the meat. Refrigerate.

4. When ready to prepare this dish, remove the duck and pick the meat off of the bone. Cut it into nice bite-size pieces.

5. In a thick-bottom pan, cook the pancetta until it is brown but not crisp. Set aside.

6. Over medium heat add the olive oil, onions, garlic and duck. Sauté them until the onions are translucent. Add the spinach and radicchio.

7. Heat the cooked pasta in hot water. Strain the pasta, shaking away the excess water.

8. Add the pasta and ham to the vegetable mixture. Toss everything together to make sure it is well coated. Season with salt and pepper.

9. Spoon the mixture into 6 bowls and sprinkle it with cheese.

**Serves 6**

## Duck Confit

This recipe is best done in 2 steps. You can cook the duck thighs in advance, and they easily keep a week in the refrigerator when covered by their own fat. This style of preparation, described in steps 1 through 3, is called a confit. (To save time, you can substitute duck breasts in place of the thighs in the recipe.)

## Pancetta Ham

Pancetta ham is basically Italian bacon coming from the belly of the pork. It is cured in brine for 3 weeks and then air cured for 4 months. Usually it comes rolled, tied and flavored with salt and herbs, such as cloves, nutmeg, peppercorns and garlic. It is easier to slice when it is half frozen.

## Wine Notes

 This dish is perfect with a Super Tuscan Italian, which is a blend of Cabernet Sauvignon and Sangiovese. Try a bold Brunello di Montalcino from the same area.

*Meats*

Veal Porter - 199
Mr. Taylor's Veal Chops - 200
Veal Betsy - 201
Veal Saltimbocca - 202
*Creamy Polenta - 203*
Osso Buco - 204
*Risotto - 205 • Gremolata - 205*
Kansas Steak with Horseradish Butter - 206
*Beet Horseradish - 206*
New York Strip Steak with Avocado Butter and Black Bean Salsa - 207
Filet Mignon - 208
*Smoked Bacon-Sweet Potato Compote - 209 • Spiced Pecans - 210*
Roasted Fillet of Beef with Blue Cheese-Horseradish Cream - 211
Twin Filet Mignons - 212
Washington Inn Tournedos - 213
Lamb Chops with Potato Pancakes and Pineapple Salsa - 214
Butterflied Leg of Lamb - 215
Cajun Roasted Pork - 216
Pork Medallions with Apple-Port Wine Sauce - 217
Pork Medallions with Cranberry-Orange Sauce - 218
*Cranberry-Orange Sauce - 219 • Mustard Spätzle - 220*

**A Family Favorite**

This is a favorite veal dish among our guests. It is named after our bartender, Bill Porter, known by many of our guests as "Coach."

# Veal Porter

*4 top round veal cutlets, 4 ounces each, pounded*
*salt and freshly ground pepper, for seasoning*
*¹/₂ cup flour*
*6 tablespoons butter*
*2 tablespoons shallots, diced*
*¹/₂ cup artichoke bottoms, sliced*
*1 cup mushrooms, sliced*
*¹/₂ pound jumbo lump crab meat*
*4 slices Monterey Jack cheese*
*¹/₂ cup Madeira wine*
*¹/₂ cup veal stock (see page 9)*

1. Season the veal lightly with salt and pepper. Dredge the cutlets in the flour.

2. Put the butter in the sauté pan and place it over medium heat. Add the veal and brown it on each side. Reserve the veal in a serving pan and keep it in a warm oven.

3. Add the shallots, artichokes and mushrooms. Sauté them for 3 minutes, then deglaze the pan with veal stock and wine.

4. Reduce for 4 minutes, until the sauce thickens slightly.

5. Spread the mushrooms, artichokes and sauce evenly over the cutlets.

6. Place the crab meat on top of this mixture. Top it with Monterey Jack cheese.

7. Place the cutlet pan in a 350°F oven just long enough to melt the cheese.

8. Using a spatula, place the cutlets onto 4 plates. Drizzle the juices over the cheese.

**Serves 4**

**Wine Notes**

 This dish is rich and delicious. A refreshing, crisp, lemony Chardonnay or a Sauvignon Blanc from California cuts through the richness of the sauce.

# Mr. Taylor's Veal Chops

*4 center-cut rib veal chops, 13 ounces each*
*salt and freshly ground pepper, for seasoning*
*3 tablespoons olive oil*
*2 cups red onions, sliced*
*8 cups spinach, cleaned and dried*
*Au Poivre Sauce (below)*
*8 ounces Stilton cheese, crumbled*
*Mashed Potatoes (see page 289)*

1.  Season the chops with salt and pepper. Place them on a hot grill. Cook them for 5 to 7 minutes on each side.

2.  In a sauté pan with the olive oil, sauté the onions and spinach. Season them with salt and pepper. Reserve and keep hot.

3.  Place the chops on 4 plates. Pour the Au Poivre Sauce on top, then sprinkle it with cheese. Serve with mashed potatoes.

## Au Poivre Sauce

*2 tablespoons butter*
*1 tablespoon shallots*
*¼ cup brandy*
*2 cups veal stock, reduced by half (see page 9)*
*1 tablespoon cracked black pepper*
*salt, for seasoning*

1.  Sauté the shallots in the butter. Carefully add the brandy, then cook off the alcohol for 2 minutes.

2.  Add the stock and cracked peppercorns.

3.  Reduce the mixture by half, or until it starts to thicken and has the consistency of a sauce.

4.  Season with salt.

**Serves 4**

**Special Friends**

This dish is named for our special friend Walt, who is part of everyone's family at the Washington Inn.

**Wine Notes**

 Match this dish with a medium-bodied Bordeaux or a Sonoma Valley Cabernet.

**A True Original**

This preparation is basically the same as the Chicken Sarah. This dish was originally on our menu when we opened up in 1978. It is named after my sister, Betsy.

# Veal Betsy

*4 top round veal cutlets, 5 ounces each, cut into halves*
*salt and freshly ground pepper, for seasoning*
*¹/₂ cup flour*
*2 ounces clarified butter (see page 181)*
*¹/₂ cup chicken stock (see page 5)*
*¹/₂ cup beef stock (see page 8)*
*¹/₂ cup dry sherry*
*8 slices of mozzarella cheese*

1. Season the veal with salt and pepper, then coat it with flour.

2. In a hot pan with the clarified butter, sauté and brown the cutlets on both sides. Reserve the veal in a warm place.

3. Sprinkle 1 tablespoon of flour into the pan, and stir until a paste forms.

4. Add the stock and sherry and cook for 5 to 10 minutes, until the sauce has thickened slightly. Season the sauce with salt and pepper.

5. Strain the sauce, then return it to the pan and keep it warm on the stove.

6. Place the mozzarella cheese on top of the veal, and place it in a 325°F oven until the cheese melts.

7. Place the veal on 4 plates and pour the sauce over each.

**Serves 4**

**Wine Notes**

 A lighter style Pinot Noir from Oregon or California works nicely. For something different, find a Mourvèdre from California or Provence.

# Veal Saltimbocca

*8 veal cutlet medallions, 2 ounces each*
*salt and pepper, for seasoning*
*¹/₂ cup flour*
*¹/₄ cup clarified butter (see page 181)*
*8 slices prosciutto ham*
*8 slices Gruyère cheese*
*¹/₂ cup veal stock (see page 9)*
*juice of 1 lemon*
*¹/₂ cup dry white wine*
*4 tablespoons fresh sage, chopped*
*1 tablespoon garlic*
*4 tablespoons olive oil*
*2 cups arugula, soaked, rinsed and dried*
*1 cup roasted peppers, peeled, seeded and sliced (see page 70)*
*Creamy Polenta (opposite page)*

1. Lightly season the veal. Dredge the cutlets in the flour.

2. Put the butter in the sauté pan, over medium heat. Place the veal in the pan and brown it on each side. Add the prosciutto ham, tossing it in the pan. Remove the veal to a baking sheet. Top it with the ham and cheese, and keep it warm.

3. In the sauté pan, add the stock, lemon, white wine and sage. Simmer this mixture for 4 minutes, until you have a nice sauce. Season it with salt and pepper.

4. Place the veal in a 300°F oven to melt the cheese.

5. In a separate pan, sauté the garlic in the oil. Add the arugula and peppers, and toss them until they are hot. Season with salt and pepper.

6. Spoon a large helping of polenta on each of 4 plates. Place the veal on top of the polenta, then pour the sauce over the top. Spoon the peppers and arugula onto the side of each plate.

**Serves 4**

## Inspired Combinations

Creamy polenta, roasted peppers and arugula are inspired accompaniments for this classic mouthwatering Roman specialty, which translates literally to "jump in mouth."

## Wine Notes

 An Italian Orvieto or a Soave has enough acidity to cut through the richness of the sage and prosciutto.

## The Color of Cornmeal

Polenta is the name given to the Italian way of preparing cornmeal—as a thick mush. The only difference between white and yellow cornmeal is the color of the corn from which the meal is ground.

# Creamy Polenta

*2 quarts water*
*3 cups polenta*
*4 tablespoons mascarpone cheese*
*1 cup heavy cream*
*salt and fresh pepper, for seasoning*

1.  Bring the water to a boil in a large thick-bottom pot.

2.  Over medium heat, add the polenta in a slow, steady stream. Use a pitcher to help you pour the polenta in nice and steady.

3.  Stir it with a whisk until it is completely blended.

4.  Turn the heat down to low and simmer for 45 minutes. Use a wooden spoon to stir occassionally.

5.  The polenta is done when it slides easily off the sides of the pot.

6.  Add the mascarpone cheese and heavy cream. Incorporate well.

7.  Season with salt and pepper.

8.  Serve with the veal.

**Serves 6 to 8**

# Osso Buco

8 pieces of veal shank, cut 2-inches thick
2 cups flour
1/4 cup butter
1 cup white wine
1 cup onions, diced
3/4 cup carrots, diced
2/3 cup celery, diced
1 teaspoon garlic
2 bay leaves
1 sprig of thyme
2 tablespoons orange zest
1 1/2 cups veal stock (see page 9)
1 1/2 cups tomato, chopped
1/4 cup olives, sliced, for garnish
Risotto (opposite page)
Gremolata (opposite page)

1. Tie each veal shank with string. If you prefer, ask your butcher to do this. Season with salt and pepper. Dredge in the flour.

2. Melt the butter in a heavy, shallow pot. Add the shanks and brown them on all sides (on their side and also standing upright). When they are nice and brown, stand them upright. Drain the fat.

3. Add the wine and simmer for 10 minutes.

4. In a separate pan, sauté the onions, carrots, celery, garlic, bay leaves, thyme and orange zest for 5 minutes.

5. Add the stock, tomatoes and sautéed vegetables to the veal. Season with salt and pepper.

6. Cover the pan and lower the heat. Simmer for 1 1/2 to 2 hours.

7. Put the risotto on a platter and place the veal on top. Spoon the vegetables with their sauce over the top.

8. Sprinkle with the gremolata and olives.

**Serves 4**

## Braising Basics

Braising is a technique for moist cooking, used for tougher cuts of meat. It involves a slow, gentle cooking in a stock or broth, which breaks down connective tissue. The juices in the meat combine with the broth that it is cooked in and concentrate its flavors.

The key to braising is browning the meat first. Browning gives the meat a sweet richness that simple poaching does not provide. After browning, the stock should be added to the skillet and brought to just barely simmering. This can be done in the oven at 350°F or on the stove top. Be sure to completely cover the pan with aluminum foil.

## Wine Notes

Big red wines from the Piedmont area of Italy work well. Try a Barolo or a Barbaresco. For a great treat, drink a reserva from these areas.

## Risotto

Risotto, or arborio rice, grows in the Po River Valley in Northern Italy. This rice has plump, long grains, and contains more starch than American rice. It holds up well during long, slow cooking. This Italian rice better absorbs the flavors in stock and wine. As the rice cooks, it releases its starch, which creates a creamy texture.

# Risotto

6 tablespoons butter
1 medium onion, peeled and diced finely
2 teaspoons garlic, chopped
2 cups arborio rice
$^{1}/_{2}$ cup white wine
2 cups water
4 cups chicken stock (see page 5)
$^{1}/_{2}$ cup cream
$^{1}/_{2}$ cup Parmesan cheese
salt and fresh pepper, for seasoning

1. Melt the butter in a heavy saucepan.

2. Over medium heat, add the onion and garlic. Sauté them until they are translucent. Do not brown the garlic.

3. Add the rice and sauté it for 1 or 2 minutes, until it looks opaque and starts to make a clicking sound.

4. Slowly add the white wine, stirring constantly until the rice absorbs all of the liquid.

5. Continue to slowly add the water and stock, stirring constantly and adding only enough liquid for the rice to absorb.

6. Continue this process until the rice is cooked al dente.

7. Add the cream and cheese into the rice. Mix well.

# Gremolata

1 tablespoon lemon peel, grated
1 tablespoon garlic, chopped
4 tablespoons parsley, chopped

1. Blend all of the ingredients together. Serve it fresh.

**Serves 4**

# Kansas Steak
## with Horseradish Butter

*6 center-cut strip steaks, 14 to 16 ounces each*
*salt and freshly ground pepper, for seasoning*
*Horseradish Butter (see page 16)*

*Beet Horseradish*
*¹/₂ cup horseradish*
*1 cup beets, peeled*
*¹/₈ cup vinegar*

1. Place all of the Beet Horseradish ingredients in a food processor. Purée them until smooth.

2. Place the Beet Horseradish in a small container and refrigerate until ready for use.

3. Season the steaks with salt and pepper.

4. Place each steak on a hot grill. Cook to your liking.

5. When finished cooking, place the steaks on 6 plates. Put a generous slice of Horseradish Butter and a dollop of Beet Horseradish on top of each steak.

**Serves 6**

**Great Grilling**

This recipe by chef Doug Gomersall was inspired by his grandfather, Joe Jurczak, who grew fresh beets and horseradish in his garden.

For better grilling, light a charcoal fire at least 30 minutes before you plan to cook. Give the coals a chance to burn and become covered with a gray ash. When this happens, the heat from the grill is radiant, so it cooks foods gradually without burning. To give your grilled meats subtle flavor, soak fresh herbs like rosemary, thyme or marjoram in water and sprinkle them over the hot coals before cooking.

**Wine Notes**

 This dish has full, spicy flavors. Try a full-bodied Hermitage or Côte Rôtie from France or a full-bodied Zinfandel from California.

## Salsas

A fresh complement to grilled foods, salsas can be made with a variety of fruits and vegetables. Some standard salsa ingredients are tomatoes, tomatillos, cilantro, cumin, peppers and onions.

# New York Strip Steak
## *with Avocado Butter and Black Bean Salsa*

*4 center-cut New York strip steaks, 8 ounces each*
*salt and pepper, to taste*
*2 tablespoons olive oil*
*4 slices Avocado Butter (see page 161)*

### Salsa
*2 teaspoons olive oil*
*1 red onion, diced small*
*3 garlic cloves, chopped*
*2 jalapeño peppers, diced*
*1¹/₂ cups black beans, cooked*
*¹/₄ cup rice wine vinegar*
*1 red pepper, roasted, peeled and diced (see page 70)*
*1 yellow pepper, roasted, peeled and diced*
*1 tomato, diced*
*1 teaspoon fresh basil, chopped*
*¹/₂ tablespoon cilantro*
*1 teaspoon ground cumin*
*salt, to taste*

1. In a large sauté pan, sauté the onion, garlic and jalapeños in 2 teaspoons of olive oil.

2. In a large mixing bowl, combine the beans, vinegar, peppers tomato, basil, cilantro and cumin. Add the sautéed onion mixture. Toss together well. Let sit for at least 1 hour.

3. Rub the steaks with 2 tablespoons olive oil. Season with salt and pepper.

4. In a hot sauté pan, sear the steaks until well browned on each side.

5. Place them in a preheated 350°F oven for 5 to 6 minutes, or until they are medium rare.

6. Place 1 steak on each of 4 plates. Top them with the Avocado Butter.

7. Spoon some salsa on the sides of each steak.

**Serves 4**

## Wine Notes

A full-bodied Zinfandel from California has the backbone to stand up to the pronounced flavors of the Black Bean Salsa. Try a Châteauneuf-du-Pape as a French alternative.

# Filet Mignon
## with Smoked Bacon-Sweet Potato Compote

*4 filet mignon steaks, 7 ounces each*
*2 tablespoons vegetable oil*
*Smoked Bacon-Sweet Potato Compote (opposite page)*
*Spiced Pecans (see page 210)*

### Filet Mignon Marinade
*1 cup molasses*
*2 tablespoons balsamic vinegar*
*2 tablespoons freshly cracked black pepper*
*2 cloves*
*1 tablespoon garlic, chopped*
*1 large shallot, chopped*
*2 teaspoons ginger, grated*
*1 teaspoon fresh thyme, chopped*
*crushed red pepper flakes, to taste*

1.  Combine the marinade ingredients in a small bowl.

2.  Reserve ¹/₂ cup of the marinade (¹/₄ cup for the compote and ¹/₄ cup for deglazing). Pour the remaining marinade over the beef.

3.  Cover the beef and refrigerate. Allow the meat to marinate for at least 6 hours.

4.  Heat the oil in a large cast iron skillet, over medium heat.

5.  Add the steaks and brown them for 3 minutes on each side. Cook to your preference of doneness.

6.  Before removing the meat, add the marinade reserved for deglazing. This creates a sauce. Let the mixture coat the filets nicely.

7.  Remove the meat from the skillet immediately.

8.  Place the potato compote on each of 4 plates. Arrange the fillets on the plates and spoon the sauce on top. Sprinkle with pecans.

**Serves 4**

---

### Deglazing

Deglazing is the practice of loosening the browned bits and caramelized drippings left in a skillet or roasting pan by adding liquid, such as wine, stock or water, then stirring and heating. The flavorful glaze produced by deglazing can then be used as a base for sauce and gravies. Deglazing the pan of your Thanksgiving turkey yields delicious flavor for homemade gravies.

### Wine Notes

 This dish needs a rich, full wine like a Cabernet Sauvignon from Napa Valley or Washington State. Bordeaux also works well with this dish.

### Rendering Fat

In this recipe, the instructions to render the fat simply mean to melt it, so that it provides a non-stick surface for cooking the potatoes and shiitake mushrooms.

# Smoked Bacon-Sweet Potato Compote

*$^1/_4$ pound bacon, diced*
*3 cups sweet potatoes, peeled and diced*
*1 cup shiitake mushrooms, stems removed and sliced*
*$^1/_4$ cup pearl onions, blanched*
*$^1/_4$ cup of Filet Mignon Marinade (opposite page)*

1. In a thick-bottom pan, over medium heat, cook the bacon and render the fat.

2. Add the sweet potatoes and shiitake mushrooms. Cook for 20 to 30 minutes, until the sweet potato is tender.

3. Add the pearl onions and cook for 5 minutes.

4. Add the marinade and cook for 5 more minutes.

5. Spoon this compote onto the plates with the filet mignon.

**Makes 3 cups**

# Spiced Pecans

*1 pound pecans, shelled*
*1/2 cup molasses*
*1/4 cup sugar*
*1/2 cup water*
*2 tablespoons fresh rosemary*
*1/2 teaspoon cayenne pepper*
*2 teaspoons salt*

1. In a pot of boiling water, cook the pecans for 15 minutes.

2. Drain the pecans. Cool.

3. In a pot of boiling water, cook the pecans for 15 minutes again. Drain the pecans, and let them cool again.

4. Preheat the oven to 250°F.

5. Dry the pecans on a sheet pan in the oven for 30 minutes.

6. Make a simple syrup by dissolving the molasses and sugar in 1/4 cup of water.

7. Add all of the remaining ingredients to complete the syrup.

8. Toss the pecans in a bowl with the syrup until they are lightly coated.

9. Place them on a sheet pan to dry.

**Makes 2 cups**

## Perfect Pecans

The pecan is a North American variety of the hickory tree, which got its name in English from the Algonquian *pakan*. The pecan tree originally flourished in Oklahoma and from there moved to Texas, where it is now the state tree.

Pecans are sold either shelled or unshelled. They have a high fat content and can easily go rancid so eat them right away.

# Roasted Fillet of Beef
## with Blue Cheese-Horseradish Cream

*1 whole tenderloin, unpeeled, 5 to 6 pounds*
*1 cup Dijon mustard*
*salt and pepper, for seasoning*

1. Trim the silverskin and excess fat off of the tenderloin. For the easiest solution, ask your butcher to make the fillet oven-ready.

2. Season with salt and pepper and rub the Dijon mustard all over the tenderloin.

3. Preheat the oven to 500°F.

4. Place the tenderloin on a baking pan and put it in the oven.

5. Roast for 35 to 40 minutes, until medium to medium rare.

6. Let it set before serving.

7. Slice the fillet into 1-inch slices, and shingle them on a cutting board or serving platter. Place the Blue Cheese-Horseradish Cream in a small bowl and serve on the side, for dipping.

## Blue Cheese-Horseradish Cream

*$^1/_2$ cup mayonnaise*
*$^1/_2$ cup sour cream*
*$1^1/_2$ tablespoons horseradish*
*$1^1/_4$ cup blue cheese, crumbled*
*juice of half a lemon*
*1 teaspoon Worcestershire sauce*
*salt and fresh pepper, to taste*

1. Mix all of the ingredients together.

2. Let the flavors blend for approximately 2 hours.

**Makes 1 small bowl**

# Twin Filet Mignons
## Au Poivre

*8 filet mignon medallions, 4 ounces each*
*salt and pepper, for seasoning*
*2 tablespoons butter*
*1 cup veal stock, reduced (see page 9)*
*¼ cup brandy*
*1 tablespoon cracked black pepper*
*½ cup heavy cream (optional)*

1. Season the filets with the salt and pepper. In a sauté pan over medium heat, in 1 tablespoon of butter, sear the filets for approximately 3 minutes on each side, until they are nice and brown.

2. Reserve the meat in a pan in a 250°F oven. Raise the oven temperature if you like your meat well done.

3. In a sauté pan, add the stock, brandy and cracked peppercorns. Reduce the mixture by half, until it starts to thicken and has the consistency of sauce. (Add the cream and reduce it further, if you would like a silkier sauce.)

4. Reduce the flame and finish the sauce by adding 1 tablespoon butter.

5. Season with additional salt, if necessary.

6. Remove the steaks and place 2 on each of 4 plates. Pour the sauce over the top and serve.

**Serves 4**

---

**A Versatile Classic**

The cream adds a new flair to a classic that the restaurant has offered for years. You can use other variations if you wish.

We frequently add mushrooms or top the filets with goat cheese or Brie, and then drizzle the sauce on top. If you like a less intense yet richer sauce, add a little heavy cream to "lighten it up."

**Wine Notes**

Try a dry French Burgundy like Pommard or Santenay. A Châteauneuf-du-Pape or a California Rhône style are fuller wines that make a good choice.

## Tournedos

Tournedos is a French word that refers to small slices of filleted beef that are round and thick. They are typically served with a sauce and garnished.

So many of our special customers remember this dish and frequently ask us to prepare it for them. One must start with a reduced beef stock in order to get the correct flavors. If using canned stock, be careful about the salt levels when you reduce.

### Wine Notes

 Try a Cabernet Franc from the Loire Valley, like Chenas, or a Bordeaux from the Graves area.

# *Washington Inn Tournedos*

*8 filet mignon medallions, 4 ounces each*
*salt and freshly ground pepper, for seasoning*
*3 tablespoons clarified butter (see page 181)*
*3 tablespoons shallots, chopped*
*2 cups mushrooms, sliced*
*1 cup beef stock, reduced by half (see page 8)*
*4 tablespoons Dijon mustard*
*3 ounces brandy*
*1 tablespoon butter*

1. Put the clarified butter in a sauté pan over medium heat. Season the filets with salt and pepper and place them in the pan. Sear the filets for approximately 3 minutes on each side, until they are nice and brown.

2. Reserve the meat in a pan in a 250°F oven. Raise the oven temperature if you like your meat well done.

3. In a sauté pan, add the shallots and mushrooms. Sauté for 2 minutes, until soft.

4. Add the stock, mustard and brandy. Reduce this mixture until it has the consistency of a sauce.

5. Reduce the flame and finish the sauce with 1 tablespoon butter.

6. Season the sauce with salt and pepper.

7. Remove the steaks and placc 2 on cach of 4 plates. Pour the sauce over the steaks and serve.

**Serves 4**

# Lamb Chops
## with Potato Pancakes and Pineapple Salsa

*8 center-cut loin lamb chops, 5 ounces each*
*salt and freshly ground pepper, for seasoning*
*Potato Pancakes (see page 229)*

### Pineapple Salsa
*1 ripe pineapple, peeled, cored and diced small*
*1 red pepper, diced*
*1/2 green pepper, diced*
*1 small red onion, diced*
*1/2 bunch of scallions, chopped*
*1/4 bunch of cilantro, chopped*
*1/2 teaspoon cumin*
*1/4 cup white wine*
*juice of 3 limes*
*salt and freshly ground pepper, for seasoning*

1.  Combine all of the Pineapple Salsa ingredients and let them sit for 30 minutes.

2.  Season the chops well with salt and pepper.

3.  Cook on a hot grill, or under the broiler, for 5 to 8 minutes.

4.  Ladle Pineapple Salsa on each plate.

5.  Place a potato pancake on top of the salsa.

6.  Place 2 lamb chops on top of each pancake.

7.  Spoon Pineapple Salsa over the lamb chops. Serve.

**Serves 4**

## Types of Lamb Meat

Chef Wayne Beck came up with this salsa recipe. It works wonderfully with the lamb.

For the most tender lamb, look for pinkish-red meat—a dark color means the meat is from an older lamb. The youngest lamb is baby, followed by spring, then yearling. Lamb cuts from the loin and rib are the most tender. Lamb chops are best served rare, with the meat still showing some pink. Loosely wrapped, lamb cuts can stay refrigerated for up to 3 days.

## Wine Notes

Fuller wines with a higher acidity work nicely with this dish. Try a mountain Cabernet Sauvignon from Sonoma or Napa.

# Butterflied Leg of Lamb

*1 leg of lamb, butterflied, 6 to 7 pounds*
*1 cup red wine*
*$^1/_2$ cup olive oil*
*2 tablespoons parsley, chopped*
*2 tablespoons chives, chopped*
*1 cup onion, chopped*
*3 tablespoons garlic, chopped*
*1 teaspoon salt*
*1 teaspoon Worcestershire sauce*
*$^1/_4$ teaspoon freshly ground pepper*
*$^1/_8$ teaspoon marjoram*
*$^1/_8$ teaspoon thyme*
*$^1/_8$ teaspoon rosemary*

1. Place the lamb, fat side down, in a shallow glass container.

2. Combine all of the other ingredients.

3. Pour them over the lamb. Refrigerate overnight or for at least 4 hours.

4. Grill the lamb slowly on an open grill. Baste it with the marinade.

5. Allow it to cook for approximately 10 to 15 minutes on each side.

6. Let the meat rest for 10 minutes before cutting it.

7. Cut the meat in thin slices on the bias.

**Serves 8**

**Wine Notes**

 A French Provence red, like a Bandol, or a red wine from the southern Rhône area stands up to this flavored marinade.

# Cajun Roasted Pork

1 boneless pork loin (approximately 5 pounds)
2 ounces butter, melted

### Seasoning
2 teaspoons black pepper
1¹/₂ teaspoons salt
1 teaspoon white pepper
¹/₂ teaspoon oregano
1 teaspoon paprika
1 teaspoon thyme
¹/₂ teaspoon dry mustard
1 teaspoon granulated garlic

1. Mix the seasonings.

2. Preheat the oven to 300°F.

3. Rub the pork roast well with the seasoning mix. Baste it with the melted butter.

4. Roast it in the oven for 2 hours.

5. Raise the oven temperature to 425°F for an additional 20 minutes, to brown the top.

**Serves 10**

## Cajun Inspiration

We prepare this dish for many parties. It was inspired by Paul Prudhomme.

## Wine Notes

Try a spicy Petite Sirah from Califonia or a Châteauneuf-du-Pape from the Rhône Valley of France.

# *Pork Medallions*
## *with Apple-Port Wine Sauce*

*8 pork loin medallions, 4 ounces each*
*salt and pepper, for seasoning*
*1/2 cup flour*
*3 tablespoons butter*
*1 1/2 cups Port wine*
*2 cups veal stock, reduced by half (see page 9)*
*1 small sprig rosemary*
*2 red onions, cut julienne style*
*12 Granny Smith apples, peeled, cored and diced*
*1/2 cup raisins*
*1 teaspoon caraway seed*
*2 tablespoons cider vinegar*
*pinch of cloves, ground*

1.  With a mallet, flatten the medallions to a thickness of 1/2 inch.

2.  Season the medallions with salt and pepper.  Dredge them in the flour.

3.  In 2 tablespoons of butter, sauté the medallions for 2 to 3 minutes on each side, until they are nicely browned.

4.  Reserve the medallions in a pan, and keep them warm.

5.  Add the Port wine, veal stock and sprig of rosemary to the sauté pan and reduce by two-thirds.

6.  In a separate pan, with the remaining tablespoon of butter, sauté the onions and apples for 3 minutes.

7.  Add the raisins, caraway, vinegar and clove. Cook them until the apples are tender.

8.  Add the apple mixture to the Port sauce and cook for 1 minute.

9.  Place 2 medallions on each of 4 plates. Spoon the sauce over the top.

**Serves 4**

# Pork Medallions
## with Cranberry-Orange Sauce

*8 pork loin medallions, 4 ounces each*
*salt and pepper, for seasoning*
*¹/₂ cup flour*
*6 tablespoons butter*
*Mustard Spätzle (see page 220)*
*Cranberry-Orange Sauce (opposite page)*

1.  With a mallet, flatten the medallions to a thickness of ¹/₂ inch.

2.  Season the medallions with salt and pepper.  Dredge them in the flour.

3.  In 4 tablespoons of the butter, sauté the medallions until they are nicely browned on each side.

4.  Reserve the medallions in a pan and keep them warm.

5.  In a separate pan, with the remaining butter, sauté the spätzle until it is brown.

6.  Divide the spätzle among 4 plates.

7.  Place 2 medallions over the spätzle on each plate. Spoon the Cranberry-Orange Sauce over the medallions.

**Serves 4**

---

**Thin, Even Meat**

Pounding the medallions gives each one an even thickness. Start at the center of each and work outward to the edges. Each medallion becomes about double its original size after it's pounded.

**Wine Notes**

 A full-bodied Napa Merlot pairs nicely with this dish. Also try a fuller Shiraz from Australia.

# Cranberry-Orange Sauce

*¹/₄ cup plus 2 ounces Port wine*
*2 ounces red wine*
*1 ounce sherry vinegar*
*1 ounce honey*
*3 ounces orange juice*
*2 tablespoons shallots, minced*
*¹/₄ teaspoon cracked pepper*
*1 bunch thyme stems*
*1 cup pork or veal jus*
*¹/₄ cup dried cranberries*
*1 orange, peeled and divided*
*zest of 1 orange, cut julienne style*
*4 teaspoons fresh thyme, chopped*

1. In a medium-weight saucepan, combine 2 ounces of Port with the red wine, vinegar, honey, orange juice, shallots, pepper and thyme stems.

2. Reduce them until the sauce is almost dry, add the jus and ¹/₄ cup Port and simmer 10 minutes. Strain.

3. Bring the Port mixture to a simmer, and add the cranberries.

4. Add the orange slices, zest and chopped thyme to the sauce. Mix and serve.

**Makes 1¹/₂ cups**

**Sweet and Sour**

The sherry vinegar used in this recipe is a perfect match for the cranberry and orange flavors. Like them, it mixes the tart and sweet sensations, which wake up and refresh the palate.

# Mustard Spätzle

*2 eggs*
*¹/₂ cup milk*
*1 tablespoon Dijon mustard*
*1 tablespoon creole mustard (if not available, use Dijon)*
*¹/₂ teaspoon mustard seed, crushed*
*salt and pepper, to taste*
*³/₄ cup flour*
*1 tablespoon butter*

1. Combine the eggs, milk and seasonings. Mix them well in a large bowl.

2. Work in the flour by hand.

3. Let the dough rest for 10 minutes.

4. Using a spätzle machine (or a colander or some other shaping technique), drop the dough into a large pot of boiling, salted water. Simmer it until it is done (approximately 5 minutes).

5. Remove the spätzle with a spider (a type of strainer), shock it in cold water, and drain it well.

6. Sauté the spätzle in the butter. Place it in a large bowl and serve.

**Serves 10**

### Making Spätzle

Instead of a spätzle machine, we use a potato ricer to make fine spätzle noodles. For larger noodles, we use a colander. We simply put the dough into the colander and push it through the holes into the boiling water.

Of course, most kitchen shops carry several types of spätzle makers. A spider is a specific type of strainer, which is also available in kitchen shops.

*Accompaniments*

## Basmati

At the restaurant we serve a wild rice blend that includes wheat berries, wild rice, brown rice and white rice. At home, you can use regular rice, since it's the seasonings that really make this delicious. We follow a classic pilaf technique when cooking this.

Among the many types of rice we use, basmati rice is a quite popular variety. It has been grown in India and Pakistan for nearly 9,000 years. When cooked, basmati doubles in length and takes on a popcorn type of aroma. It cooks up fluffy and delicious and is best when cooked pilaf style.

# Washington Inn Rice

*3 tablespoons butter, melted*
*1 cup onions, diced*
*1 bay leaf*
*2 tablespoons dried thyme*
*2 cups wild rice blend*
*5 cups vegetable stock (see page 6) or chicken stock (see page 5)*
*salt and pepper, for seasoning*

1. Sauté the onion in 1 tablespoon of butter. Add the bay leaf and thyme. Cook for 5 minutes.

2. In a baking dish, toss the rice with 2 tablespoons of butter.

3. Preheat the oven to 350°F.

4. In a saucepan, bring the stock to a boil and add the onion mixture.

5. Season it well with the salt and pepper.

6. Pour the hot stock over the rice in the baking dish.

7. Spread out the rice evenly.

8. Cover the dish with a lid or aluminum foil and bake in the oven for 45 minutes.

9. Remove the pan and its covering. Fluff the rice with a large spoon and serve.

**Serves 6 to 8**

# Garlic Custard

*1 cup heavy cream*
*1 clove garlic, finely chopped*
*2 eggs*
*1 egg yolk*
*5-8 roasted garlic bulbs (makes ¹/₂ cup purée) (see page 4)*
*salt and pepper, for seasoning*

1. Preheat the oven to 300°F.

2. Mix all of the ingredients together.

3. Place them in a square baking dish.

4. Place the dish in a water bath and put both dishes into the oven.

5. Bake for 75 minutes, until a toothpick comes out clean.

6. Cool. Cut into squares to serve.

**Serves 4**

## What's a Water Bath?

When baking custard, use a water bath, or bain marie. The water moderates the heat in the oven when baking. You need a deep pan that holds the baking dish or ramekins comfortably.

## Miniature Dumplings

Spätzle are a very simple form of egg dumplings. They probably originated in Germany, but are also popular in Switzerland and Austria. Made from a basic batter and pushed through a sieve into boiling water, they are done cooking when they rise to the surface. They are always drained, then sautéed in butter.

# Spätzle

*2 eggs*
*3 ounces milk*
*pinch of garlic, to taste*
*salt and pepper, to taste*
*3/4 cup flour*
*1 tablespoon butter*

1. Combine the eggs, milk and seasonings. Mix them well in a large bowl.

2. Work in the flour by hand.

3. Let the dough rest for 10 minutes.

4. Using a spätzle machine (or other shaping technique), drop the dough into a large pot of boiling, salted water. Simmer it until it is done, approximately 5 minutes.

5. Remove the spätzle with a sieve, shock it with cold water, and drain it well.

6. Sauté the spätzle in butter for approximately 4 minutes. Serve.

**Serves 10**

# Roesti Potatoes

*3 pounds large baking potatoes, peeled*
*4 tablespoons clarified butter (see page 181)*
*salt and pepper, for seasoning*

1. Boil the potatoes for 15 minutes, until they are almost cooked.

2. Let them cool, then dry and cover them.

3. Grate the potatoes with a large-size cheese grater.

4. Put the butter in an 8-inch non-stick sauté pan.

5. Fill the pan with the potatoes. (Do not pack down the potatoes.) Season with the salt and pepper.

6. Sauté 1 side of the potatoes for 6 minutes on medium heat, until they are a nice golden brown. (As the potatoes start to brown, keep turning the pan so that they do not stick.)

7. Using a spatula, turn the cake over. Cook for 5 minutes on the other side. (Remember to turn the pan regularly.)

8. Serve the cake on a platter. Cut it like a cake.

**Serves 4**

---

**Really Roesti**

These Swiss potato cakes are delicious, and a great accompaniment to steaks and chicken. Be creative. Add cheese, ham, bacon—just about anything.

Also called rosti, these classic Swiss potato pancakes get a delicious crispy golden crust when sautéed in butter. Like hash browns, roesti potatoes can be made with raw or boiled potatoes. The boiled method is used here, as it is easier to grate the potatoes and quicker to cook them. Try them garnished with snipped fresh chives and a dollop of sour cream.

# Potatoes au Gratin

*6 large baking potatoes, peeled and sliced $^1/_4$-inch thick*
*$^1/_4$ cup cheddar cheese, shredded*
*$^1/_4$ cup Parmesan cheese*
*$1^1/_2$ cups heavy cream*
*salt and pepper, for seasoning*

1.  Layer the slices of potato, alternating them with cheese. (Add shredded cheddar first, then sprinkle with Parmesan.)

2.  Season the cream with the salt and pepper. Pour this mixture evenly over the top.

3.  Bake in a preheated 375°F oven for 75 minutes, until the potatoes are tender and the cream is reduced.

**Serves 6**

# Roasted New Potatoes

*4 pounds small new potatoes, cut into quarters*
*4 tablespoons olive oil*
*1 tablespoon fresh thyme, chopped*
*salt and pepper, for seasoning*

1.  Toss the potatoes in the oil and fresh thyme. Season with the salt and pepper. Place this mixture in a baking dish.

2.  Roast in a 400°F oven for 30 to 40 minutes. While roasting, toss the potatoes occasionally so that they do not stick to the pan.

**Serves 6**

# Baked Stuffed Potatoes

4 large Idaho potatoes
2 tablespoons butter
3 tablespoons milk
1 tablespoon Parmesan cheese
2 tablespoons cheddar cheese
3 tablespoons fresh chives, chopped
salt and pepper, for seasoning
paprika, for sprinkling

1. Wash the potatoes well. Prick them with a fork to allow the steam to escape.

2. Bake at 425°F for 90 minutes, until the potatoes feel soft.

3. Remove them and allow them to cool long enough to be able to handle.

4. With the potato positioned lengthwise, cut a hole in the center and top of each. The hole should be large enough to allow you to scoop out the pulp, approximately 1¹/₂ inches in diameter.

5. Remove the skin from the hole. Put the remaining pulp from the hole into a bowl. Then scoop out most of the pulp inside each potato and add that to the bowl. (Be gentle! Do not break the skin on the shell.)

6. Add all of the other ingredients—except the paprika. Mix well.

7. Spoon the pulp mixture back into the potatoes. Sprinkle the paprika over the top of the stuffing in each potato.

8. Bake at 375°F for 15 minutes, until the top of the stuffing is golden brown.

**Serves 4**

## Classic Favorites

For years our stuffed baked potatoes were a popular part of our menu. Twice-baked potatoes are again very popular at restaurants, just as mashed potatoes have made a comeback. Both are classic comfort foods. You can vary stuffed potatoes to include your favorite cheeses and herbs. Blue cheese, Gruyere or goat cheese all make interesting variations.

# *Potato Pancakes*

*¹/₂ cup onions, grated*
*1¹/₂ pounds russet potatoes*
*1 egg*
*2 tablespoons fresh parsley, chopped*
*¹/₂ ounce flour*
*¹/₂ ounce matzo meal*
*salt and freshly ground pepper, for seasoning*
*oil or rendered chicken fat, for cooking*

1. Peel the onion and grate it through large holes. Place it into a strainer.

2. Mix the grated potatoes and onion in the strainer. Press them against the strainer to extract as much moisture as possible.

3. In a mixing bowl, add the remaining ingredients—except for the oil. Mix well and season with salt and pepper.

4. Heat the oil (or chicken fat) in a non-stick pan.

5. Pour enough batter into the pan to make a 3-inch cake (approximately 3 tablespoons).

6. As soon as each cake turns golden brown on one side, turn it.

7. When browned on both sides, place the cakes on a platter. Bake at 350°F until crisp, approximately 5 minutes. Serve.

**Makes 12 pancakes**

# Lighthouse Sweet Potato Chips

*3 large sweet potatoes (yams), peeled*
*8 cups vegetable oil*
*Horseradish Cream (see page 41)*

1. Using a slicer, mandoline or food processor, slice the sweet potatoes crosswise, to the thickness of a potato chip.

2. In a thick pot, heat the oil to 275°F. (The oil should not be too hot, as that darkens the chips before they are crisp.)

3. Fry the chips in 3 batches. Watching carefully, cook the chips until golden, approximately 10 minutes. (The chips do not crisp completely until they are out of the oil.)

4. Remove the chips and place them on paper towels.

5. Serve them in a bowl with Horseradish Cream.

**Serves 4**

## Amazing Mandolines

A mandoline makes fast work of slicing firm, crisp fruits and vegetables like potatoes, apples, carrots, onion and beets into perfect thin or thick slices. This slicing tool usually comes with two adjustable cutting blades—one straight and one rippled. It is ideal for julienne-style vegetables or cutting French fries. Better models have a carriage that holds the food and protects your fingers while slicing.

*Desserts*

## Divine Decadence

Chocolate ganache, a rich chocolate icing made of semisweet chocolate and whipping cream that gets whipped to twice its volume, is what makes this dessert so decadent. A water bath is used for the cake. Known as a bain marie, a water bath surrounds food with gentle heat while cooking, either on top of the stove or in the oven. A water bath allows delicate custards and mousses to cook without breaking or curdling and also can be used to keep foods warm.

# Chocolate Oblivion Torte

*2 pounds dark chocolate*
*8 ounces butter, chilled and cut into cubes*
*12 large eggs*
*¹/₂ cup sugar*
*1 pound Dark Chocolate Ganache, for topping (see page 235)*

1. Chop the chocolate into small pieces. Melt it in a double boiler.

2. When all of the chocolate is melted until it is smooth, stir in the chilled butter cubes.

3. Cool the chocolate and butter mixture to approximately 86°F. (The cold butter cools the chocolate faster.)

4. Preheat the oven to 425°F.

5. At room temperature, beat the eggs and sugar until they are light and fluffy (approximately 3 times their original volume).

6. Fold the egg mixture, all at once, into the cool chocolate mixture. Pour this mixture into a 10-inch springform pan.

7. Place the pan in a water bath. Bake it in the oven for 25 minutes.

8. Refrigerate the pan and its contents overnight.

9. To unmold, place the pan in warm water to loosen the cake.

10. Place the cake on a cardboard cake round. Cover with the ganache.

11. To serve, cut it with a very hot knife, otherwise the cake will tear.

**Serves 6 to 8**

# *Chocolate Pâté*

*2 cups heavy cream*
*8 ounces bittersweet chocolate*
*4 ounces butter*
*whipped cream, fresh, for serving*
*Raspberry Sauce, for serving (see page 25)*
*1 cup (or as needed) fresh fruit, for serving*

1. Scald the cream in a thick-bottom saucepot.

2. While the cream is heating, chop the chocolate into small pieces, to speed the melting process.

3. After the cream comes to a boil, remove it from the heat and blend in the chocolate until it is smooth.

4. Stir in the butter and blend it until the mixture is smooth.

5. Pour the pâté into a plastic-lined loaf pan or any desired mold.

6. Place the pan in the freezer overnight.

7. When ready to serve, drop the pâté out of the mold, remove the plastic and slice it ¹/₂-inch thick with a hot, dry knife.

8. Serve it with fresh whipped cream, Raspberry Sauce and fresh seasonal fruit.

**Serves 6**

**Serving Suggestions**

Rich and satisfying, a little chocolate pâté goes a long way. You can use a decorative mold to create a beautiful presentation or a loaf pan to give the pâté its traditional rectangular shape. Drizzle Raspberry Sauce in a design on a plate, then place a slice of pâté on it. Finish with a dollop of whip cream and a sprig of mint.

## Chocolate Cream Dream

Our pastry chef, Jeff Space, was a great innovator. He developed many of our signature desserts. The Chocolate Mousse Tower and our Crème Brûlee are just a few. These desserts look wonderful on a Viennese table and taste delicious.

This dessert can be made as a large tart, which can be sliced with a hot, dry knife and served, or go in the opposite direction to make mini tarts for passing around.

This dessert looks like you went to a fancy patisserie, but it's actually easy to assemble. The tart or pastry shells are prepared, you simply fill them and decorate with a drizzling of chocolate ganache made to look like a spider web. Try this trick to decorate the top of a cake or pudding.

# White Satins

*4 ounces raspberry jam, preferably seedless*
*4 4-inch pastry shells (or 1 full-size pastry shell)*

### White Chocolate Ganache
*8 ounces white chocolate*
*3 ounces heavy cream*

### Dark Chocolate Ganache
*2 ounces semisweet chocolate*
*1 ounce heavy cream*

1. To make the ganache, scald the cream in a heavy saucepot.

2. Chop the chocolate.

3. Separate 3 ounces of cream and add the white chocolate. Over medium heat, stir the chocolate into the hot cream and continue stirring until it is smooth.

4. To the remaining ounce of cream add the semisweet chocolate. Over medium heat, stir the chocolate in the hot cream and continue stirring until it is smooth.

5. To make the tarts, spoon the jam into the bottom of the tart shell(s), dividing it if necessary.

6. Cover the jam with the white chocolate ganache.

7. Place the dark chocolate ganache in a pastry bag with a very small, round tip. (If you don't have a pastry bag handy, place the ganache in a zip lock baggy and cut a small piece out of one of the corners.)

8. Make a spiral on the top of the white chocolate ganache. With the tip of a knife, lift up the white chocolate from the bottom, moving in lines from the center out to create a spider-web pattern.

9. Chill and serve.

**Makes 4 mini tarts or 1 large tart**

# Chocolate-Pecan Pie

*1 9-inch frozen pie shell*

*Filling*
*2 ounces unsweetened chocolate*
*2 ounces sweet (unsalted) butter*
*4 eggs, large*
*1 cup granulated sugar*
*1¼ cups dark corn syrup*
*1 teaspoon vanilla extract*
*2 tablespoons dark rum*
*2 cups pecan halves, shelled*

1. Preheat the oven to 350°F.

2. Bake the shell partially, for 15 minutes. Remove and set aside.

3. Melt the chocolate and butter over a double boiler or in the microwave. Stir it until it is completely melted and smooth.

4. Beat the eggs, sugar and syrup, just enough to mix.

5. Add the vanilla, rum and melted chocolate, and mix.

6. Mix in the pecans.

7. Pour the mixture into the pie shell, making sure that you do not pour batter on the edges or overfill it. Discard any excess filling.

8. Bake for 50 minutes. Do not overbake: The middle should be soft and "wiggly."

9. Remove the pie and place it on a rack. Cool it completely before cutting it.

**Serves 6 to 8**

## Quick and Easy

The convenience of a frozen pie shell and ingredients you're bound to have on hand lets you whip up this fantastic dessert at the spur of the moment. Fresh whipped cream and/or good vanilla ice cream make perfect accompaniments.

# Kristi's Sugared Pecans

*4 cups pecans, shelled*
*1 stick butter (8 tablespoons)*
*2 egg whites, room temperature*
*1 cup sugar*
*$^1/_2$ teaspoon salt*

1. Preheat the oven to 250°F.

2. Bake the pecans on a cookie sheet for 30 minutes.

3. Remove the pecans from the pan, and put the butter on the cookie sheet.

4. Increase the oven temperature to 300°F.

5. Melt the butter on the cookie sheet in the oven.

6. Beat the egg whites until they have soft peaks. Slowly add the sugar and salt, while continuing to beat.

7. Beat until the egg whites are thick.

8. Fold in the pecans.

9. Spread the mixture evenly on the cookie sheet with the butter.

10. Cook for 45 minutes, tossing every 15 minutes.

11. Cool the pecans, then store them in a sealed cookie container.

**Makes 4 cups**

# Caramel Pot de Crème

*2 cups heavy cream*
*1 cup milk*
*1/2 teaspoon espresso powder*
*8 egg yolks*
*1 cup sugar*
*1/4 cup water*
*whipped cream, for serving*
*powdered chocolate or cinnamon, for serving*

1. Combine 1 cup of heavy cream, the milk and espresso powder, and scald.

2. Slowly add this cream mixture to the egg yolks, and mix well.

3. In a heavy saucepan over medium heat, combine the water and sugar.

4. Cook until this mixture caramelizes to a golden brown.

5. At the same time heat the other cup of cream in a saucepan.

6. Preheat the oven to 200°F.

7. Slowly add the warm cream to the caramel to stop the cooking.

8. Add this caramel mixture to the egg mixture. Mix well.

9. Pour the custard into 6 coffee cups.

10. Place the cups in a flat pan and put it into the oven.

11. Cook for 40 minutes.

12. Turn the pan 180° and cook for another 40 minutes.

13. Turn the pan 180° again and cook for another 15 minutes.

14. Chill in the refrigerator overnight. When ready to serve, top with whipped cream and sprinkle with powdered chocolate or cinnamon.

**Makes 6 cups**

**Carameled Cream**

French for "pot of cream," this creamy rich custard is traditionally made and served in small, individual covered porcelain pots. Ramekins or tea cups work just as well in this recipe—just be careful not to scald the cream in the oven. A candied violet on top of a cooled pot de crème adds a wonderful touch.

# Crème Brûlee

*4 cups heavy cream*
*1 vanilla bean*
*pinch of salt*
*8 egg yolks*
*³/₄ cup plus 2 tablespoons granulated sugar*
*8 tablespoons light brown sugar*
*¹/₄ cup Amaretto (optional)*

1. Preheat the oven to 300°F. In a heavy medium saucepan, combine the cream, vanilla bean and salt. Warm them over moderate heat until the surface begins to simmer, about 5 minutes.

2. In a large bowl, stir the egg yolks and sugar with a wooden spoon until they are blended. Pour in the hot cream and stir it gently (to avoid forming air bubbles) until the sugar dissolves. Strain the custard into a large measuring cup and skim off any bubbles. Add ¹/₄ cup of Amaretto, if desired.

3. Place 8 ³/₄-cup ramekins in a roasting pan. Pour the custard into the ramekins, filling them to the rim. Place the roasting pan in the oven and pour in enough warm water to reach halfway up the sides of the ramekins. Cover the roasting pan loosely with foil.

4. Bake for 75 minutes, or until the custard is firm around the edges.

5. Remove the ramekins from the water bath and let them cool. Cover them and refrigerate until they are cold.

6. Preheat the broiler. Set the ramekins on a baking sheet. Use a sieve to sprinkle 1 tablespoon of brown sugar over the top of each custard.

7. Broil the custard as close to the heat as possible until the sugar is caramelized, approximately 30 seconds. Watch carefully so that the sugar does not burn.

8. Cool before serving.

**Serves 8**

# Brown Butter Bread Pudding

*6 ounces stale white bread*
*cinnamon, for sprinkling*
*2¹/₂ cups milk*
*1 stick butter (8 tablespoons)*
*5 eggs*
*³/₄ cups granulated sugar*
*1 tablespoon vanilla*
*Butter Rum Sauce, optional (see sidebar)*
*cream, optional*

1. Cut the bread into large cubes. Lightly sprinkle them with a dusting of cinnamon.

2. In a saucepan, begin to heat the milk.

3. In another saucepan, cook the butter over medium heat, until it is brown. Add the butter to the milk.

4. Mix the eggs and sugar in a bowl. When the milk has come to scalding, add it to the egg mixture slowly.

5. Add the vanilla.

6. Pour the mixture over the bread and let it soak thoroughly.

7. Preheat the oven to 400°F.

8. Grease and sugar a glass baking dish. Pour in the mixture, and cover it with a lid or aluminum foil. Place it in a water bath, and bake it in the oven for 40 to 50 minutes.

9. Cool.

10. Serve, warm or cold, with Butter Rum Sauce or cream.

**Serves 6 to 8**

## Butter Rum Sauce

*¹/₂ cup butter*
*¹/₂ cup brown sugar*
*¹/₄ cup milk*
*Rum or extract, to taste*

1. Melt the butter in a saucepan.

2. Stir in the brown sugar. When completely combined, remove from the heat.

3. Add the milk and rum.

4. Serve warm. Do not refrigerate this sauce. Covered, it keeps in a cool, dark place for up to 1 week.

**Makes 2 cups**

# Brown Butter Tart

*6 ounces salted butter*
*$^1/_2$ vanilla bean, split (approximately 3 to 4 inches)*
*3 whole eggs*
*1$^1/_4$ cups sugar*
*1 tablespoon lemon zest, finely grated*
*$^1/_2$ cup flour*
*Sweet Pastry Dough (see page 26)*
*2 cups fresh fruit*
*Raspberry, Vanilla, or Caramel Sauce (see pages 24 and 25)*

1. Combine the butter and vanilla bean in a heavy skillet. Over medium heat, brown the butter, then remove it from the heat. Discard the bean.

2. Whip the eggs, sugar and zest together.

3. Add the browned butter and mix.

4. Add the flour and mix.

5. Preheat the oven to 300°F.

6. In a tart pan, make a crust with the Sweet Pastry Dough.

7. Pour the batter into the crust, and place the tart pan in the oven.

8. Bake the tart for 35 to 45 minutes. Use a cake tester to check for doneness.

9. Top with fresh fruit. Serve warm with Berry, Vanilla or Caramel Sauce.

**Makes 1 9-inch tart**

# Fresh Fruit Clafouti

1 pound cherries, peaches, nectarines, plums or other fruit
1¼ cups milk
4 eggs
½ cup granulated sugar
1 teaspoon salt
1 cup all-purpose flour
1½ tablespoons butter, melted
2 cups whipped cream, for serving
confectioners sugar, for sprinkling (optional)


1.  Preheat the oven to 350°F.

2.  Clean the fruit. Peel it, remove the pits and slice, if necessary.

3.  Arrange the fruit in the bottom of a shallow, 10-inch rectangular or
    round baking pan.

4.  Combine the milk, eggs, granulated sugar, salt, flour and butter. Mix
    them with a whisk or in a food processor.

5.  Pour the batter over the fruit and place it in the oven. Bake it until the
    batter forms a firm, custard-like consistency, approximately 30
    minutes.

6.  Remove the dish from the oven, spoon the clafouti into 6 dishes and
    serve it warm. Add generous dollops of whipped cream. Sprinkle with
    confectioners sugar, if desired.


**Serves 6**

---

**Fruity Clafouti**

Clafouti is a country French dessert made with a creamy batter that's poured over fruit. When it bakes, the batter creates a custard-like cake top. Clafouti is traditionally made with cherries, but plum, peaches and pears are popular variations. It is usually served warm from the oven, topped with whipped cream and sprinkled with sugar.

# Joyce Gould's Deep Dish Apple-Sour Cream Pie

*Crust*
*1 9- or 10-inch prepared Ritz pie crust*
*plain bread crumbs, as needed*

*Filling*
*6 Golden Delicious apples, peeled, cored and sliced*
*1²/₃ cups sour cream*
*1 cup sugar*
*¹/₃ cup flour*
*1 egg*
*2 teaspoons vanilla*

*Topping*
*1 cup walnuts, chopped*
*¹/₂ cup flour*
*¹/₃ cup brown sugar, firmly packed*
*pinch of salt*
*1 stick butter (8 tablespoons), room temperature*

1.  Preheat the oven to 450°F.

2.  Mix the filling ingredients in a large bowl. Add the apples.

3.  Sprinkle the bottom of the crust with the bread crumbs (to absorb moisture).

4.  Spoon the filling into the crust.

5.  Bake for 10 minutes at 450°F, then reduce the heat to 350°F. Bake for an additional 40 minutes. The filling becomes puffy and golden brown.

6.  Mix the dry ingredients for the topping. Blend them with butter until the mixture is crumbly.

7.  Spoon the topping over the pie and bake an additional 15 minutes at 350°F.

**Makes 1 pie**

# Frozen Key Lime Pie

*12 egg yolks*
*12 ounces condensed milk*
*14 ounces evaporated milk*
*3 limes, preferably Key limes*
*12 ounces Key lime juice*
*1 quart heavy cream*
*1 pound granulated sugar (2 cups)*
*3 graham cracker pie shells, ready-made*

1. Zest and juice the limes. Set aside.

2. Combine the yolks and milk in a large bowl. Mix until they are incorporated.

3. Slowly whisk in the lime juices and zest until the acid starts to thicken the yolk mixture (which is what you want).

4. In a separate bowl, whip the cream and sugar into stiff peaks.

5. Gently fold the cream into the thickened yolk mixture until they are incorporated. Do this gently, as you do not want to lose the air in the cream.

6. Pour the mixture into the pie shells. Freeze them overnight.

7. Slice with a hot knife and serve.

**Makes 3 full-size pies**

## Key Limes are Key

This dessert is light, cool and refreshing. It is perfect in the summer. You need real Key lime juice for this recipe. Key limes are more yellowish than regular limes and are very tart. You can sometimes find true Key limes outside of Florida at specialty food markets, but they all come from the same place—the Florida Keys.

# Pumpkin Cheesecake

## The Crust
1 cup graham cracker crumbs
*1/3 cup butter, melted*

## The Batter
*1 1/4 pounds cream cheese, room temperature*
*1/2 cup sugar*
*1/2 cup brown sugar*
*1 teaspoon cinnamon*
*3/4 teaspoon cloves, ground*
*1/2 teaspoon nutmeg*
*2 cups unsweetened canned pumpkin*
*5 large eggs*
*1/4 cup heavy cream*
*1/4 cup sour cream*

1. Make the crust by combining the crumbs and butter, then pressing them into a 9-inch springform pan.

2. To make the batter, beat the cream cheese until it is light and fluffy. Add the sugars and spices, and continue to beat until they are well incorporated.

3. Add the puréed pumpkin.

4. Preheat the oven to 350°F.

5. One at a time, add the eggs. Scrape the bowl well.

6. Put the batter in the pan and bake it for 1 hour.

7. Turn off the oven and let it stand in the oven for 1 more hour.

8. Cool on a rack.

9. Refrigerate for a minimum of 2 hours.

10. Unmold and serve.

**Makes 1 9-inch cake**

## Not Just for Ghouls

Although pumpkins are usually associated with the pilgrims, they were used as food throughout the world long before America was discovered. This member of the gourd family is one of the oldest vegetable varieties used by humans. It was traditionally used as a main ingredient in soups, but Americans have made it famous for its use in pumpkin pie.

Many different types of pumpkin are available. It is most popular in its canned form, which you can find year-round in supermarkets.

Pumpkin has a mild sweetness that is enhanced by the addition of spices such as nutmeg, cinnamon, and allspice…all traditional spices for pumpkin pie. We use several classic pumpkin pie spices in our cheesecake recipe.

# Biscotti

$^1/_4$ pound butter (8 tablespoons), softened
$1^4/_5$ cups granulated sugar
5 eggs
1 teaspoon vanilla extract
$^1/_2$ teaspoon lemon extract
1 teaspoon almond extract
dash of anise extract
$^1/_8$ teaspoon anise seed
$^3/_4$ cup all-purpose flour
$^3/_8$ tablespoon salt
$^1/_4$ teaspoon baking powder
$^1/_2$ cup almonds, sliced

### Correction
**Biscotti Recipe** on page 246
calls for 3 3/4 cups of all-purpose flour
not 3/4 cup of all-purpose flour

1. Cream the butter and sugar.

2. Incorporate the eggs slowly.

3. Add the extracts and blend the mixture, then stir in the seeds.

4. Sift the flour, salt and baking powder and mix it in.

5. Add the almonds last, to prevent them from being crushed. Be sure to scrape the bottom of the bowl.

6. Roll the dough into 4 logs. Place them on an ungreased baking sheet.

7. Bake them in a preheated oven at 350°F, until they are golden and semi-firm, approximately 30 minutes.

8. Cool the logs and then slice them on a bias.

9. Spread out the slices on the baking sheets and rebake them until they are golden brown and semi-firm, approximately 20 minutes.

10. Cool. Place the biscotti in an airtight container.

**Makes 2 trays**

### Irresistible Anise

Anise, known for its licorice-flavored overtones, enhances the bittersweet appeal of this irresistible biscotti recipe. Anise seeds are commonly used in cookies, and the oil is popular when making sponge cake.

*Brunch*

## Quiche Made Easy

Quiche has its origins in the Alsace-Lorraine area of France. The basic custard filling can be flavored with just about anything.

We use a ratio of 7 to 8 eggs per 1 quart of light cream or half-and-half. This ratio makes a nice custard and can take any type of filling.

Remember to partially cook any vegetables before adding them to the mixture. If you don't, the water from the vegetables dilutes the custard.

Use a frozen pie shell as the crust for added convenience. Partially baking the shell ahead of time ensures its doneness.

# Crab Meat and Cheese Quiche

*1 9-inch pie shell, partially baked*
*1/2 pound jumbo lump crab*
*3 eggs*
*2 tablespoons Sherry*
*3/4 cup milk*
*1 1/2 cups light cream*
*1/2 teaspoon salt*
*1/2 teaspoon white pepper*
*pinch of cayenne pepper*
*1/4 cup fresh chives, chopped*
*1/2 cup Swiss cheese*

1. Preheat the oven to 375°F.

2. Spread the crab and cheese evenly over the bottom of the pie shell.

3. Whisk together all of the remaining ingredients to make a custard.

4. Pour the custard over the pie shell to reach 1/2-inch below the rim of the crust.

5. Bake approximately 30 to 35 minutes, until a toothpick comes out clean.

6. Allow it to set. Serve warm or at room temperature.

**Serves 6**

# Sausage and Cheese Strata

*1 pound sausage, ground (breakfast type, flavored with sage)*
*butter, for greasing pan*
*12 slices of bread*
*1 pound sharp cheese, grated*
*6 eggs*
*1¹/₄ cups milk*
*1 tablespoon dry mustard*
*1 teaspoon Worcestershire sauce*

1. Cook the sausage and drain it. Let it cool.

2. Grease a small baking dish with butter.

3. Create layers in this order: bread, sausage, cheese; bread, sausage, cheese.

4. Whisk the eggs, milk and seasonings.

5. Pour the mixture evenly over the top of the bread layers.

6. Cover with aluminum foil and refrigerate overnight.

7. Preheat the oven to 350°F.

8. Bake for 35 minutes.

9. Pull the dish out of the oven. Let it set for 10 minutes.

10. Serve.

**Serves 4 to 6**

**Sunday Morning Serenade**

In the late 1980s we served a Sunday jazz brunch—champagne, a Dixieland band and great food. What could be a better way to start your Sunday morning?

# Ham and Cheese Soufflé

*butter, for greasing pan*
*16 slices of Pepperidge Farm bread, crusts removed*
*16 slices ham, smoked*
*1 pound Swiss and/or American cheese, grated*
*6 eggs, beaten*
*3 cups milk*
*1/2 teaspoon onion salt*
*1/4 teaspoon dry mustard*
*1/2 cup butter, melted*
*3 cups cornflakes, crushed*

1. Grease a 9- x 12-inch baking dish with butter.

2. Create layers in this order: bread, ham, cheese; bread, ham, cheese.

3. Whisk the eggs, milk, salt and mustard.

4. Pour this mixture evenly over the top of the layers.

5. Cover with aluminum foil and refrigerate overnight.

6. Preheat the oven to 400°F.

7. Melt the butter and mix it with the cornflakes.

8. Spread this cornflakes mixture over the top of the soufflé.

9. Bake for 45 minutes.

10. Pull the dish out of the oven. Let it set for 10 minutes.

11. Serve.

**Serves 8**

# Eggs Washington

*3 quarts water*
*¹/2 cup white vinegar*
*12 slices Canadian bacon*
*12 slices ripe tomatoes*
*12 English muffin halves*
*12 eggs*
*1 tablespoon chives, chopped*
*1 tablespoon parsley, chopped*
*1¹/2 cups Hollandaise Sauce (opposite page)*

1. In a shallow pan, bring 3 quarts of water to a simmer. Add the vinegar (to help keep the poached eggs together).

2. Preheat the oven to 300°F.

3. Bake the bacon on a baking sheet for 5 minutes. Place the tomatoes on top and bake for 5 more minutes.

4. Toast the English muffins. Place the bacon and tomatoes on top. Keep them warm.

5. Carefully crack the egg shells and drop the eggs into the water. Make sure to keep them separated from each other. Cook 3 minutes for soft and 5 minutes for hard poached eggs, depending on your preference.

6. Use a slotted spoon to place the eggs on the muffins.

7. Mix the herbs into the Hollandaise Sauce and ladle it over the top.

**Serves 6**

**Timing Tip**

Make the Hollandaise Sauce for this recipe before you start making the eggs and muffins.

# Hollandaise Sauce

*4 egg yolks*
*2 tablespoons lemon juice*
*1 tablespoon water*
*1 tablespoon white wine*
*1 cup clarified butter (see page 181)*
*salt, for seasoning*
*dash of Tabasco, for seasoning*

1. Combine the yolks, lemon juice, water and wine into a stainless steel bowl. Whisk vigorously.

2. Fill a pot with water and bring it to a boil.

3. Place the stainless steel bowl on top of the pot, securing it so that it does not move around.

4. Start whisking the yolk mixture. (Make sure that you scrape the bottom of the bowl so that no part of the yolk turns to scrambled eggs.)

5. Whisk the mixture until it becomes fluffy and light. Taste the mixture: It should not have too much egg taste.

6. Place the warmed butter in a measuring cup. Pour its oil slowly into the yolk mixture while you continue whisking.

7. When all of the oil is added, season with the salt and Tabasco. Add more lemon juice, if desired.

**Makes 1¹/₂ cups**

## Quick Fix Hollandaise

In a pinch? A blender version of this sauce can be made easily. Place the yolks, lemon and water into a processor and process it for 5 minutes. Bring the butter to almost boiling. Carefully and slowly add the butter to the processor, which should be on. When complete, thin with water if necessary. Season.

# Frittata

*2 tablespoons olive oil*
*$^1/_2$ cup onion, sliced*
*$^1/_4$ cup zucchini, cut julienne style*
*$^1/_4$ cup red pepper, sliced*
*$^1/_4$ cup mushrooms, sliced*
*$^1/_2$ teaspoon garlic*
*salt and pepper, for seasoning*
*$^1/_4$ cup Monterey Jack cheese*
*2 tablespoons fresh basil, chiffonade*
*12 eggs, mixed*

1. Sauté the vegetables and garlic in the olive oil for 2 minutes. Season them with salt and pepper. Remove them from the heat and let them cool slightly.

2. Preheat the oven to 375°F.

3. Rub the bottom and edges of a round baking dish with some olive oil. Put it in the oven for 3 minutes.

4. Remove the baking dish and place the vegetables, cheese and basil in the bottom of it.

5. Pour the eggs on top and place the baking dish on the middle rack of the oven for 20 minutes, until it looks cooked and golden brown.

**Serves 8**

## Italian Ingenuity

This tasty treat is considered an Italian version of its much more famous cousin, the French omelet. But the Italian version uses the oven to allow a much thicker layer of eggs and a much longer cooking time.

# French Toast

*12 slices French bread, crust on
vegetable oil for frying, as needed*

*Egg Mixture*
*4 eggs*
*1 tablespoon sugar*
*$1/2$ teaspoon cinnamon*
*pinch of nutmeg*
*$1^1/2$ cups milk*
*$1/4$ cup Grand Marnier (optional)*
*1 tablespoon orange rind, grated*

*Garnish Mix*
*$1/8$ cup confectioners sugar*
*1 teaspoon cinnamon*

1. Mix all of the egg mixture ingredients together in a mixing bowl.

2. Dip a slice of bread in the egg mixture, until it is nice and soaked.
   Repeat this process with each slice.

3. In a heavy skillet, cook several slices of toast at once, until they are
   puffed and brown on each side.

4. Place 3 slices on each plate. Sprinkle with the garnish mix.

**Serves 4**

# Brunch Potatoes

*3 pounds red bliss potatoes*
*1 stick butter (8 tablespoons)*
*1 cup onions, sliced*
*½ tablespoon black pepper*
*salt, for seasoning*

1. Cut the potatoes in quarters. Parboil or steam them until they are tender. Cut them into ¾-inch pieces.

2. In a warm cast iron pan, add the butter and allow it to heat.

3. Add the onions and sauté them for 2 minutes. Then add the potatoes.

4. Add the black pepper and season with the salt.

5. Cover the pan with a lid and cook for 15 minutes, until brown. Turn the potatoes over and cook for another 15 minutes.

**Serves 8**

# Smoked Salmon Cream Cheese

*1 pound smoked salmon, chopped*
*¼ cup green onion, chopped*
*1 pound cream cheese, softened*
*juice of half a lemon*
*1 tablespoon lemon zest*
*1 tablespoon capers, drained and chopped*
*fresh pepper, to taste*

1. Combine all of the ingredients in a mixer. Blend well.

2. Place in a bowl and serve with assorted bagels.

**Makes 1 bowl**

**Perfect Potatoes**

Red bliss potatoes are ideal for this type of cooking technique. Their moist insides adapt well during parboiling or steaming, which prevents them from becoming overly sticky during cooking.

**Supreme Cream Cheese**

This spread is fantastic with bagels. Guests devour it when we serve it on our buffets.

## Amazing Mint

Mint adds a refreshing and cool aftertaste to many foods. The most commonly known versions are peppermint and spearmint, but apple, orange, and even pineapple flavors of mint are available. In addition to enhancing fruit dishes, such as this one, mint also complements various meats, vegetables and candies, including chocolate.

# Chunked Melons
## with Fresh Mint

*1 large canteloupe, ripe*
*1 large honeydew, ripe*
*¹/₄ cup fresh mint, chiffonade*

1. Cut off both ends of the melons.

2. On a cutting board, place a melon upright on one of its cut ends.

3. To cut the rind off, carefully take a knife and cut along the inside of the rind straight down toward the cutting board.

4. Repeat, going around the melon until all of the rind is off.

5. Repeat this process for the second melon.

6. Cut the melons in half, removing the seeds. Then cut them into 2-inch chunks.

7. Place the chunks in a bowl and toss them with fresh mint.

**Makes 1 bowl**

# Blueberry Crumb Coffee Cake

*Topping*
1 cup light brown sugar
$^1/_4$ cup all-purpose flour
$^1/_4$ cup unsalted butter, cold

*Cake*
2 cups flour
1 teaspoon baking powder
1 teaspoon baking soda
$^1/_4$ teaspoon salt
$^1/_2$ cup unsalted butter, softened
1 cup sugar
3 eggs, lightly beaten
1 cup sour cream
2 cups blueberries, fresh or frozen

1. Sift together the flour, baking powder, baking soda and salt for the cake. Set aside.

2. Cream the butter and sugar for the cake in a mixer.

3. Add the eggs and mix well.

4. Add the dry ingredients in small amounts, alternating with the sour cream.

5. Fold in the blueberries.

6. Pour the batter into a greased 9 x 11-inch rectangular baking pan.

7. Preheat the oven to 325°F.

8. Mix the topping ingredients and sprinkle them evenly over the top.

9. Place in the oven, and bake for 30 minutes.

**Makes 1 cake**

### Coffee Cake

Coffee cake gets its name from the time and occasion when it's served—usually at breakfast or with afternoon coffee or tea. Coffee cake typically is not frosted or decorated, but sometimes—as with this cake—is sprinkled with a topping before baking, which adds a little crunch.

# Poppy-Seed Lemon Pound Cake

*1 cup flour*
*1 teaspoon baking powder*
*1 1/2 sticks butter (12 tablespoons)*
*1 cup sugar*
*3 large eggs*
*1 teaspoon lemon extract*
*juice from 1 lemon*
*1 tablespoon lemon zest*
*1 tablespoon poppy seeds*

1. Preheat the oven to 350°F.

2. Sift together the flour and baking powder. Set aside.

3. Beat together the butter and sugar until they are light and fluffy.

4. Add the eggs, 1 at a time, to the butter mixture. Incorporate well.

5. Add the extract, lemon juice, zest and poppy seeds. Mix.

6. Fold the flour into the batter in small amounts: Do not fold in all of the flour at once.

7. Pour the batter into a large greased loaf pan.

8. Bake it for approximately 30 minutes.

9. Unmold the cake. Cool.

**Makes 1 large loaf**

# Zucchini Bread

*3 tablespoons butter, unsalted*
*1¹/₂ cups sugar*
*3 eggs*
*1¹/₄ cups oil*
*2 cups flour*
*2 teaspoons baking soda*
*1 teaspoon baking powder*
*1 teaspoon salt*
*1 teaspoon cinnamon*
*1 teaspoon cloves, ground*
*2 cups zucchini, grated on a cheese grater*
*1 teaspoon vanilla extract*
*1 cup walnuts, chopped*

1. Preheat the oven to 350°F.

2. Butter 4 small loaf pans (3 x 5 x 3 inches).

3. Cream the butter and sugar in a mixer until it is light and fluffy. Add the eggs and oil. Beat well.

4. Sift the flour, baking soda, baking powder, salt, cinnamon and cloves together. Mix into the egg mixture.

5. Add the zucchini, vanilla and nuts.

6. Pour the batter into an ungreased baking pan.

7. Bake for 1 hour. Test for doneness with a toothpick.

**Makes 4 small loaves**

### Baking Soda or Powder?

This recipe calls for both baking soda and baking powder, which are used for leavening. Baking soda is more basic, and is acutally contained in baking powder. To make your own baking powder, mix 1 teaspoon of baking soda with 2 teaspoons of cream of tartar.

## A Great Combination

The combination of bananas and walnuts, which contain a high amount of oil, makes this sweet bread extremely moist—and delicious!

# Walnut Banana Bread

*1 stick unsalted butter (8 tablespoons), softened*
*1 cup sugar*
*2 eggs*
*1¹/₂ cups flour*
*1 teaspoon baking soda*
*1 teaspoon salt*
*1 cup ripe bananas, mashed*
*¹/₂ cup sour cream*
*1 teaspoon vanilla extract*
*¹/₂ cup walnuts, chopped*

1. Preheat the oven to 350°F.

2. Butter 4 small loaf pans (3 x 5 x 3 inches).

3. Cream the butter and sugar in a mixer, until they are light and fluffy. Add the eggs and beat well.

4. Sift the flour, baking soda and salt together. Mix them into the egg mixture.

5. Add the bananas, sour cream, vanilla and nuts.

6. Pour the batter into the loaf pans.

7. Bake for 1 hour. Test for doneness with a toothpick.

**Makes 4 small loaves**

# Cranberry-Orange Muffins

2 cups flour
1$^1$/$_2$ teaspoons baking powder
$^1$/$_2$ teaspoon baking soda
4 tablespoons unsalted butter
1 cup sugar
1 egg, beaten
zest of 1 orange, grated
$^3$/$_4$ cup fresh orange juice
1 tablespoon Grand Marnier
2$^1$/$_2$ cups cranberries, fresh or frozen
vegetable oil spray, for coating

1. Preheat the oven to 350°F.

2. Sift together the flour, baking powder and baking soda.

3. Add the butter and sugar until the mix is crumbly.

4. Add the egg, zest, orange juice and Grand Marnier. Mix gently.

5. Fold in the cranberries.

6. Spray the muffin tins with a vegetable oil spray.

7. Pour the batter into the muffin tins.

8. Bake for 15 to 20 minutes. Test for doneness with a toothpick.

**Makes 12 muffins**

## Muffin Magic

Because they appear as miniature, individual cakes, muffins can add a quaint feeling to even the simplest of meals. Yet they are wonderfully easy to make. The trick to making great muffins is to mix the ingredients just until they are moistened—any longer can create a texture that's too compact.

8

## Apple Appeal

These apple fritters use a special apple for baking—Granny Smith. This tart and firm green apple originally came from New Zealand. Its juicy quality gives the fritters additional moisture—so they easily melt in you mouth!

# Fresh Apple Fritters

1 egg, beaten
1 cup milk
4 tablespoons butter, melted
1 teaspoon vanilla
1 orange
1 large Granny Smith apple, peeled, cored and chopped
3 cups flour
1/2 cup sugar
1 teaspoon baking powder
1/2 teaspoon salt
confectioners sugar, for sprinkling
oil, for frying, approximately 2 cups

1. In a bowl, whisk together the egg, milk, butter and vanilla.

2. Finely grate the orange zest into the egg mixture. Squeeze the juice of the orange into the egg mixture, then add the chopped apple. Set aside.

3. In a large bowl, sift the flour, sugar, baking powder and salt. Make a well in the center of the bowl and add the egg mixture. Beat them together until they are smooth.

4. Heat a generous amount of oil in a frying pan. Spoon in level tablespoons of the fritter mixture and fry them until they are golden brown (approximately 10 minutes). Remove the fritters and let them drain on paper towels.

5. Dust the fritters with confectioners sugar after draining off the oil. These are best served warm.

**Makes 12 fritters**

# Jeff's Best Scones

8 ounces flour
2 teaspoons baking powder
1/2 teaspoon kosher salt
1 tablespoon sugar
4 ounces butter, cold
3/4 cup buttermilk
egg wash (see page 187)

1.  Mix together all of the dry ingredients.

2.  Cut the butter into the dry mix with a pastry blender.

3.  Add the buttermilk and mix gently, until the dough barely holds together.

4.  Preheat the oven to 350°F.

5.  Roll out the dough. Cut it into 2-inch rounds with a biscuit cutter.

6.  Use an egg wash to brush the tops of the scones.

7.  Bake them on a greased baking sheet for approximately 15 minutes, until golden.

**Makes 20 2-inch scones**

## Buttermilk Basics

Many people think that buttermilk is high in fat. It is actually skim milk to which a culture has been added. The milk takes on a slightly acid-flavored taste.

Originally, buttermilk was the thin liquid left over after the butter had been churned.

Buttermilk adds zip, flavor and lightness to cakes, scones, muffins and pancakes. It also makes a good substitute for oil or cream in dressings.

Entertaining

*G*reat food, good organization, careful planning and a beautiful setting are all very important ingredients in entertaining. However, the key word in our family for having a successful get-together is fun for everyone! Your guests feel it, your food represents it, and the host is able to enjoy it too.

*W*ith today's more relaxed approach to life, entertaining can be as casual or as formal as you like. There are no hard and fast rules anymore. The real criteria for success is how many good memories you've made when gathering your family and friends.

# Planning is Everything!

- Pick a date and time. Remember that many people prefer daytime for driving. Sunday afternoon or evening is a great time for entertaining.

- Put together your guest list. Don't be afraid to invite people who don't know one another. A party atmosphere brings out the best in all of us.

- Take into consideration the amount of space you have available. Allow enough room for people to be comfortable. This also determines the type of party you plan.

- Choose the style of entertaining you'll do for this celebration. Below are the main options you can consider. Throughout the rest of this chapter, we offer advice on how to host each type of event, complete with menus, recipes and serving suggestions. Enjoy!

## Cocktail or Wine Party

This type of party can be inexpensive to prepare. Your equipment is minimal: glasses, napkins, bar stock, trays and a bar table.

## Buffets

Buffets allow the most versatility. You can have a country brunch or a fancy dessert party, with simple single-plate servings.

## Sitdown Dinners

Sitdown meals are more intimate celebrations. At a dinner table, 6 to 10 people can make for a comfortable grouping and good conversation. Rented tables and chairs can increase the party size to as large as you desire.

# Choosing a Menu

Taste and simplicity are always the best combinations for parties. Take into consideration the season, so you can serve the freshest food available at the time. Balance the foods for color, texture and substance. Pick some of your favorite foods to make, and include them in your menu.

Choose foods and combinations that can be made ahead, then simply heated, sliced, or cooled right before the party. This has the added advantage of allowing easy clean-up—before the party even begins.

## Those Wonderful Lists...

After making your guest list, get a notebook for your other party lists. Your lists should include:

- What you are serving and the quantities you need

- Wine varieties and quantities

- Drink varieties and quantities

- Where to find the recipes for everything you are serving

- A shopping list based on the menu

- Serving pieces to be used for each item

- Flowers needed.

### Decorating Ideas

You should buy or pick (preferably from your own yard) as many flowers as your house can hold. Use containers that are unusual, but fit your theme. For example:

- As a country brunch centerpiece, you can tie raffia around a quart jar then fill it with flowers.

- Fill a pretty glass pitcher with some stones, fresh ivy and water.

- Put a mirror in the center of the buffet table and scatter flower petals over it.

- Place 3 candles of different sizes on the buffet.

- Add herbs or flowers to a serving tray to create a special touch.

# Cheese Displays

We prepare quite a few cheese displays for our catered events and weddings. Here are some helpful hints.

- Three pounds of cheese serves 15 people.

- To highlight and bring out the delicious flavors of cheese, always serve it at room temperature. It is best to pull the cheese out of the refrigerator at least 2 to 3 hours before serving. As with wine, cold temperatures hide the delicious nuances of its flavor.

- Refrigerate cheese in an airtight container. Well wrapped cheese can last a month in the refrigerator.

- Cutting hard cheese is easy with a cheese knife or cheese wire.

- Don't cut cheese far ahead of time because the slices dry out.

- A cheese course after your meal prepares the palate for dessert. Use light cheeses if the meal is hearty, and rich cheeses if it's light.

- Be creative in the presentation. Cheese can be very visually appealing. Use triangles or long rectangles. You can leave a nice wedge whole, with just a few slices or dices set off.

Use any combination of these arrangements. They make a great conversation topic at cocktail parties.

Cheese can be displayed on anything—plates, silver, marble slabs, old pottery or wicker. Use your imagination! Garnish for the cheese can be nuts, crackers, olives, cornichons or roasted peppers…along with fruit, berries, grapes, apples or plums. Anything with color adds appeal to your cheese display.

We try to use specialty crackers and bread sticks to enhance the cheeses. Don't forget a nice cheese knife and cocktail napkins.

---

## Delicious Diversity

When putting together a cheese display, choose one of each type of cheese so that the flavors and textures are varied. Use hard, semi-firm, blue and semi-soft, or triple cream types. Here is a sample cheese selection:

- One type of Brie cheese, or Camembert.

- One smoked cheese, such as mozzarella, provolone or Gouda.

- One hard sharp cheese, like cheddar, Swiss or Gouda.

- One blue cheese, like Gorgonzola, Roquefort or Stilton.

- One goat cheese, rolled in peppercorns, ash or marinated with fresh herbs.

- One semi-soft cheese, like Bel Paese, Munster, or Port-Salut.

- One herbed cheese, such as Boursin.

# Our Favorite Cheeses

At the Washington Inn we use small, scrap pieces of marble to display each cheese. The marble really highlights the cheese. Grape leaves, even made of paper, also add a nice touch.

## Brie Cheese

Absolutely delicious with crusty French bread and a glass of Merlo, this French cheese is a soft, ripened cheese made from cow's milk. Brie should be creamy and a bit runny at room temperature. Good Bries have a butterfat content of 50 to 60%. If Brie is chalky and hard, you don't want it. The skin on the outside has a neutral flavor and is fine for eating.

## Aged Gouda

This Dutch cheese has incredible complexity and flavor. A hard aged Gouda can be used similarly to fresh grated Parmesan.

## Gorgonzola

This Italian blue is great in dressings, on salads, in soups and with pasta. Try mixing it with cream cheese or mascarpone, then stuffing it in a fig. It can be wrapped with bacon and baked. Gorgonzola can be young and sweet or aged. Both types have a pronounced strong flavor.

## Roquefort

The king of blue cheeses, this cheese is made only in France. It comes from sheep's milk and is aged in caves. It's simply perfect with salad and crusty French bread.

## Triple Cream Cheeses

These rich and silky smooth cheeses owe their essence to their high quantity of butterfat, which can be as much as 75%. Their appearance resembles Brie cheeses, with an outer brine and off-white interior. The type we serve most often is Saint-André.

---

**Wine and Cheese Pairing**

Matching wine and cheese is a matter of personal choice. But with so many cheeses available, a few guidelines might help:

**Flavor and Body:** Fuller-bodied red wines go well with rich cheeses. They stand up to, but don't overpower, the cheese. A rich Pinot Noir matches a Camembert or Brie. Brunello di Montalcino or a Chianti Reserva work with Taleggio or Reggiano Parmesan cheeses.

**Acidity:** Try to match high acidity cheeses and wines. A goat cheese works well with a crisp Vouvray or Sauvignon Blanc. For red wines, try a French Burgundy, such as Côte de Beaune or Givry.

**Fruitiness:** Fruity red wines go well with mild, creamy cheeses. Fruity Zinfandel, Beaujolais or Merlot pairs with cheeses such as Port Salut, Bel Paese or Fontina.

**Contrasting Combinations:** Two of the best wine-and-cheese matches have completely contrasting flavors. Roquefort and Sauterne make a beautiful pair. The salty sharpness of the blue cheese is mellowed by the sweetness of the dessert wine. Also, try a Port with a Stilton to create a caramel-vanilla taste.

# *Crudités*

Nothing says fresh like a display of colorful, cut-up vegetables, sweet ripened pieces of fruit and a smooth array of cheeses. By adding dips, spreads, creams and breads you have a healthy and satisfying buffet table that can be a meal in itself or a beautiful addition to a cocktail party.

The beautiful colors of the different vegetables can be used to make a visual impact. Large or small, crudité displays always attract interest. Even though crudités are typically raw vegetables, blanching vegetables such as broccoli, string beans, sugar peas, cauliflower and baby carrots brings out their vibrant colors, which makes the display all the more appealing.

We use different vessels to hold and display our crudités. Baskets, silver trays, flower pots and crystal dishes. Virtually anything you can think of can be used. Use linens in draping the table but keep them simple. If there is too much of a print on the cloths that you use for display, everything can appear too busy. The colors from the vegetables should catch and hold the eye.

# Dips for Crudités

## Honey Mustard Dip

$^1/_4$ cup Dijon mustard
$^1/_4$ cup honey
1 tablespoon soy sauce
1 tablespoon parsley, chopped
1 teaspoon fresh ginger, minced (optional)

**Makes $^1/_2$ cup**

## Green Peppercorn Parmesan Dip

1 cup mayonnaise
$^1/_4$ cup Parmesan cheese, grated
1 teaspoon green peppercorns, drained (available in supermarkets)
salt, to taste

**Makes 1 cup**

## Sun-dried Tomato-Olive Dip

4 sun-dried tomatoes, moistened
1 tablespoon anchovy paste
2 tablespoons olive oil
$^1/_4$ cup black olives, pitted
2 tablespoons fresh parsley, chopped
2 tablespoons chives, chopped
10 fresh basil leaves
1 cup mayonnaise

1.  Put everything but the mayonnaise in a food processor. Purée until smooth. Fold into the mayonnaise. Mix well.

**Makes 1$^1/_2$ cups**

## Horseradish Cream (see page 41)

## Balsamic Blue Cheese Dressing (see page 19)

### All in the Timing

Green peppercorns come from the same vine as black and white ones—they're just picked earlier, when they're underripe. These berries are often preserved in brine or wine vinegar, and can be bought in supermarkets.

As the berries ripen, they are harvested and dried to become black peppercorns. If the berry further matures, the outer skin is removed to reveal a kernel, which is dried to become white peppercorn.

# Cocktail Party Menu
### • Serves Several Guests •

## Cheese Selection
Saga Blue • Aged Gouda • Vermont Cheddar • Brie Cheese
Assorted Crackers

## Roquefort Grapes
Recipe on page 58

## Risotto Cakes with Tzatziki Sauce
Recipes on pages 57 and 47

## Grilled Chicken Saté with Peanut Dipping Sauce
Recipe on page 54

## Grilled Shrimp with Horseradish, Mustard and Bacon
Recipe on page 45

## Mediterranean Canapés
Recipe on page 35

## Roasted Eggplant Croutons
Recipe on page 33

# Spring Buffet Menu
### • Serves 8 Guests•

## Jicama Salad
Recipe on page 116

## Grilled Vegetable Salad
Recipe on page 275

## Randall's Greek Salad
## with Pasta and Feta Cheese
Recipe on page 276

## Poached Salmon with Mustard-Dill
Recipe on page 277

## Roasted Fillet of Beef
## with Blue Cheese-Horseradish Cream
Recipe on page 211

## Fresh Berry Shortcake
Recipe on page 278

## Grilled Veggie Tips

Grilling vegetables is easier than you think…if you keep a watchful eye. Don't wander off or daydream, because veggies burn fast. Below are more tips:

Most veggies don't need oil added before grilling…just a clean grill. Grill the veggies just until they are marked: They will continue cooking after removed from the grill. Cook each type of vegetable separately and season them just before combining them with the other types. For seasoning, try variations of simple oil and vinegar, lemon juice, fresh herbs, salt and pepper. The general rule of thumb is: Keep seasoning simple! The fresh, natural flavors are the highlight.

For veggie tips on this recipe: Grill onions until they are caramel brown and then finish them in the oven. Do not salt the eggplant before grilling. Afterward, stack the slices on top of each other so that they continue steaming. Squash marks quickly, so turn it over soon. Peppers take longer to cook, so quartering them helps. For mushrooms, season them with a little oil and spice mix before grilling. Enjoy!

# Grilled Vegetable Salad

*2 red onions, sliced thick*
*1 large eggplant, cut into rounds*
*3 zucchini, sliced ¹/₄-inch thick*
*3 yellow squash, sliced ¹/₄-inch thick*
*1 green pepper, cut into fourths*
*1 red pepper, cut into fourths*
*1 yellow pepper, cut into fourths*
*2 cups mushrooms, tossed with any Cajun seasoning*
*1 bunch green onions, sliced*

## Marinade
*¹/₄ cup red wine vinegar*
*¹/₄ cup balsamic vinegar*
*3 tablespoons Dijon mustard*
*2 cups olive oil*
*salt and fresh pepper, to taste*

1. Grill the vegetables as described in the sidebar.

2. After grilling, cut the eggplant into strips.

3. Toss together the marinade and vegetables.

4. Allow them to sit for at least 1 hour. Serve.

**Makes 1 large bowl**

# Randall's Greek Salad
## with Pasta and Feta Cheese

2 pounds cooked fusilli or penne pasta, cooked al dente
4 cups fresh plum tomatoes, chopped
$1/2$ pound feta cheese
1 bunch scallions, sliced
1 cup black olives, sliced
$1/4$ cup red wine vinegar
$3/4$ cup olive oil
5 tablespoons dried oregano
1 tablespoon dried basil
$1/4$ cup parsley, chopped
salt and freshly ground pepper, for seasoning


1.  Combine all of the ingredients.

2.  Season with salt and freshly ground pepper.

3.  For the best results, refrigerate overnight.


**Makes 1 large bowl**

### Salting Cold Dishes

Remember that flavors in a cold dish are more muted than in a hot dish. You need to add more salt and pepper when seasoning. Taste before and as you season it to prevent over salting. Always pour salt from your hand—not from the box.

# Poached Salmon
## *with Mustard-Dill Sauce*

*2 salmon fillets, 14 ounces each*
*2 to 3 quarts court bouillon (poaching broth) (see sidebar)*
*2 tablespoons shallots, chopped*
*1 tablespoon butter*
*2 tablespoons Dijon mustard*
*1/2 cup dry white wine*
*1/4 cup chicken stock (see page 5)*
*2 cups heavy cream*
*1/4 cup fresh dill, chopped*
*salt and pepper, for seasoning*
*sprig of dill, for garnish*

1. To make the sauce, use a saucepan to sauté the shallots in the butter until they are soft.

2. Add the mustard, white wine and chicken stock. Reduce by two-thirds.

3. Add the heavy cream. Reduce until you have a sauce-like consistency. (Be careful not to let the cream boil over.)

4. Add the fresh dill. Season with salt and pepper.

5. To make the salmon, strain the poaching broth into a roasting pan. Bring it to a slow simmer.

6. Place the salmon in the broth. Cook it for approximately 10 minutes.

7. Carefully remove the fillets. Pat them dry and place them on a plate.

8. Spoon the sauce over the fish. Garnish with a fresh sprig of dill.

**Serves 8**

# Fresh Berry Shortcake

*³/₄ cup butter, softened*
*1¹/₂ cups plus 1 tablespoon sugar*
*2¹/₄ cups cake flour*
*³/₄ cup milk*
*2¹/₄ teaspoons baking powder*
*1¹/₂ teaspoons vanilla extract*
*¹/₃ teaspoon salt*
*3 eggs, large*
*1¹/₂ cups whipping cream*
*1¹/₂ cups strawberry purée, sweetened*
*1¹/₂ pints blueberries*
*³/₄ pint strawberries*
*1¹/₂ pints raspberries*

1. Preheat the oven to 350°F. Grease and flour 8 5-inch round cake pans.

2. In a large bowl, beat the butter at low speed. Add 1 cup of sugar and blend well. Beat for 5 minutes, until the batter is light and creamy.

3. Reduce the speed and add the flour, milk, baking powder, vanilla, salt and eggs. Beat until well mixed, frequently scraping the bowl.

4. Increase the speed and beat for 2 minutes.

5. Divide the batter equally into 6 pans. Bake for 25 to 30 minutes, or until a toothpick comes out clean.

6. Cool the cakes on a cake rack.

7. Whip the cream and 1 tablespoon of sugar into stiff peaks.

8. Cut each cake in half to create 2 thinner circles out of each one.

9. Place 1 cake layer on each plate. Drizzle some strawberry purée onto the cake layer. Top it with the mixed fruit. Add a dollop of whipped cream.

10. Place the other cake layer on top. Repeat.

**Makes 6 servings**

### Shortcake? Sure!

Shortcake is a dessert made of short, sometimes sweetened, biscuit dough that is split in layers and filled with toppings, usually of fruit. It is usually made with a large amount of butter or other shortening.

# *Summer Sitdown Dinner Menu*

**• Serves 6 Guests •**

## *Crab Pillows with Butter Sauce*
Recipe on page 280

## *Chilled Two-Melon Soup*
Recipe on page 113

## *Jersey Tomatoes with Pesto Vinaigrette*
Recipe on page 115

## *Pan-Seared Cajun Tuna*
## *with Shrimp, Corn Salsa and Fettucini*
## *and New Orleans Butter Sauce*
Recipe on page 282

## *Fresh Berry Temptation*
Recipe on page 284

# Crab Pillows
## with Butter Sauce

*1 egg*
*2 tablespoons cold water*
*6 puff pastry squares, 5 x 5 inch*
*1½ pounds jumbo lump crab meat, picked over for shells*
*6 tablespoons Lemon Butter (opposite page)*
*Butter Sauce (opposite page)*

1.  Beat together 1 egg and 2 tablespoons of cold water to make an egg wash.

2.  Lay out the puff pastry and place one-sixth of the crab meat in the center of each square.

3.  Top each square with a slice (1 tablespoon) of Lemon Butter.

4.  Brush the edges of the pastry with the egg wash, then seal the edges together to form a pillow. Make sure that you have a good seal.

5.  Place the pastries seam-side down on a cookie sheet and bake in a preheated 450°F oven for 15 minutes.

6.  Serve with the Butter Sauce—an ideal match because it is so light.

**Serves 6**

**Make-Ahead Magic**

These crab pillows can be made ahead, refrigerated for up to 2 days and then baked when you are ready. They also can be frozen: The only difference is that the crab meat sometimes gets a bit of a stringy character.

**Wine Notes**

Try a medium-bodied Australian Chardonnay or a crisp Oregon Chardonnay with just a hint of oak.

## Lemon Butter

1 cup white wine
$^1/_4$ cup shallots, chopped
juice of 3 lemons
1 pound butter, softened
salt and pepper, for
    seasoning
2 tablespoons fresh parsley,
    chopped
zest of 1 lemon, chopped

1. In a small saucepan, blend the white wine, shallots and lemon juice.

2. Bring them to a boil, then reduce the heat. Simmer until the mixture is nearly dry. (A few tablespoons of syrupy liquid should be left in the pan.)

3. Place the softened butter in a mixing bowl, then beat in the cooled wine and shallot mixture.

4. Season with the salt, pepper, parsley and lemon zest.

5. Place the butter on a sheet of waxed or parchment paper and roll it into a log. Refrigerate it until it is firm.

**Makes 2 logs**

# Butter Sauce

3 tablespoons shallots, chopped
$^1/_4$ cup fish stock (see page 7) or clam juice
2 tablespoons white wine vinegar
$^1/_4$ cup white wine
$^3/_4$ cup cream
3 tablespoons butter
salt and freshly ground papper, for seasoning
1 tablespoon Dijon mustard

1. Put the shallots, stock, vinegar and wine in a small saucepan. Bring them to a simmer. Reduce until the shallots are just moist.

2. Add the cream and simmer. Reduce until it has a sauce-like consistency.

3. Lower the heat and swirl in the butter.

4. Season with the salt, pepper and mustard.

**Makes 1 cup**

# Pan-Seared Cajun Tuna
## with Shrimp, Corn Salsa and Fettucini and a New Orleans Butter Sauce

*6 tuna steaks, 8 ounces each*
*³/4 cup Seafood Seasoning (see page 139)*
*3 tablespoons butter*
*12 jumbo shrimp (16-20 count)*
*1¹/2 pounds fettucini pasta, cooked al dente*
*New Orleans Butter Sauce (see sidebar)*
*Corn Salsa (opposite page)*

1. Preheat the oven to 350°F.

2. Season the tuna with the Seafood Seasoning. Make sure that the tuna is coated well with the spice mix.

3. Heat the butter over medium heat in a large sauté pan. Add the fish and sear it for 4 minutes on each side.

4. Halfway through the cooking, add the shrimp to the pan. Make sure that you cook the tuna until it is pink inside.

5. Place the pasta on 6 plates. Place the tuna steaks on the pasta.

6. Ladle the New Orleans Butter Sauce over the pasta and tuna.

7. Place the shrimp on top of the tuna. Spoon the Corn Salsa on the side of the pasta. Serve.

**Serves 6**

## New Orleans Butter Sauce

*2 sticks (1/2 pound) plus 3 tablespoons butter*
*3 shallots, chopped*
*3/4 cup white wine*
*1/2 cup heavy cream*
*3/4 tablespoon Seafood Seasoning (see page 139)*

1. Place 3 tablespoons butter, the shallots and white wine in a small saucepan.

2. Reduce over a medium flame to two-thirds.

3. Add the cream and reduce by half. Remove from the heat.

4. Cut the 2 sticks of butter into small pieces and whisk them into the reduction.

5. Season with the Seafood Seasoning, adjusting the amount to your taste.

**Makes 1¹/2 cups**

### Wine Notes

 Many flavors come together in this dish. Try a dry Rosé or sparkling wine from California. A full-bodied Vouvray also holds up to the complexity of this dish.

# Corn Salsa

*18 fresh ears of corn, roasted, cooled and kernels cut off the cob*
*2 cups tomato, diced*
*1 red pepper, finely chopped*
*1 bunch green onions, chopped*
*$1/2$ cup celery, finely chopped*
*2 dried pasilla chilies, seeds removed, soaked and finely chopped*
*4 jalapeño peppers, seeds removed and chopped*
*1 bunch cilantro, chopped*
*1 teaspoon cumin*
*$1/8$ cup olive oil*
*dash of rice vinegar*
*juice of 1 lime*
*salt and fresh pepper, to taste*

1.  Mix all of the ingredients together.

2.  Allow the flavors to blend for approximately 1 hour.

**Makes 1 large bowl**

# Fresh Berry Temptation

*1 package phyllo dough*
*¹/₄ cup butter, melted*
*¹/₄ cup granulated sugar*
*1 cup Raspberry Sauce (see page 25)*
*¹/₄ cup Hershey's Syrup*
*2 cups strawberries, sliced*
*1 cup fresh raspberries*
*1 cup blueberries or blackberries*
*whipped cream, as needed*

*heavy oven-proof bowl*

1. Preheat the oven to 400°F.

2. Cut the phyllo into 4 x 4-inch squares.

3. Brush each square with melted butter and then lightly sprinkle it with sugar.

4. Stack them, criss-crossed, into 4-inch baking ramekins. Make each stack 4 sheets thick.

5. Put the ramekins in the oven and bake the dough until it is brown and crisp (approximately 10 to 15 minutes). Remove them and set them aside.

6. Ladle some Raspberry Sauce onto each of 6 plates.

7. Pour the chocolate syrup into the bottom of each baked phyllo cup.

8. Fill the cups with fresh fruit and top them with whipped cream.

9. Place the cups on top of the Raspberry Sauce on each plate.

**Serves 6**

## Tempting Tips

Simple to make and easy to adapt as a lowfat dessert, Fresh Berry Temptation can be made with any variety of berries, depending on what you have on hand. For a nonfat dessert, do not use the butter and sugar between the phyllo sheets. The phyllo cups also can be used to hold other fruits or a light pudding or mousse.

# Victorian Holiday Menu
## • Serves 8 Guests •

### Scalloped Oysters
Recipe on page 286

### Watercress and Beet Salad with Raspberry Vinaigrette
Recipe on page 114

### Roast Pork Loin
Recipe on page 287

### Cornbread-Apple Stuffing
Recipe on page 288

### Mashed Potatoes
Recipe on page 289

### Baked Pears in Custard Sauce
Recipe on page 290

# Scalloped Oysters

*4 pints shucked oysters and their liquor*
*12 ounces unsalted butter*
*4 tablespoons olive oil*
*1 tablespoon garlic, chopped*
*1 cup unseasoned cracker crumbs*
*1 cup coarse fresh bread crumbs*
*6 tablespoons fresh parsley, chopped*
*6 tablespoons green onions, green part only, sliced thin*
*salt and freshly ground pepper, to taste*
*¼ teaspoon cayenne pepper*
*2 lemons, cut into wedges, for garnish*

1. Preheat the oven to 400°F. Drain the oysters and pick out any visible shells.

2. In a large sauté pan over medium heat, mix the butter and olive oil together.

3. Add the garlic and cook until softened, but not browned. Add the crumbs, parsley and herbs.

4. Remove from the heat and add enough oyster liquor to moisten the mixture.

5. Season with the salt, pepper and cayenne.

6. Butter 8 individual baking dishes and distribute half of the mixture in the bottom of the dishes.

7. Divide the oysters and place them on top of the mixture.

8. Sprinkle with the remaining mixture.

9. Dot each dish with butter and bake for 10 minutes, until the mixture is bubbling around the edges.

10. Serve with lemon wedges.

**Serves 8**

**Oyster Tips**

The best time for harvesting and buying oysters is late fall, winter and early summer. Once purchased, oysters can be stored in a plastic bag in the refrigerator for 3 to 4 days. Be certain to rinse them well in cold water before opening them.

**Wine Notes**

Match this dish with a crisp Chardonnay from Carneros or the Anderson Valley in California.

## Testing Doneness

The best bet for testing a roast for doneness is to use a meat thermometer. More confident cooks can do it by feel—measuring doneness by the indentation their finger makes in the meat.

# Roast Pork Loin
## *with Cornbread-Apple Stuffing*

*1 pork loin roast, 4 pounds*
*$^1/_3$ cup dry white wine*
*$^2/_3$ cup chicken stock (see page 5)*
*salt and pepper, for seasoning*

*Spice Mix*
*2 garlic cloves, minced*
*$^1/_4$ cup parsley, chopped*
*2 tablespoons fresh sage, chopped*
*1 teaspoon dried thyme*
*1 tablespoon salt*
*$^1/_2$ teaspoon black pepper*

1. Preheat the oven to 350°F. Mix all of the spices together to make a paste.

2. Rub the spices all over the pork roast.

3. Roast the pork in an uncovered pan for 2 to $2^1/_2$ hours or until the roast reaches 155°F.

4. Deglaze the pan with the wine and stock. Scrape all of the drippings from the bottom of the pan. Reduce this to intensify the flavor.

5. Strain the liquid and season it with salt and pepper. Serve it as an accompaniment with the roast.

6. Let the roast stand on a platter for 15 minutes before serving.

**Serves 8**

## Wine Notes

 A spicy Zinfandel from California or a Syrah from Australia goes nicely with this dish.

# Cornbread-Apple Stuffing

*1 stick butter (¹/₂ cup)*
*2 cups onions, chopped*
*2 cups Granny Smith apples, cored and diced*
*3 tablespoons dried sage*
*2 tablespoons dried thyme*
*2 cups breakfast sausage, cooked and crumbled*
*¹/₂ cup pecans, chopped*
*6 cups cornbread, crumbled*
*2 cups white bread, cubed*
*salt and pepper, for seasoning*

1. Sauté the onions in the butter until they are soft. Add the apples, sage and thyme and continue to cook for 3 minutes. Keep the apples crunchy.

2. Cool the mixture.

3. Preheat the oven to 350°F.

4. Toss in the dried herbs, cooked sausage and pecans.

5. Add the cornbread and white bread. Toss well.

6. Moisten the mixture with water if it is too dry.

7. Season with the salt and pepper, to taste.

8. Place the stuffing in a buttered casserole dish and bake it in a 350°F oven for 30 minutes.

**Serves 8**

## Yummy Year-Round

Since stuffing is so tasty, it's surprising that we only enjoy it once a year at Thanksgiving. This recipe for traditional stuffing is so simple, you'll want to make it again and again.

If you can't get Granny Smith apples, use Golden Delicious instead. This stuffing is great with chicken breasts, as well as pork roast.

# Mashed Potatoes

$1^1/_2$ gallons water
1 tablespoon salt
3 pounds Red Skin or Yukon Gold potatoes
$^3/_4$ cup sour cream
$^3/_4$ cup heavy cream
$1^1/_2$ teaspoons garlic powder
$1^1/_2$ tablespoons fresh horseradish
$1^1/_2$ sticks butter, melted
$^1/_3$ cup Parmesan cheese
$^1/_3$ cup Monterey Jack cheese
3 teaspoons salt
$1^1/_2$ tablespoons pepper

1. Put the water in a large pot and bring it to a boil. Add the salt and return it to boiling. Add the potatoes and boil them until they are fully cooked (approximately 30 minutes).

2. Mash the potatoes in a food mill or with a potato masher.

3. Mix in all of the other ingredients until they are smooth.

**Serves 8**

# *Baked Pears in Custard Sauce*

*8 ripe pears*
*8 tablespoons sugar*
*3 egg yolks*
*3 cups heavy cream*
*2 tablespoons Licor 43 (a Spanish vanilla liqueur)*

1.  Preheat the oven to 400°F.

2.  Peel the pears. Cut them in half and core out the seeds.

3.  Fill each pear cavity with $^1/_2$ tablespoon of sugar.

4.  Arrange the pears in 1 layer in a baking dish.

5.  Place the uncovered dish on the middle shelf of the oven for 45 minutes.

6.  In a large bowl, beat the egg yolks until they are thick and have a lemony color.

7.  Whip in the cream and add the liqueur to create a custard.

8.  Remove the pears from the oven when the edges are golden brown and the sugar has caramelized.

9.  Pour the custard around the sides of the pears while they are still in the dish.

10. Turn off the oven and let the pears sit, uncovered, in the oven with the door closed for 20 minutes, so that the custard can set.

11. Serve immediately.

**Serves 8**

## Quick Custard

This technique for making custard requires less effort than cooking on top of the stove. Because custard can easily curdle, it needs to be checked constantly when it's in a saucepan. With this recipe, that timing trouble is taken care of.

# About the Authors

**MICHAEL CRAIG** has been general manager of the Washington Inn for the past 12 years. After graduating from Cornell University in Hotel Administration, he gained work experience in London, Switzerland and Atlantic City. Wine is one of his passions, which he and his brother David have developed into an outstanding wine program at the restaurant. Michael resides in Cape May, New Jersey, where he grew up. He and his wife Elaine have two daughters, Maddie and Natalie.

**MIMI WOOD,** a member of the Washington Inn family since 1991, has been Executive Chef of the Inn since 1996. Originally from the greater Philadelphia area, Mimi received hands-on training in Classic French cooking techniques and has, over the years, combined those skills with her personal flair for creating light, flavorful foods. Her stops along the culinary trail include stints in California, St. Croix, Switzerland, Pennsylvania, and now Cape May. Mimi resides in West Cape May with her husband, Chris.

# About the Artist

**ALICE STEER WILSON** has been painting Cape May scenes for more than 30 years. She discovered her love for painting early, and finds joy in teaching as well as creating. Her work is included in collections throughout the United States, Europe and Japan. All of her work that appears in this edition was originally painted in watercolor, including: